Also by Bruce Campbell
If Chins Could Kill: Confessions of a B Movie Actor
Make Love the Bruce Campbell Way

BRUCE CAMPBELL

WITH CRAIG SANBORN

THOMAS DUNNE BOOKS ⚏ NEW YORK

ST. MARTIN'S PRESS

THOMAS DUNNE BOOKS.

9\17 An imprint of St. Martin's Press.

HAIL TO THE CHIN. Copyright © 2017 by Bruce Campbell. All rights reserved. Printed in the United States of America. For information, address St. Martin's Press, 175 Fifth Avenue, New York, N.Y. 10010.

See pages 305–308 for known image credits.

www.thomasdunnebooks.com
www.stmartins.com

The Library of Congress Cataloging-in-Publication Data is available upon request.

ISBN 978-1-250-12560-6 (hardcover)
ISBN 978-1-250-15098-1 (signed edition)
ISBN 978-1-250-12561-3 (e-book)

Our books may be purchased in bulk for promotional, educational, or business use. Please contact your local bookseller or the Macmillan Corporate and Premium Sales Department at 1-800-221-7945, extension 5442, or by e-mail at MacmillanSpecialMarkets@macmillan.com.

First Edition: August 2017

10 9 8 7 6 5 4 3 2 1

For Joanne

CONTENTS

INTRODUCTION
BY JOHN HODGMAN

When I first got access to decently fast internet, I did what everyone did: I typed in my own name. It was twenty years ago. I was an assistant at Writers House, an accredited literary agency in New York City, and we had just gotten a T1 line. Prior to this my internet experience had been walled in by the slow, screeching garden of dial-up AOL. Now I had the World Wide Web – indeed, the world – on my desktop. And with new and remarkable speed, Alta Vista told me I did not exist in it.

The next thing I did was to type in "Bruce Campbell."

I knew about Bruce because in high school Nicholas McCarthy showed me *The Evil Dead*. Then in college, I watched *The Adventures of Brisco County, Jr.* with Jonathan Coulton before it was briskly cancelled. Bruce was already a cult celebrity by this time, but it is both important and difficult to remember that this time, before Internet had meaningfully saturated our lives, cults still met in the dark. Before YouTube, social media, even blogging, nerds only found their fellow cult members in slow motion, via letter columns and yearly regional conventions. They had not yet mobilized via the Web into a massive, cranky, demanding, and inspiring consumer and cultural force. Since I didn't exist on the internet, I wanted to know if there was anyone else out there like me. So like any nerd, I typed in some code words – a single ping into all that darkness – and waited for what echo came back. What came back was Bruce.

Along with a half dozen Bruce Campbell fansites was bruce-campbell.com. It didn't look that great. The design was unflashy and homegrown. There may have been some Comic Sans in use. But because it was so cheesy and charming and great at the same time, I knew it could only be real Bruce behind it. And it was. I am usually right.

Aside from posting the dates of his appearances at upcoming horror movie conventions, Bruce told stories on his Web site. He wrote about the tedium of leaving his family to live in Mexico for months to shoot his few scenes in a movie that no one would remember (unless you happen to be the nerd who runs a Tumblr devoted to Tom Arnold's interpretation of *McHale's Navy*). He wrote about the sweat and fake blood that he and Sam Raimi and Rob Tapert had to pour into *The Evil Dead* to get it, impossibly, made. He wrote about the strangeness of being like unto a God within the hotel ballroom that is hosting this small horror movie convention, only to step into the hotel lobby, a suddenly anonymous, unfamous Shemp. He wrote about a fox he saw one day when he went out for a bike ride.

I thought it would all make an interesting book. (Well, not the fox part, though I still love that story. There is something unmistakably Bruce – his openness to the world and small pleasures – in his turning to the Internet to report that he saw a cool fox that day). I clicked on the link that was an e-mail address. I typed a few more words into the darkness, and then forgot about it. Until

Bruce wrote back.

Of course Bruce checked his own e-mail. At least then he did, because he could. He knew how few of us weirdos were out there – enough to delight with his Web site and fox tales, but not enough to bother him with too much attention or money. I did not understand this at the time. I thought I had hit a gusher. Someone had just sold a Whoopi Goldberg book for almost a million dollars. And since I had the cultural face-blindness of the young nerd that could not differentiate between the fame of Bruce Campbell and Whoopi Goldberg, I thought Bruce's sudden blind trust in me was not only A) astonishingly kind, but also B) well-placed, and C) the start of a very successful career as a professional literary agent. Only A was true.

Bruce mentioned casually in his own afterword to *If Chins Could Kill* that it was not easy to find a publisher for that book. I will be less casual: it was rough. Bruce wrote an amazing proposal along with the help of his incredible assistant Craig (who I am thrilled to see back in the byline with this book). But as I called around, I realized I had underestimated how many New York book editors loved *Army of Darkness*; and equally, I underestimated the sniffy contempt so many New York book editors would have for those nerds who did. *Army of Darkness* was a cult movie, beloved by a few weirdos, but dismissed by the mass mono-culture that could only be reached by big publishers and studios and record labels and broadcast TV, the same mass mono-culture that was the only way to make money and which would go on forever and ever. The rejections poured in, each a humiliating gut punch: I was not only failing, I was failing my hero.

In 1999 or 2000, I went with Bruce to a horror movie convention at the New Yorker Hotel near Penn Station. Conventions were still like Bruce's old web site: small, a little ramshackle, and summer-campy. No one was coming to launch a major media property there. It was weirdos who loved weird things, including Bruce Campbell. Seven hundred or so people crowded into the room for his Q&A. Bruce answered every question. He reassured the crowd that they should not be worried: his old high school pal Sam Raimi was the perfect person to bring Spider-Man to the screen. He encouraged them to get out there and make movies just like he and Sam had done. He pointed out that the most profitable movie of that year had been *The Blair Witch Project*, which had been self-produced, shot on consumer grade equipment, and home-publicized using the Internet. Things are changing, Bruce pointed out.

I had sent out a videotape (a videotape!) of an appearance like this, from an earlier convention, with each proposal. Who knows if the publishers watched it, and if they did, whether they were impressed. All of them rejected the proposal except one, Barry Neville, of St. Martin's Press.

Barry was there with me now at the New Yorker Hotel. It was the spring before *If Chins Could Kill* would be published. We watched the fans line up, hundreds of them, to bring their T-shirts and Ash figurines and bared chests for Bruce's signature. In a few months they would come back with books in their hands. This would happen in dozens of cities across the country. I'm sure its sales did not rival Whoopi Goldberg's, but it was enough to put it on the *New York Times* bestseller list. And I guarantee it made the publisher a profit, because I know what the advance was.

Barry was brave to have fought to acquire the book, but his was a bravery of love, not of business. Neither of us knew the book would succeed. We only guessed based on what Bruce had told and shown us: you can cultivate a good and profitable artistic career by knowing your audience and keeping them close; that soon we would all have to do that, because mass mono-culture was largely not going to exist anymore; and that Sam Raimi would do a good job at *Spider-Man*. By the time *Spider-Man* opened to almost 100 million dollars in one weekend, it was becoming clear: what mass culture would remain would be nerd culture.

Was Bruce ahead of his time? Yes. But the success of *Chins*, like all his successes, stems more from the fact that he is an old-fashioned good dude. Before he signed with me I had to meet his manager. It was a hot summer Sunday. He was in town for some premiere, and I had just bought a blazer to make myself look like a grown up. It just made me sweat, and that sweat grew cold in the a/c of the Au Bon Pain where we sat as I tried to figure out how I was going to convince this man to put his client into my soft, inexperienced hands.

But I didn't have to worry. The manager was bemused, a living sigh of "what's Bruce gotten into now?" He told me a story about how a major director wanted Bruce for a big mini-series, but Bruce turned him down. He had promised Rob Tapert he would do *Xena* this year, and Bruce kept his word. So when Bruce was armed with the technology to reach the whole world, of course he would keep it personal, straightforward and groovy. To help people reach out to him, and to give people chances. If some kid wrote to him about writing a book, he'd take it seriously. And if he went insane or got drunk and accidentally agreed to let John Hodgman represent him, he wouldn't go back on his word now.

When Nicholas McCarthy showed me *The Evil Dead* in high school, all he wanted to be was a horror director. He is that now (his movie, *The Pact*, is one of my favorites). When I watched *Brisco County, Jr.* with Jonathan Coulton in college, all he wanted to be was a musician who wrote songs about technology and feelings. He is that now. All I ever wanted to do was become a semi-famous person like Bruce Campbell. Bruce's hard work and legacy of awesomeness and decency allowed this to happen, and we are but three data points among the people he has inspired.

I am grateful, always, for his faith in letting me join him at the beginning of his book-writing career, and also for his understanding when, once *Chins* was published, I realized I would be a terrible literary agent and thus had to quit. I looked back on the book this morning and remembered all of this and wrote it down, and I am grateful to you for letting me air these memories out. I also noticed in the latest edition of *Chins* Bruce corrected the spelling of my name from HODGEMAN to HODGMAN. I guess I'm grateful for that too, though it did rob me of a chance to make fun of him.

Thanks, Bruce.

That is all.

John Hodgman

PRE-RAMBLE

Back in 1997, a literary agent named John Hodgman contacted me and asked if I had ever considered writing an autobiography. I guess he read a few early, primitive "blogs" on my Web site and found them amusing. But writing a book about myself? No, I hadn't ever thought about it, but it was an intriguing possibility. I did love reading biographies about actors, but there weren't too many out there about the so-called B-listers.

"That's exactly the point," John explained. "Tell the story of the underexposed working stiffs of the silver screen."

I set about scrawling outlines, anecdotes and notes on the backs of screenplays. Within a few years, I had managed to come up with enough words and dig up enough old photographs to tell the story of my life. *If Chins Could Kill: Confessions of a B Movie Actor* was unleashed upon the literary world in 2001, and I'm proud to "confess" that it became a *New York Times* bestseller.

That was fifteen years ago. As I looked back I realized that if this were a movie, the first book would really only be Act One, where you meet your hero and follow him through his formative years. This might very well be part two of a three-act story. This book has a little more of the "meat" of my life as an experienced actor, with more "adult" experiences.

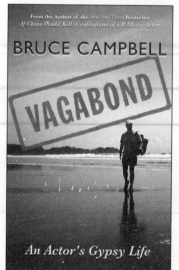

From the Author of the *New York Times* Bestseller
If Chins Could Kill: Confessions of a B Movie Actor

BRUCE CAMPBELL

VAGABOND

An Actor's Gypsy Life

I had originally intended to write a travel memoir titled *Vagabond: An Actor's Gypsy Life,* but my stories were so intrinsically tied to my ongoing career that it all just worked better as my "further confessions."

If you've already read *If Chins Could Kill,* the following few pages are a breezy reminder of my life from my childhood in Michigan to my "legendary journeys" with a "warrior princess."

If you've never read *If Chins Could Kill,* your life is as dull as toast, but it's still available in four different editions: the hardcover, trade paperback, audiobook (read by yours truly) and full-color, gently updated e-book.

Regardless, I'm about to recap my first tale at the beginning of the new one. Why not? It worked for *Evil Dead II* and *Army of Darkness…*

PREVIOUSLY ON…

The youngest son of Charlie and Joanne, I was born in 1958 outside of Detroit, Michigan. I spent my happy childhood digging tunnels, building forts and creating UFO scares with my brothers, Mike and Don. I was your typical suburban kid until one fateful day in 1966 when I saw my father performing onstage as part of a local theater troupe. The thespian seed was planted and it wasn't long before I landed my first acting role in *The King and I* at our beloved St. Dunstan's Theatre.

Local theater was only the beginning. There was something else brewing during my adolescence. Over the years, I met and amassed a tight group of friends, like-minded "Shemps" who rallied together under the banner of Super-8 filmmaking. Super-8 was a grainy, primitive medium, but it was a shared passion in my group (along with the Three Stooges) and we all took turns with the various duties making numerous screwball comedies.

My buddies Mike Ditz, Scott Spiegel, Josh Becker, John Cameron and Dave Goodman were all serious about pursuing the dreams we cultivated together, but one kid named Sam Raimi was "a different bird entirely." Sam and I met in drama class in 1975 and bonded immediately over our embarrassing failures at improv. He brought a lot to our filmmaking troupe, including a creative fire, a devilish sense of humor, a goofy little brother and a 1973 Oldsmobile Delta Royale.

High school ended and, thanks to my mother's encouragement, I interned at the Cherry County Playhouse. A valuable learning experience, this was my first time working among professional actors, with all their wisdom and quirks. My college career lasted all of six months because I already knew what I wanted to do. I believed the best education would be to actually start working in the entertainment industry. I became a production assistant for local commercials and got to see how a "real" film set operated.

The "boys" and I continued to get together at every opportunity to make more Super-8 shorts. Only now we had a new member: Sam's roommate, Rob Tapert. As we grew, so did the scope (and cost) of our projects. Sam and Rob's "The Happy Valley Kid" cost $700 but actually made about $5,000 at the box office / college's campus theater. We began to think that our films might actually be able to make some money.

Up next was Sam's ambitious flop, *It's Murder!* This time, he wanted to produce a feature-length story, complete with a large cast, stunts – even a car chase. It cost over $2,000, which was a huge amount of money in 1978. Alas, for all our effort and expense, *It's Murder!* bombed, but within the film was a surprising silver lining that sealed our fates. In one scene, a character lurched forward from the backseat of a car so unexpectedly that it scared the audience – every time we showed it. Maybe pratfalls and slapstick weren't the keys to success. What if the path to fortune and glory was paved with shock and horror?

Sam, Rob and I started officially working toward making a feature-length horror film. We started with the production of a "proof of concept" short called "Within the Woods" that we could screen for potential investors. For all of our inexperience, we were committed to getting our feature funded, made and distributed.

After many months of shooting and several years of effort, expense, injury and near-sex experiences, our film was finished. With the help of marketing guru Irvin Shapiro and the endorsement of horror authority Stephen King, we were a hit at the 1982 Cannes Film Festival. Soon after, *Evil Dead* was released in England, but a domestic distributor had yet to be found.

Thankfully, the movie took off across the big ditch – second only to the blockbuster *E.T.* in some areas – and it awoke New Line Cinema's interest here in the United States. The film was released in 1983 and did very well – for New Line Cinema. We got an "advance" of $125,000 and it was the last penny we ever saw.

The emergence of home video came to the rescue and *Evil Dead* ultimately sold more than a million VHS tapes through Thorn EMI, an astonishingly reputable video distributor. None of this happened overnight. The film was shot in 1979, released in 1982/3 and took six years to break even. In this case, it was the rights fee to make *Evil Dead II* that put the original movie partnership in the black.

Based on the strength of foreign sales for the first film, the sequel came together very quickly. We were happy to get back to a world we understood after our second film, *Crimewave*, died a thousand deaths.

You are cordially invited to a screening
of
The Ultimate Experience in Grueling Terror...

EVIL DEAD

AVCO III, WEDNESDAY, MARCH 31st, 11:00 A.M.
Worldwide representation, Irvin Shapiro, FILMS AROUND THE WORLD
At the American Film Market, Westwood Plaza Hotel (AFM Headquarters)
Room 1018, 1020, 1022

Fishing for distributors.

Evil Dead II was so sought after, partner Rob Tapert walked on the set during pre-production and announced that the film was already in profit due to pre-sales of various rights around the world.

When *Evil Dead II* came out in 1987, it did moderately well at the box office, but it didn't seem to matter – we already made what we were going to make, profit-wise.

By then, I was a working actor, living in Los Angeles with my family: wife, Cristine, daughter, Rebecca and son, Andy. The *Evil Dead* movies had established me as a "horror guy" and I was cast in a slew of B movies, ranging from psycho slasher flicks to sci-fi adventures.

As the 1990s approached, I joined Josh Becker and Dave Goodman in producing Josh's indie comedy *Lunatics: A Love Story*. Alas, with repeated extended absences, the film industry can be brutal to families and I returned home from shooting *Lunatics* to discover that Cris wanted a divorce.

Despondent, I burrowed back into my B movie pigeonhole. There, on the set of *Mindwarp*, I met a feisty costume designer named Ida who took pity on me and my rusty efforts to woo her. Ida and I were married in 1991 and are still going.

The next time *Evil Dead* reared its ugly head was that same year, when Sam, Rob and I convinced Dino De Laurentiis and Universal to team up and make *Army of Darkness*. This third installment was, to us, epic in proportions. The budget went from 8, to 11, to 13 million. In the process, we put a boatload of our own money in the flick, lost creative control of the editing and generally had a miserable time making the thing.

Army of Darkness made about $13 million at the box office. In order to recoup our inflated budget, we would have to make *three times* that. The Evil Dead franchise, if you could even call it that, was officially dead in the water. But, hey, I couldn't expect to play *Evil Dead*'s Ash character for the rest of my life, could I? (wink)

I moved into television, landing the lead role in a Fox Western called *The Adventures of Brisco County, Jr.* Although fans loved it, the ratings failed to impress the network and Fox canceled it after one season. Honestly, though, I was a bit relieved. Being a leading man in an hour-long episodic series was exhausting and I shifted my sights toward supporting characters and one-off TV movies. Roles on *Lois & Clark, Ellen, The X-Files, The Love Bug* and other TV gigs mingled with more B movie roles and the occasional A-lister.

It's not too late...

In the meantime, Sam and Rob kept busy, starting up a syndicated action show called *Hercules: The Legendary Journeys*. I directed a few episodes, but my most memorable contribution to the series was my recurring role as Autolycus. As *Hercules* headed toward the end of its six-season run in the late 1990s, I began to direct and appear in its successful spin-off, *Xena: Warrior Princess*. I can honestly say that working on those two shows was one of the most enjoyable experiences of my career.

And that – in a B movie nutshell – was the first forty years of my life. Still on board? Still interested in reading what I've been up to between then and now?

If so, groovy.

If not, no refunds.

EXODUS

My mom, even though raised in the Midwest, was a huge fan of Westerns and had a deep fondness for the world to the west of Detroit. As a boy, I'd doodle little flip book animations in the corners of her Zane Grey books. The author had written more than fifty Westerns, but I only knew him as the guy who wrote books that I used to draw cartoons.

Michiganders had a long-standing tradition of heading south to Florida when weather got bad or the holidays were upon us. My mother broke that tradition. She didn't want to go south – she wanted to go west.

"This Christmas, let's go to Phoenix instead," she offered.

The family looked at her in unison. "Phoenix…Arizona?" we asked.

"Yep."

"Do they even have Christmas in Arizona?"

The takeaway from our "Western" holiday wasn't about fake snow being blown on entire neighborhoods to replicate the season – it was about staring at the vast, empty expanses outside my airplane window on the way to Phoenix. I was transfixed by large areas of desert that still didn't have any roads.

How is that even possible? I'd ask myself.

It wasn't like I grew up in a really crowded area, but there were always people around. My neighbors, while not packed in tenement-style, were everywhere. Every road – and most were paved – had cars on it, any time of day. Humanity was a constant.

The only respite, and one that I really took to, was property my parents bought outside of Gladwin, Michigan. At 160 acres, it was a quarter-mile square of woods, meadows and bogs – classic Michigan terrain. My mother designed and oversaw a small but fully functional cabin on a bluff overlooking the lower acreage. Many a weekend was spent at this wonderful getaway.

When my parents divorced in 1980, the property was sold as part of the settlement. This turn of events haunts me to this day. When Mom and Dad split, I was still struggling to complete *Evil Dead* and didn't have a pot to piss in monetarily, so I had to watch, helplessly, while my personal slice of paradise slipped away. That harrowing experience planted a seed that would grow twenty years later.

Post-divorce, Mom moved west to start a new life. She remarried, a rancher, and they migrated from one piece of western property to another. Whenever I wanted to see Mom, I'd make my way to wherever she lived at the time – Sequim, Washington; Nevada City, California or Humbug, Oregon. I loved seeing the new places she found and it really cemented my idea that the West was different – in almost every way.

The first time I saw the Milky Way was out west, while working on *Sundown: A Vampire in Retreat* in Moab, Utah. I was astounded. It was real. I felt like I was starting to reconnect a little bit with the natural world. While making that movie, I explored the Utah outback at every opportunity when I wasn't working.

It was the first time in my entire existence, while at the Navajo National Monument, when the only sound I could hear was the crunch of gravel under my feet on a remote trail. A crow passed by across the canyon and I could hear its wings flap, so distant was any traffic or ambient, human-created noise. Solitude was something I began to crave.

When I moved to Los Angeles to pursue acting more seriously, I threw myself into a sea of humanity. Los Angeles has been described many ways: The City of Angels, The Big Orange, La-La Land. I call it the City of Sloppy Seconds.

Ironies abound – the guy with the fancy sports car can't get it over 45 miles per hour because of all the traffic; the "health nut" unknowingly sucks the equivalent of half a pack of Camels in particulate matter every day; the "Mellow" Californian doesn't exist – not in Los Angeles anyway.

About ten years into my L.A. "residency," I was returning from a trip with Ida – my wife and co-conspirator for twenty-five years – late in the afternoon. Through the airplane window, we could see the unmistakable pale orange band of smog blanketing the city. This wasn't "marine layer" or anything atmospheric – this was pure, big-city smog. Ida and I glanced at each other. I extended my right hand.

"Let's make a deal to get out of here in five years."

She took my hand and shook it firmly. "Deal."

To assuage her that we wouldn't starve if we moved out to the boonies somewhere, I drew up a "where did I work in

1997?" chart. It turned out that 70 percent of my movie or TV work took place outside of Los Angeles. With better rebate deals being offered by New Zealand, Canada, Bulgaria and others, film production left California at an alarming rate.

Only 30 percent of my work was in Los Angeles? Why was I still here?

Our five-year escape plan came to fruition within a year.

GO NORTHWEST, YOUNG MAN!

By this time, my mother lived in Ashland, Oregon, and she dabbled in real estate. Mom was an early "flipper." She loved buying places for cash, fixing them up and selling them whenever she and her new husband, Bob, got bored.

In an exploratory phase, Ida and I were looking for a house that wasn't in a standard neighborhood or even a small town – we wanted a place that was farther out, ideally with land.

Oregon seemed like as nice a place as any. It encompassed anything from high desert to mountainous forest to desolate coastline. Oregon was on the same coast as Los Angeles, so the whole time zone thing would be the same – and there was a two-hour direct flight from Medford to Los Angeles once a day.

This could work.

Ida and Ma scouting our "next location."

I asked Mom to fax me some real estate listings and a few of them seemed promising. Ida and I headed north.

Oregon in the fall is grand – it's a mix of still-warm days, breezy sunshine and fall colors. The day we accompanied Mom to see the Applegate Valley property was the kind of day real estate agents pray for: sunny, crisp with the slightest of breezes to remind us that it was fall. This particular piece of property was situated on a hill with spectacular south-facing views of the Siskiyou Mountains.

The setting was very appealing, but the ownership map told me everything I needed to know – our property was surrounded on three sides by land administered by the Bureau of Land Management (BLM – more on them later) and our mountainous view was also either BLM or National Forest Service land.

A mountain range with no lights on it. Where do I sign up?

I immediately turned into a lousy house negotiator because I instantly wanted the place.

"Ida, you know when you buy a house, you're supposed to pretend that you're not really that interested?"

"Yeah?"

"Well, I don't care. I want to buy this place. I want to whip out a check right now to hold it."

Ida was a little stunned. "Really?"

"Really."

We put a check in the owner's hand as a deposit and bought the place. Just like that, Ida and I were done with Los Angeles. Our new life in the wilderness had begun!

JACK OF ONE SEASON

The irony of being a working actor was that I was so busy globe-trotting that I barely got to spend any time in my new home. In 1998, I made a deal to appear in ten episodes of *Hercules* and *Xena* and direct two of them.

I regard the *Hercules* and *Xena* time period as a blast because of the creative nature of it. Rob Tapert and the other producers trusted us, and because it was syndicated we didn't have the overbearing infrastructure of a studio with endless, nitpicky notes. Alas, *Hercules* and *Xena* ran their course after six seasons each.

After almost a decade in the Land of the Long White Cloud, Rob Tapert had cultivated not only an impressive episodic TV machine but also an important reputation in syndicated televi-sion. When the Warrior Princess made her exit, an hour-long hole was left in the schedule and Universal Studios (and Rob) had every intention of filling that slot. They were looking for another action-y set of shows to replace swords and sandals, ideally without pause. For better or for worse, the next two shows came together very quickly.

BACK-TO-BACK ACTION HACK

When a show like *Hercules* or *Xena* airs for five or six years, it is eventually going to lose viewership – that's just a fact of TV life. When viewership declines, the studio can't command the number-one time slot anymore or get the highest advertising rates. Shows then get moved to less desirable slots. Therefore, *some* replacement shows started their run in "downgraded" slots – the harbinger of cancellation, in my opinion. Such was the case with *Jack of All Trades* and *Cleopatra: 2525*.

Nevertheless, the producers still wanted to continue the successful pairing of a "guy show" with a "girl show," so they developed *Jack* and *Cleopatra*, two half-hour action comedies, dubbed the "Back-to-Back Action Pack." It was a very rare, very strange combo that Rob somehow managed to sell to the syndicators.

Because we were no strangers to the Auckland setup, Rob tapped both myself and Josh Becker to help participate in the two shows. Mine was *Jack of All Trades*, a period piece about America's first international spy. I was intrigued by the concept. The story took place in 1801 and was set the West Indies, where the United States had sent a spy to keep an eye on Napoléon (ultimately played by the great two foot eight Vern Troyer).

Jack was basically what Zorro – one of my favorite characters as a kid – would be like if he had been played by comedian Bob Hope. The approach of the material was very much my sensibility. I like borderline vaudeville humor. I enjoyed making fun of Thomas Jefferson, kings and rich people in general.

The model Rob had in mind was *Hogan's Heroes*. To Rob, the series should be confined to just one French-controlled Caribbean library of sets, props, costumes and creatures. The now-seasoned crew had become specialists in the production of adventure entertainment. Then something happened that decimated Rob's resources and left his studio in much worse shape than it should have been…

Orcs invaded New Zealand!

Peter Jackson started production on the Lord of the Rings trilogy in 1999, promptly engulfing and employing every able-bodied specialist in the production of adventure entertainment. Seemingly, every armorer, best boy, focus puller and four-foot-tall stand-in responded to Jackson's muster, including the effects team at Weta Workshop and Ngila Dickson, costume designer of the trilogy (and Academy Award winner).

The masked alias of my "Batman of the West Indies" character was the Daring Dragoon. A dragoon was a member of the mounted cavalry – an imposing soldier, laying waste upon his impressive steed. Yeah, nice to want – our beleaguered crew couldn't find a proper horse because *The Fellowship of the Ring* happened to prominently feature nine "Black Riders." As a result, every black or dark brown horse in New Zealand, Australia and Papua New Guinea had been acquired by Jackson – who paid as much as a quarter-million dollars for the most photogenic equine. All we could manage for the Daring Dragoon was a bony nag I sarcastically nicknamed Lightning.

My ass still hurts.

People ask me all the time what I think about the Lord of the Rings movies. My response is always the same: "I hate 'em."

"But, Bruce, these are Academy Award–winning, billion-dollar-box-office movies!" fans would breathlessly explain.

"I wouldn't know," I would clarify. "I've never seen them."

"Then how could you hate them?" the crestfallen fans would ask.

island and focus only on the ongoing conflict between the heroes and the island's goofy commandant. At the time, Josh and I objected to the rule that the show was never to leave the island of Pulau-Pulau and we tried to convince Rob that the show should take place along the Barbary Coast instead.

Drumming along to the opening theme.

From 1801 to 1805, the United States engaged in the First Barbary War against four North African states, targeting the predatory pirates that captured American ships and held their crews hostage. One of the earliest deployments of the U.S. Marine Corps was to the Barbary Coast and the opening lines of the "Marines' Hymn" (not to mention the chorus of Joe LoDuca's *Jack of All Trades* theme song) pays homage to this Barbary baptism: "From the Halls of Montezuma / To the shores of Tripoli…"

Beyond the battles between marines and pirates, the region was rich with possibilities – sultans, princes, Dutch captains, tribal intrigues – which could have provided a sweeping, colorful canvas for a series. Alas, Rob shot it down. In this case, I think his production team feared the multiple sets and large cast that our "angle" might demand.

While I feel the show was therefore doomed to claustrophobia, we at least tapped into the era by incorporating real historical characters such as Thomas Jefferson, Napoléon, Ben Franklin and Blackbeard (even though the latter two were technically dead by 1801).

Meanwhile, Josh had pitched Rob *Tumithak of the Corridors*, based on a 1932 Lovecraft-inspired public domain story. Set in an uninhabitable future occupied by spider-aliens, humankind had to burrow underground progressively deeper to survive. Ultimately, they had been underground for thousands of years and there were completely different civilizations on each layer.

Like the story, the series would center on Tumithak, one guy who sees the light from way up top and thinks, Hmmm, what's up there? Josh's *Tumithak of the Corridors* would have been this guy's journey to the surface of the Earth, with each season being a new layer with a whole new civilization. Finally, as a possible end of the series, he'd emerge onto the surface through a manhole in Manhattan and get promptly flattened by a taxicab.

Rob was intrigued, but he wasn't sold. He needed a "girl" show. As series development is known to do, each component of the original concept was individually removed, reworked and replaced until only morsels of the original concept remained. In went *Tumithak of the Corridors*; out came *Cleopatra 2525* – a series about a stripper who goes in for a boob job and wakes up in the twenty-sixth century.

[long pause]

Not exactly what the author had in mind.

Somehow, a subterranean serial about survival got mixed up with the true story of an actress friend of mine who got a botched boob job in Canada, and became one of the most ridiculous concepts ever recorded.

In spite of all common sense or creative logic, "*Hogan's Heroes* of the West Indies" was produced along with "Boob Job of the Corridors." Thus, this odd, Back-to-Back Action Pack premiered with a roaring sigh on the shitty time slot left by a waning warrior princess.

CO-EXEC OF ALL TRADES

If I was going to be the star of a TV show again, I wan[t] be under the right circumstances. The big kahuna Rob T[apert] pal for decades now, trusted me and I always enjoyed the "creative lenience" on the shows he produced in New Z[ealand] One of the other big men on campus was Eric Gruender[man] veteran of *Herc* and *Xena* and someone who had been tolera[ting] since my "temp sound" days on *Darkman*. Eric was a con[summately] sane producer – a rare delight – so I knew that working w[ith] wasn't really going to feel like work.

Part of my deal was that I was also a coexecutive p[roducer] which meant I wasn't powerful enough to stand up [to] the studio, but I had *almost* enough power to make a [costume] designer do what I said. The title gave me a voice tha[t people] had to pretend to listen to and it allowed me to work wi[th] impunity.

I had much more control on *Jack* than I did on *The Adve[ntures of]* *Brisco County, Jr.*, where I was just an actor for hire on so[meone] else's show. Carlton Cuse was a very strong show runner[. I] rarely disagreed with any dialogue on *Brisco* because it w[as good] writing. *Jack* was always a more creative environment for [me and] we would improvise and collaborate until everyone was [happy.]

One sequence in particular had never been fully rea[dy by] the time we shot it, so we had no choice but to make it u[p on the] spot. That day, we improvised every gag, every bit, ever[y poke in] the eye, every ass slap. As co-exec, I was free to shoot fro[m the hip] without having to call the studio for permission, and cr[eatively] that's exactly where I wanted to be.

ROB IS ROBBED!

Rob Tapert had spent the latter part of the 1990s cultiv[ating his] "backlot," refining its infrastructure and amassing an im[pressive]

"Because Peter Jackson stole our whole Kiwi crew."

Jack's brash character needed a vocal, headstrong counterpart to keep him in check. This came in the form of the British spy Emilia Rothschild, played by New Zealand actress Angela Dotchin. As with many in the

The only reason I'm lounging is because the cape is so damn heavy, I can't actually get up.

Kiwi talent pool, Ange cut her teeth in the New Zealand soap opera *Shortland Street*, then graduated to appear in one or two episodes of *Young Hercules* and *Xena*. In fact, we both appeared in the *Xena* episode "Tsunami," during which I saved Ange's life – as she put it.

In the episode, a massive ocean storm capsizes a ship carrying Xena, Gabrielle, Autolycus and various guest characters. To simulate the underwater aspect of the story, a submerged set was constructed inside a giant water tank. Life imitates art and the tank cracked open without warning, spilling more than five thousand gallons of water in a virtual ocean storm of our own.

Water flows in the opposite direction in the Southern Hemisphere. Perhaps that's why Angela ran *toward* the rupturing tank. I shoved her in the opposite direction and my "gallant heroism" was hailed. The truth is, Angela probably would have gotten more dampened than drowned, but I milked her praise for all it was worth.

The *Jack* production benefited from a combined twelve seasons of *Herc* and *Xena* – notably in executing fight scenes. Countless brawls and scuffles had been staged over the course of both shows, but I was never satisfied with the way they had been filmed. The procedure of the day, one that I bristled against, was to shoot the fights all in one uninterrupted piece, just like the stunt guys did. That's fine if you have months to rehearse a complicated fight, but on a TV schedule you're learning the fight the morning of the scene, so there isn't time for all the moves to sink in. I felt that the longer fight takes lasted, the sloppier and more dangerous they became.

When *Jack* rolled around, we worked out a very straightforward formula for shooting fight sequences that I still use today. We broke each fight into a series of smaller, easier to execute, beats. Each chunk, now shorter, could be shot with more safety and confidence and didn't take any more time to complete.

To their credit, *Herc* and *Xena* established a rule that "actors don't fight other actors." That may seem both obvious and absurd at the same time, but it was actually a very safe and successful guideline. Stunt guys are not known for their acting prowess and actors are not known for their flawless stunt work.

The master and wide shots for the fight scenes of *Jack of All Trades* were all staged with stunt people. In closer shots, if the Daring Dragoon was the focus the French soldier fighting him was a stuntman and vice versa. We ultimately got everything down to a nice, efficient science. No actors or stuntmen were injured during the season.

RIDING INTO THE SUNSET...AGAIN

Six years had passed since I headlined *The Adventures of Brisco County, Jr.*, my first "one-season wonder." *Jack of All Trades* was to be my second. At the end of the day, *Jack* was a woulda, coulda, shoulda scenario. There were a lot of good elements in place, but the show was hamstrung by its own self-imposed limitations. Crappy time slots didn't help, either.

When you're a young actor, your reaction to a failure is egocentric: *It's me. It's my fault. They didn't like me. I guess I didn't try hard enough...*

Getting canceled after such a short burst can make an actor think that people only want you as a little spice and sizzle – not as the whole meal. But, after you've been around a while, you realize that it's not all about you – you're just a little cog in a larger set of wheels.

Whatever the reason, I was faced with my second failure in a row as a leading man of a TV series. The saving grace for me was feeling confident that on both *Jack* and *Brisco* really good work was done by all participants. Both shows have "aged" well in the eyes of the public and have since become "Cult TV" – a somehow fitting end.

GNOME, SWEET GNOME

Ida and I bought a very funky house, knowing that we could always "fix it up." True vision must come from complete blindness, because we had no idea what we were getting into.

For starters, the house, if you could call it that, was essentially the shape of a Quonset hut, but not all aboveground – it was about half-submerged, with eighteen inches of dirt on the roof.

I personally had never lived in a Hobbit house, but there were many pluses. The arch was a very sound structure and allowed for open spaces within the home. Because of the dirt above, the hottest summer day had virtually no effect on the interior temperature, and the same applied to winter. A single wood-burning stove was sufficient to heat the entire house and there was no need for air-conditioning of any kind.

If you're a noise freak and like peace and quiet, a dirt roof is for you. Ida and I have slept through numerous wind, rain and thunderstorm events because the natural insulation was such an effective barrier.

Having said that, the place was very cave-like. The lower level, mostly underground, swallowed light. It was not unusual to have two or three lights on at 1:00 in the afternoon. The curved shape is a square-footage cheater as well. Furniture can never be placed too near the wall, because you'd bang your head on the arched ceiling above you.

The eleven-hundred-square-foot house had been built ten years previously by an eccentric Englishwoman and she lived alone. In retrospect, the house was perfect for one person – one bathroom (if you exclude the "country" toilet in the pantry), one main bedroom that was attached to a small greenhouse, a very tiny second room and a mostly open upper floor, with the exception of cheesy cabinetry that blocked a million-dollar view out the windows.

There were no building codes in Oregon until the seventies, and it allowed for some odd results. Because there were so many hippies in my neck of the woods (and still are), there are many single pieces of property with six or seven habitable dwellings. Oregon locals are a hearty, self-sufficient bunch and they like to build their own garages, pour their own concrete and rewire their own electricity. Permits? Deal with that when you sell.

Our house was not a model of building code compliance. A lot of new age "Pioneering" had been done since the initial construction phase. By definition, I mean: *work performed by unskilled laborers, whereby a proprietor hopes to save money but ultimately wastes even more in the end because the crappy work never lasts and has to be redone.*

Evidence of Pioneering was everywhere in our house, from the keep-the-spirits-away quartz-laden wall in the greenhouse to the stove, which was attached via a bare copper tube to a barbecue-sized propane tank outside.

Every sink, faucet and showerhead had to be replaced – not so much to suit our tastes, but because they had become so calcified from the well water that they no longer functioned properly. Item by item, we began to rip out, replace and upgrade the house to the twentieth century.

GREEN ACRES, OREGON-STYLE

One of the more challenging projects was upgrading the telephone system. Two lines came into the house, with one jack upstairs and one down. In my world of home/office, I needed a six-pair line installed to meet my immediate needs.

Easier said than done.

For the sake of technological reference, my valley was using telephone party lines up until the eighties. Getting extra lines in the Oregon backcountry wasn't as easy as calling up the phone company and deciding whether it would be a morning installation or an evening one. Here is a letter I later sent, outlining the odyssey:

> *Dear US West,*
>
> *Let's turn back the calendar to May, 1998. I placed an order to add additional phone lines and voice mail. The installation was to be fulfilled approximately July 15th. Several days after that date, realizing that no US West phone company representative had shown up, I placed a call to a Customer Service Representative – let's call him Leo – and asked why. The answer that came back was simple, yet astounding: "The area of concern utilized an 'older' system, and doesn't provide the switching to*

connect a missed call to Voice Mail, or provide the additional lines that you need."

"Leo" from the Home Office Consulting Center in Phoenix (very far from where I live) didn't even know what systems were available in my quiet little valley before he placed the order.

Recommendation #1: Introduce the left hand to the right hand. Maybe throw a mixer.

Together with Leo, I formulated Plan B, which was simple but challenging: "Your company would dig a trench up the length of my property – seven-tenths of a mile – lay a shiny new six-pair line, and I would pay for it."

Quick update:

The work was completed in January of this year. In case you don't have a calendar handy, that's nine months after the order was placed. I heard that there was a nasty little strike within your company during that time. Everything work out okay?

In June of this year, the sub-contractors returned to bury the remainder of the exposed cable. That was the good news. The bad news was that in the process they "stretched" it in one area and snapped the line.

Then there was the water thing.

After a temporary splice reconnected the phone line, the diligent trench-digging men scraped an old steel pipe several times. Undaunted by this, they continued their course until they hit the pipe again, this time severing it. To our mutual horror, this turned out to be the main water supply for approximately three families across the road.

Imagine the angry phone calls I got. You probably have a record of them somewhere.

Recommendation #2: Update The Trench Digger's Guide to Trench Digging by encouraging diggers to "change course" when encountering "obstacles."

Eventually, the severed line was repaired and all was well again in my happy valley – until I wanted to get call waiting. I lost count of how many times I was told "next day by six" or "tomorrow by noon for sure."

A Customer Service Representative in Salt Lake City – let's call her Doris – informed me that I would have to call Repairs if I wanted something done. I became perplexed: How can something be repaired if the service hasn't even taken place?

Recommendation #3: Take Team Phoenix and Team Salt Lake to a US West corporate retreat for trust exercises and charades.

Eventually, Doris said that the call waiting problem was caused by a Centraflex system that had been on my line all along. In order to use call waiting, she instructed, I had to hit the flash button, then dial *9. The only odd thing about this conversation was that the programming solution came from Doris – in *Repairs*.

Recommendation #4: Close down Customer Service and let the repair department do everything. Corporations

*are always looking for ways to cut operational expenses,
right? I'll give you that one for free.*

*Over the last year or so, I tried to calculate exactly
how much time I have spent on the phone, talking to
various representatives from both Sales and Repairs.
After much tabulation, I realized that it was enough time
to read How to Trench Responsibly, Companies That Are
Too Big for Their Own Britches and Waiting for Call
Waiting cover to cover.*

*If US West were my child, I would send it to the finest
attention deficit disorder clinic in the nation. If you were
my employee, I would fire you. If you were my employer,
I would quit.*

Yours in eternally crabby regret,

Bruce "I can't hear you" Campbell

Granted, verbal battles with corporate giants aren't anything
new, but rural areas are even more neglected because equipment
upgrades and service calls are always last on the corporate list.

After much documented heartache, my damned six-pair line
was trenched. Installation to the actual house was next, but an
insurmountable obstacle halted the progress: hunting season.

Norm, the phone guy, warned me after he came over the first
time for a look, "This is gonna be easy, Mr. Campbell, but I gotta
warn ya – I'm not gonna be around from the third through the
seventeenth."

"Oh, going on a vacation?" I asked.

"Nope. Elk season – high desert."

"Ah, yeah." I nodded like I knew what he was talking about.
"Right. Of course."

So, a couple weeks after elk season the phone lines were
installed and I could get on the Internet. As I type this now, I

laugh at how easy it has all become since. After all the aggravation, money and corporate incompetence, about a year later Satellite Internet was introduced to my area, and being situated on a hill, facing south, I was a prime candidate. The installation took one day and there wasn't a trench in sight. Internet: done. Today, though I still have no cellular service, I make calls via satellite as well. Phone service: done.

By the time Ida and I declared construction "sort of over," we had added an entry with level, connecting walkways, poured concrete steps from one building to another, built a carport, carved out a park and a café and rerouted the driveway in order to create a more pleasing oak savannah backyard.

What we should have done, Ida and I reasoned later, was drop a bomb on the house and start from scratch.

Footnote: It only took us eighteen years, but Ida and I finally did just that – we destroyed the hippie haven and built us a proper house.

"I'VE GOT WHAT ON MY PROPERTY?"

Lavender. Specifically, *Lavendin grosso*. It's a combination of cold-hearty English and heat-tolerant Portuguese varieties. As it turns out, lavender has many medicinal uses aside from its beautiful violet-blue flowers. During WW I, it was used in hospitals as an anti-bacterial agent. Today, it is promoted for its soothing properties and pleasing, not overpowering, smell.

Ida: Lavender Lady.

Go figure. This was all news to me as Ida and I surveyed the acre or so of lavender at the lower end of our property.

Southern Oregon is a lavender-friendly part of the world, as it has hot, dry summers, and this mature crop was still doing very well. We decided to figure out this whole lavender thing and see what could be done with it.

It turned out that the prep, harvest and processing of lavender wasn't that big of a deal. It's a once-a-year harvest, usually late July. Other than that, you keep the plants drip-irrigated, as they are not particularly thirsty and everything lies fallow in the winter. The harvest is done with hedge trimmers and you cut where the stalk meets the "ball" of the plant. The stalks are gathered and tossed into the back of a U-Haul truck, destined for the distillery.

Distillation is the fun part. Harvesting is just hot and backache inducing, but distilling is where the sweet science of essential oils comes into play. Our lavender is loaded into a large, locking metal trailer with ventilated tubes fixed along the bottom. Once the cooking process begins, it's kind of like steaming broccoli – you keep a lid on it and crank up the heat. A couple hours later, the oil is skimmed off the top of a separate container and voila – you've got lavender essential oil.

"Okay, Ida, that all sounds great," I said. "Where should we distill?"

"How about Steven Seagal's ranch?"

"Steven Seagal has a distillery?"

"I guess so," she explained. "In researching lavender, I came across his ranch manager. They grow all kinds of botanicals."

I never would have used "botanicals" and "Steven Seagal" in the same sentence otherwise, but perhaps "Bruce Campbell" and "lavender" are a bit incongruous as well. Either way, off Ida and I went to distill our first batch of lavender.

Over the years, as Ida did more research and development on what you can do with lavender, we began to make gifts for the cast and crew of various shows I worked on. Lavender products were particularly popular with the Miami-based *Burn Notice* crew. Quite literally, because of the unusually high heat index, combined with long hours of manual labor, they tended to smell worse than any other crew. As a joke one year, Ida and I gave away lavender soap, made from our oil. The response was swift and favorable, so yearly we expanded our offerings to include lotions, balms, ointments and dried lavender sachets.

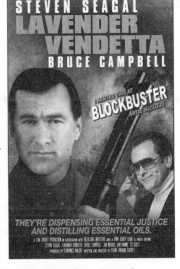

I knew we were on to something when our low-end products became addicting. One day during the *Burn Notice* shoot, a burly teamster lumbered up to me, invading my personal space. He was sweaty, of course, and he smelled "just okay."

"Hey, Bruce, where's my fuckin' lavender this year? I'm startin' to smell like shit over here. C'mon!"

If you're expecting this chapter to go all "Newman's Own," where Ida and I build a lavender empire from our humble beginnings, you can stop there. This was a losing venture from the start and it always will be. We just do it for fun.

RECONNECTING: BLADE RUNNER

When you're an actor, you have a lot of things done for you. You get driven to the filming location. You get your meals prepared for you on set. Chances are you even have someone to run your errands, answer your phone and feed your cats. Over time, you begin to feel like you've forgotten how to do anything.

It's not necessarily the consequence of ego or wealth – there is definite professional value in having others handle the distracting aspects of life so you can concentrate on your work. Rehearsing dialogue or writing screenplays takes focus and it helps to know that certain things are off your plate entirely.

Still, occasionally an actor finds himself stranded in the boonies of his own acreage without a personal assistant or teamster anywhere to be found. After I recovered from the initial shock of self-reliance, I embraced the new responsibilities of being a woodland landowner.

One of the most pressing concerns was our driveway, which was seven-tenths of a mile long, steep and unpaved. If it became impassable, we'd be marooned.

If you listen closely, you can hear the sounds of hippie marriages falling apart.

There were plenty of married retirees living in the valley and one thing rural, isolated couples discover over time is that they can't stand the sight of their spouses anymore. Shockingly, long marriages imploded all around us, and I was opportunistic enough to buy a John Deere tractor from a neighbor who was liquidating his life during just such a divorce.

With the tractor, I'd be able to "blade" the driveway, smoothing out all the ruts and packing down the loose dirt. The reason an unpaved driveway needs to be bladed is because of the "washboards." Scrambling for traction, every two-wheel-drive vehicle that trudges up the hill tears the road apart.

The only problem with my new tractor was that I had no clue how to use it, so I did what people from the Midwest do: I called Sears.

Fooled into thinking it was just a "general service call," Sears would send out a technician to take a look at my tractor. Once he was there, I deftly weaseled the operating instructions out of him.

"Hey," I asked, "is this the lever for the front loader thing?"

"Yeah," the Sears tech would explain, "but make sure the loader is engaged when you use it."

"Of course! And, now, this thing is the uh…"

"Oh, that's the electrohydraulic hitch control," the tech said, getting suspicious. "You ever drive this before?"

"Sure, plenty of times!" I would assure him.

You may be wondering why I didn't just admit I had bought a tractor without the slightest idea of how to make it work. Well, when you're best known for mounting a chainsaw on your hand and building "deathcoasters" people just assume you're an expert in landscaping equipment.

Over the course of three different "service visits," I figured out how to operate my tractor. It wasn't all that different from a riding mower and I finally worked up the courage to blade the driveway all by my big-boy self.

At first, I was primarily concerned with making it *look* nice and flat. The problem was that flat roads provided absolutely nowhere for rain to go. Water just pooled into puddles and turned my flat driveway into a craggy, uneven mess.

After a few tries and the advice of a veteran blader, I finally discovered what road builders have probably known since ancient Rome: Roads need to be slightly higher in the middle. Eureka! Now, rain had somewhere to go and my hard work wouldn't wash away immediately. With that simple innovation, I went from having to blade my road weekly to only having to do it two or three times a year.

I knew I had finally nailed it when we were hosting a party for the valley residents during our lavender harvest. Anticipating a parade of guests, I gave the driveway a fresh John Deere makeover.

During the festivities, Scotty, a big, tough rancher, moseyed

Actor Tractor.

over to me and asked, "Who did your driveway, son?"

"Uh, I did, sir," not sure what his response would be.

Scotty put a grizzled hand on my shoulder and smiled appreciatively. "That's a hell of a blade job, son."

And with that, my initiation to Oregon was complete.

A HUNK OF BUBBA LOVE

"So, Don, are you gonna see it? Are you gonna see the dick?" I asked.

"No," Don Coscarelli replied. "It's implied."

Both the question and the answer were important, because in Don's new movie, *Bubba Ho-Tep*, the story revolved around a sixty-eight-year-old Elvis Presley in an East Texas rest home who was dying from cancer – on his penis.

I was asking Don because in considering the role of Elvis in this whacked-out story by Joe R. Lansdale I wanted to know how far Don was going to go. Was he going John Waters far? *Pink Flamingos* far? If so, the movie would become something you couldn't take back – it would be knocking on the door of taste-lessness, and although I've been in unrated movies and plenty of edgy stuff, that wouldn't be something I was looking for.

Once I had cleared that major hurdle, the next question concerned my litmus test for low-budget productions: "How long is the shoot?"

I didn't ask that because I was lazy and hoped for a mercifully short shooting schedule so I could golf more. I asked because in the *movies-without-budgets* world I tend to inhabit, shooting length can be the difference between "doable" and "no fuckin' way." If Don was hoping to bang this thing out in two or three weeks, like a lot of ultra-low-budget filmmakers, I knew it would be time to *walk away, Ray.*

"Six weeks," Don said, reassuringly. "We gotta get this right."

That was all I needed to hear. "Great!" I exclaimed. "I'm in."

I knew *of* Don Coscarelli, but I didn't really *know* him before shooting *Bubba Ho-Tep.* Don, like we did with *Evil Dead,* started in the world of nano-budget genre movies – very handmade stuff – and his first effort, *Phantasm,* became a cult classic.

I've always had respect for people who go their own way creatively and Don fit the bill quite nicely. Joe Lansdale, by my way of thinking, also had an enviable career writing pretty much anything he damn well pleased. When not penning mostly dark, homespun material, Joe is a martial arts expert, dog lover and small-town Texas man who has mostly shunned mainstream Hollywood. My kind of guy.

The elements were in place. Now I had to get ready to play The King. Although the Elvis character in this story was a geriatric sixty-eight, a few flashbacks featured Elvis performing live, late in his career. Terrified that I actually had to get onstage and emulate a performer – whose live acts were astonishing – I tracked down an Elvis impersonator and scheduled a session ASAP.

My "session" with – let's go with "Ken" – wasn't as long and exhausting as you might expect. In fact, it was rather short, mostly because Ken gave up on me halfway through. It all started innocently enough, with Ken regaling me about the time he wore a jumpsuit that Elvis actually wore.

"I was doin' this charity gig, see – on the Vegas Strip. I called up the jumpsuit company that made the outfits for Elvis. There's only one company in the whole country that makes 'em. But dig this," Ken continued, using vernacular like The King. "If they made a jumpsuit for you, they owned it. You had to give it back. Even Elvis."

"Sounds draconian," I remarked, wondering where his story was going.

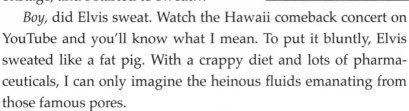

"So, anyway, I asked if I could wear an actual suit Elvis wore for this charity deal and they say, 'Okay.' Me and the King were similar in size, so it fit me like a glove."

I still wasn't sure if the story was cool or creepy.

"So, there I was, baby, doing my thing onstage, and I started to sweat…"

Boy, did Elvis sweat. Watch the Hawaii comeback concert on YouTube and you'll know what I mean. To put it bluntly, Elvis sweated like a fat pig. With a crappy diet and lots of pharmaceuticals, I can only imagine the heinous fluids emanating from those famous pores.

"Now," Ken explained, "because of all the sequins on the jumpsuits, they couldn't really wash those things; they could only steam 'em – so ol' Elvis, he would get a little ripe, see? To cover up the smell of B.O., or whatnot, Elvis would use Brut. He'd dump the shit all over himself."

By this time, I was pretty sure Ken's story was gonna turn creepy. I was right.

"Well, I'm doin' my thing onstage and I start to heat up real good," Ken elaborated, his eyes widening at the magical memory. "Next thing I know, the smell of Brut (albeit thirty years old) starts to come out of the suit. It was the same smell as The King.

I knew it was legit. I was channeling Elvis Damn Presley. Best show I ever gave."

Desperate to avoid becoming entwined in another slightly homoerotic story, I cheerily clapped my hands together. "Great story, Ken. Hey, wanna try some moves?"

Ken ran me through the particulars of stage posture, microphone-holding techniques and general hip-thrusting gyrations, but it didn't last long. After about five minutes of watching me attempting to thrust my pelvis, Ken threw up his hands. He had seen enough.

"Look, man, you're never gonna get it. Let's call it quits."

As far as research goes, I was on my own.

By the time I became aware of Elvis Aaron Presley, he was a washed-up, bloated ghost of his former self – touring mindlessly to support his over-the-top lifestyle and avoid dealing with the ruins of his life. But Elvis, in his heyday, was *something*. Frank Sinatra was the first singer to drive teenagers insane, but nobody drove them as insane as Elvis.

Bubba Ho-Tep, even with a ridiculous plot (an aging Elvis teams up with a black man – who thinks he's JFK – to save a rest home from a soul-sucking mummy), had a sweet core. Deep inside all the crazy antics, there was an engaging, redemptive story lurking. *Bubba* was ultimately a quiet meditation about aging and usefulness. This is what I connected with and tried to get across in the characterization.

I watched a lot of footage of Elvis. YouTube is the modern actor's research library. Wanna see Elvis' last concert? It's there. Wanna see his "posse," drunk and crying in an interview a decade after Elvis' passing? It's there. My takeaway was that Elvis had it all and lost it all – fame, fortune, relevance – and it pushed him over the edge. Ultimately, he was a supremely talented, not fully formed human being who found out too soon that the dream of riches and fame could easily become a nightmare.

In addition to "learning" how Elvis moved, talked and sang, I had to try to look like him. Thankfully, my Elvis was mostly sixty-eight years old in the movie, so we were in uncharted territory. To sell the main illusion of Elvis, two things were critical – the hair and the almost ever-present sunglasses.

"We could use your actual hair," makeup wiz Melanie Tooker explained, "but if we use a wig, we can match it perfectly." She was right. Even without doing anything else, the wig got me halfway home. Elvis' sunglasses took it the rest of the way. There is something so iconic about them, you just start talking like Elvis the second you put them on.

Don Coscarelli got in touch with the aforementioned jumpsuit manufacturer, which amazingly still made elaborate outfits – and still wanted them back when we were done! For the flick, I ended up with three bitchin' outfits: white, black and a vibrant blue. What I wouldn't give to have those suckers hanging in my closet now. Drunken karaoke nights would never be the same.

Some locations don't need a lot of work to be camera ready. This ancient WW II era veterans' facility in Downey, California, was one such place. Used to house countless vets after a devastating war, then abandoned due to neglect and consolidation, the sprawling compound already had dank, interminable hallways, peeling lead-based paint and banks of un-flushable toilets. The smell alone made the location all too real.

Shooting *Bubba* wasn't much different from other low-budget movies, but after a brief chat with the boom man, the person responsible for recording every word out of my mouth, it dawned on me how low-budget this movie actually was.

"So, Mike, you excited to work on this whacky flick?" I asked, using my most pleasant, first-day-of-filming vocal inflections.

"I sure am," Mike said, fairly beaming. "This is the first movie I ever worked on."

I went pale. "So, Mike, you've never held a boom pole in your hand before?"

"Nope. But I'm sure excited to learn."

I'm not usually an asshole on set, but I raised a finger and pointed it at Mike's face. It wasn't a threatening gesture, but it wasn't a friendly one either.

Years ago, the American public was asked to vote for the official Elvis postage stamp.

"Now, you listen to me, Mike. I don't like looping. You don't even know what that means, so I'll tell you: Looping is what actors do if they haven't been recorded properly, you understand?"

I have found that performances always suffer in the looping process. Granted, with wind machines and talkative directors there are cases where you can't avoid replacing some dialogue, but to me looping means we failed on set.

"We can't fail, Mike," I concluded sternly. "You have to record every one of my lines like your life depended on it." I said it with a smile, but Mike knew, deep down, that I was not kidding. Mercifully, Mike did a great job and 99 percent of my dialogue was recorded perfectly.

Ossie Davis was a revelation. By the time he worked on *Bubba*, he was already eighty-three years old. This was to be his second-to-last performance. You could tell that Ossie was a guy who didn't have bad habits. He didn't smoke; it didn't seem like he was a drinker; his mind was still very sharp. Ossie was a good steward of his instrument.

The first time I met him was on set.

"Ossie, I know why *I'm* in this movie, but what are *you* doing in this movie?"

"When I got the script, I showed it to my grandkids," he explained. "They said, 'Oh, Grandpa, you got to do this!' "

Apparently, the youngsters were fans enough of *Evil Dead* to recommend the gig. We were grateful to have him. Ossie lent a huge amount of overall credibility to the film, just by being there. An actor of tremendous poise and charm, he "classed up the joint." Lest we forget, Ossie's first film was around 1945. He has since been honored with lifetime achievement awards, Kennedy Center awards, a Grammy, a daytime Emmy. I could go on. Most substantially, he was an ardent civil rights activist, who delivered the eulogy of Malcolm X. Mr. Ossie Davis was an impressive man.

When you shoot a horror movie, a lot of things will never change – creepy locations, working at night, fake fog, fake blood, prosthetic makeup and, inevitably, monsters. In those respects, *Bubba Ho-Tep* was no different, and the shoot plodded along. Horror movies don't "race," they plod, because all of the aforementioned elements take more time to do.

Don Coscarelli was slow and methodical in his prep and execution. He's a meticulous director and ultimately I appreciated that. I say "ultimately" because while I tend to be more "ready to go" in my approach to filmmaking, Don tends to be more ponderous in his. This was an adjustment for me, being inherently impatient, but once I could see what Don was up to, how he was crafting these scenes, I calmed down and we got into a good rhythm. Ossie and the rest of the cast – including *Phantasm*'s Reggie Bannister, who did a great cameo – brought their best under the low-budget conditions and we walked away feeling like we had at least done something a little different.

Don, being the truly independent filmmaker that he is, basically disappeared for a year to edit the film. I admire Don for his dogged determination to make movies by hand. Every frustration I ever had with him was always erased by knowing how much personal time, effort and money he puts into each of his projects.

Don finally emerged and showed us the final product. I thought *Bubba* was funny, unique and strangely touching. I was very happy with the results and very happy to help promote it.

Big-budget motion pictures have big PR machines behind them. *Bubba Ho-Tep* had Don Coscarelli. In an impressive feat of personal tenacity, Don began the horrifying process of self-distribution – fronting the money for making film prints, placing local ads, booking theaters and then *collecting*. On *Evil Dead*, we had much of the same independent spirit, but thankfully, we never had to self-distribute. The concept of dealing with bookers and theater owners, notorious for taking forever to pay, makes me shudder.

On my end, I agreed to appear at some local L.A. theater screenings and ended up introducing the film in half a dozen cities – all to very good reception. The midnight screening at the Toronto Film Festival will always remain with me as a treasured experience. The audience response was almost rapturous. Joe Lansdale's very original story walked a fine line between absurdity and pathos and it really connected with audiences.

Bubba worked its way into numerous film festivals and the reviews were crazy good. Eventually, after a respectable run in theaters, Don made a deal with iconic MGM to handle the DVD and ancillary rights.

Just recently, now fifteen years after its initial release, I taped an interview for the updated, Blu-ray release. It's always great when a film you worked on decades ago remains popular enough to be reissued and preserved for generations to come. At the end of the day, that's really all us entertainment types can hope for – relevance.

Hey, it's Ossie Davis!

One of my favorite, lasting images of *Bubba Ho-Tep* was in Nacogdoches, Texas, home to writer Joe Lansdale. The local theater was showing *Bubba* and I was in town for a Q&A with Joe after the show. As I walked up to the theater, I could see two long lines of patrons, each snaking out the door and into the adjacent parking lot. One line was waiting for *Bubba* and the other line was for Mel Gibson's wildly successful *Passion of the Christ.* I enjoyed contrasting the type of people in each line. While visually very different (*Bubba* fans had more tattoos), I guess you could say each group shared strong "passion."

As I walked by, a *Bubba* fan spotted me. "Hey, look!" he shouted, gesturing to dueling lines of devotees. "We're all here to see The King!"

T.C.B.

HELLO, NEIGHBOR!

The perception of Californians is that they are all a bunch of wackos, living the bohemian life, but after I met my new neighbors north of the border Los Angeles seemed dull as dust in comparison.

The day Ida and I moved in, I was checking to see which mailbox was ours and I ran into my first neighbor – Cowboy Kenny. He was tall, wiry, and had a slightly nasal twang in his voice.

"I'm just an old cowboy," he said, extending a weathered hand, "but I got me a younger wife!"

Kenny worked for Sam and Melinda – a former food broker and lawyer, respectively. Ten years ago, they cashed in the chips for a Black Angus cow-calf operation in the middle of nowhere. Naturally. Kenny and his "younger wife" Gidget stayed in separate ranch quarters with two teenage kids from different marriages.

Later that same afternoon, a mid-eighties Lincoln Continental chugged up our long, steep driveway. Gidget jumped out, cradling a tall can of Bud in one hand and Dude, a terrier, in the other.

"Howdy, I'm Gidget," she said, shaking my hand like she was running for office. "Now, I know that this is your first day here – we saw the moving van – and you're not going to have anything ready to eat, so Kenny and me want you to come over for dinner tonight. We're right across the road."

I couldn't help but smile. "Then I guess we're coming to dinner, Gidget."

That night, Cowboy Kenny squinted at me from the end of the rustic dinner table.

"I unnerstand you played a cowboy in a TV show."

"That's right," I said, stuffing my face with local Oregon beef.

"Can you ride?"

"Hell yeah, I can."

"Well, I'm runnin' a hundred head of cattle up the road on Saturday," Kenny said, wiping butter from his mouth with a sleeve. "Why don't you get your ass on a saddle and help us out?"

"Got an extra horse?"

"Sure do."

"I'll be there."

That Saturday, Ida brought her new video camera, I wore the gaudiest Hawaiian shirt in my collection and damned if we didn't herd a hundred head of cattle from one pasture to another. Granted, the cattle ran along the road, not the open range – and they followed a hay truck – but my job of keeping heifers from wandering into lawns and gardens seemed absolutely indispensable at the time.

On that same drive, easily half of our immediate neighbors were also there, helping in various ways, and I met more people in one morning than I had the three years prior in Los Angeles.

There are many clichés about people who live in the country: They're less educated, more paranoid, God-fearing but gun-loving, with more connection to the earth, more dirt on their boots, more dust on their trucks – which are jacked up to keep their knuckles from dragging on the ground.

Granted, those sensibilities were very much in evidence in our new neighborhood, but the locals I met the morning of my first cattle drive were, in reality, an incredibly diverse group.

There was Reggie, an English-born former insurance executive; Dilbert, a Merchant Marine now on disability after getting a leg smashed between two boats; the Baron and Baroness of Buncom, really Gil and Patty, who live on a former mining camp; Brenda, owner/operator of a lesbian co-op; Jervis, a right-wing ex-executive; Baxter, a former Southern California rocket scientist (I would have no reason to make that up), now returning to his cowboy roots with a vengeance. For the cattle drive – and every other time I saw him – Baxter looked like a modern-day Tom Mix, complete with vintage Western gear (jeans tucked in tall boots, a red scarf, vest and tilted, crumpled hat), a dog named Slick and a ratty Toyota pickup truck with a gun in the glove box, "Just for good measure."

Cowboy Kenny, leader of the cattle drive, was something of an anomaly himself. He had spent as much time in Los Angeles as he had on any ranch and his last management gig was at a marina on one of those behemoth man-made lakes in the desert.

What I discovered in the hinterlands of Oregon was more of a "new" country, which tended to turn much of Western lore on its head. Traditionally, people who worked the land stayed in one place for generations and passed the family trade down the line. City folks, conversely, tended to move around all the time. But with development knocking at the doors of farmers and ranchers, many are selling their large spreads to people who are often relocating for reasons other than necessity.

Ironically, it is now the "city folks" who want to settle down to a simpler life, while rural Americans often hit the road in search of something more exciting – like a city.

Y2K OR BUST!

Ida and I moved to Oregon in 1998 – what turned out to be a very fortuitous time period. After settling in, we attended any and all events, parties, breakfasts and other assemblages of humans in order to meet the people of our area. We enjoyed the process, but among the retirees, self-made and local folks we met, there was a small percentage of couples who ultimately moved to the middle of nowhere fearing a Y2K disaster.

It only dawned on me after-the-fact why Dr. Dome (an affectionate name I gave to Glen, a former crisis counselor) had retrofitted his geodesic dwelling for the End of Days and planted a particular ratio of apple to nut trees in his backyard – so "when

Y2K hoarding, Oregon-style.

civilization falls" he'd have something of value that the surviving community would be in need of. Yikes.

Two sisters relocated their husbands to build an off-the-grid home on a beautiful, remote hunk of land for the same semi-survivalist reasons. But when the world didn't collapse, their nirvana – and Dr. Dome's – began to unravel. Having long since divorced and moved out of the valley, the doctor is no longer in the house.

JOIN US

One of the downsides of living a gypsy life is that it's hard to "join" anything – even a bowling league on Tuesdays. I just can't predict where I will be or when – or for how long. In an effort to be a part of *something*, I finally broke down and joined my local Ashland, Oregon, Elks, Lodge #944, and it has since been a wonderful lifeline to what I consider "normal."

Being an actor makes me the perfect Elk. In 1868, in order to evade the laws of New York City regarding the opening hours of public taverns, a group of minstrel show performers formed a "private" club and ultimately named it The Elks. It made practical sense. By the time performers were "off the clock" late at night, everything was closed. By forming a private club, they could stay open as they pleased. Interestingly, as a result there is at least one bar in each Elks Lodge.

The Ashland Lodge Induction Hall was enormous. It was built at the turn of the century, when membership in organizations like this was robust – much more so than today – hence the disproportionate size. The induction process was ritualistic, as one would expect with a fraternal organization, with pledges to each side of the room, representing Charity, Brotherly Love, Justice and Fidelity. At each turn, the Chair Officer runs you through an oath that you repeat.

It's all very noble and altruistic, but I must admit that I was stoned out of my gourd throughout the induction, so it was all pretty amusing. With right hand raised, my pledges were repeated loudly and with staccato – not unlike a certain William Shatner – and I powered through the induction like James T. Kirk himself.

Afterward, the Exalted Ruler approached me with a tight smile. "Welcome to the Elks, Mr. Campbell."

"Thanks, Exalted Ruler!" I exclaimed, pumping her hand excitedly.

"Sure seemed like you were having fun up there…"

"Oh yes, ma'am!" I assured him.

"…Almost like you were mocking the affair."

"Oh no, ma'am," I said solemnly. "You have to remember, unlike most of your members, I'm an actual actor, so I'm prone to be a bit more 'theatrical.' "

Another Elks lodge in nearby Medford also made for a great filming location.

The Exalted Ruler wasn't thoroughly convinced, but I've been a dutiful member ever since. If you're thinking of joining the Elks – please do. Aside from being old-fashioned and a little kitschy, the organization donates a lot of money to charity and the drinks are really cheap!

CARS, CRASHES AND CLASHES

They say that moving to the country is good for your health – the air is cleaner, the pace is slower, and you pass your golden years in peace and quiet. Well, "they" don't always know what "they" are talking about.

During my time in Oregon, I totaled four cars. In the thirty-nine years prior to arriving in Oregon, I wrecked exactly zero cars. I maintain that suburban and urban driving, the style I'm accustomed to, is often less disastrous on vehicles because streets are far more apt to be paved, straight, speed regulated, more than two lanes and lit at night. Country roads, like those carved into the foothills of the Siskiyou Mountains (known for their serpentine soils), are just plain dangerous.

The early roads in southern Oregon were put in to extract minerals and get the hell out, so miners weren't concerned about shoulders, grade or pitch – they just blasted a road and moved on when they were through.

The Campbell party of two arrived in Oregon with a Saturn sedan and a Nissan minivan – two of the least appropriate vehicles imaginable for where we now lived. Driving around, I was amazed at how many big rigs populated the road – and these weren't the shiny, Hollywood-premiere types; these were mud-spattered Jeeps, logging trucks, dualies, Rural Fire District trucks, ratty pickups, SUVs, some sporting winches on the front or flatbeds on the back. In these parts, the average two-wheel-drive city car was, by far, in the minority and they kept to their side of the not-quite-wide-enough road.

After a year of tearing up our rural driveway with suburban automobiles, we decided to swap out the minivan for a Subaru Forester – its all-wheel-drive capacities proven by the brazen car salesman who drove the car into a gully and out again to prove his point. The brand had a good overall safety record and generous headroom for a full-sized guy like me.

About a month later, the Forester was put to the test – a crash test. On Christmas Day, we decided to visit my mom, who lived in nearby Ashland.

"Let's take the scenic route," I said, full of holiday cheer (not the liquid kind). "What could possibly go wrong?"

That route was, in fact, down the backside of a mountain – the side that doesn't get any sun – and it wasn't maintained in the winter.

I was at the wheel and the Subaru was doing rather well on the snowy back roads, but as we dropped over the backside of

Griffin Lane everything changed. Snow underneath the car had been pliable, almost slushy on the south-facing, sunny side, but now that we were north-facing, the car was traveling on a sheet of ice atop packed snow.

I took the first of four nasty switchbacks a little too fast and it proved to be the point of no return. I knew from driving in icy conditions in Michigan that if you jam your brakes on ice the car is destined to tailspin. That didn't seem like a good idea on this steep descent, with alternately wicked drop-offs, so I decided not to brake at the next curve – I'd try to hydroplane my way around. The Subaru made it, with some wild fishtailing, but because my speed kept increasing I knew there was no way to stop this vehicle – and the next curve was arriving quickly.

"Ida, hang on; we're not going to make it!" I shouted hastily, like the lead actor in a disaster film and slammed on the brakes anyway.

The Forester hit the lip of the next turn sideways, sideswiped a pine tree, which flipped it upside down almost immediately, and we proceeded to plummet down the slope, tires in the air. From inside the careening car it was a point of view I hadn't seen since wiping out on a toboggan as a teenager – a snowy landscape turned upside down, racing at me from all sides.

Halfway down the hill, the Subaru was mercifully stopped dead by a large pine tree. Out of breath, we hung upside down in our seat belts, trying to get our bearings. The car was still running, so my first instinct was to turn it off.

"Are you okay, hon?" I asked.

Ida nodded, her face red from the inversion. "Yeah...yeah... let's get out of here."

We unbuckled and dropped with a thud on the roof of the car. Looking back, I noticed that the rear window had been blown out in the crash, so we crawled out and stood up on the steep slope to survey the damage. As was touted by the Subaru salesman, the roof hardly collapsed while upside down and Ida and I essentially walked away without a scratch.

After a really scary incident like that, people react in different ways – some bemoan the loss of their car, others shiver at the what-ifs – but Ida pumped her fist in the air.

Are the trees supposed to be upside-down?

"Whoooo!" she shouted with genuine glee. "We made it! Whooo!"

I hadn't thought of celebrating at that particular instant, but there was much to be grateful for. A car could be replaced – we couldn't.

Just a few days later, several weird things happened. The first was a phone call from the Subaru dealership.

"Hello, Mr. Campbell, this is Joyce from Subaru. We have a thing we do with all new car owners. We do a commercial, and we get them on tape saying how much they enjoy their car. Is this something you'd be willing to do?"

"Well, sure, if I still had the car…"

"I'm not sure what you mean," Joyce said, confused.

"I just totaled it."

"Oh my God!" she exclaimed. "I am *so* sorry."

"No, no, it's okay," I assured her. "My wife and I are fine. In fact, you know, we'd be willing to do an ad, next to the wrecked car, and talk about the car's safety."

"Uh, oh, well, that would certainly be different. Could I call you back?"

"Sure."

About a week later, Joyce did call back and cheerfully announced that Subaru would be happy to do a safety commercial. A film crew met Ida and me where the totaled Subaru lay in state and we made our first local commercial. I say "first" commercial, because Ida and I turned right around and bought another Subaru Forester, which tickled the dealership so much they decided to make a second, "sequel" commercial.

I had been fairly anonymous in this area until those damn ads started running. Between them, I got more local airplay than any *Xena* episode I ever did.

I have since gotten the occasional nod from a passerby. "Hey, you're that Subaru guy…"

At least it was a new one.

The second strange thing I alluded to was an instant message I got while surfing online the day after the wreck. The back-and-forth went something like this:

"Is this Bruce?"

"Who wants to know?"

"I just wanted to make sure he was all right. My name is Jewel. I am Native American. I had a dream last night that Bruce went upside down in a car – and there was a woman with him."

I stared at the computer screen. Nobody knew about this incident, apart from Ida, a tow truck driver and my mother. I began to type again.

"Okay, you're scaring me…"

"Are you Bruce?"

"Yes. And I did go upside down in a car. My wife was with me."

"Oh my God! Are you all right?"

"Yeah, we hit a tree before it got ugly."

"This is freaking me out."

"No shit, sister."

Jewel went on to explain that she sometimes gets dreams and premonitions. I told her not to tell me if she had any more. It sounded like one of those tabloid-type stories, but it was true enough to be very unsettling. The odd coincidence could mean a lot or nothing at all, but I took it as a hint that people are more connected than we think.

That and $1.50 will buy you a cup of coffee.

You know you're a yuppie living in the country when your caretaker hits your housekeeper head-on. This episode was next in the Vehicular Insanity line, and the tragedy of the situation, aside from a few missing teeth and a torn friendship, was that it destroyed my newly resuscitated, 1973 Ford F-150 truck.

Like any city boy turned redneck, I felt it was important to have a ratty old truck for working around the property, so I scoured the local *Nickel* newspaper, found what sounded like a cool truck and bought it for $1,750 from a local rancher. Three thousand *additional* dollars later I had a workable truck, but that's another story – I had me a genuine workhorse that was jacked up, tuned up and ready for servitude.

Apparently, the accident all happened on a blind curve. Seat belts are optional in the countryside, so everyone involved got the crap rattled out of them. The housekeeper's daughter bit the dash of her mom's car and donated a few teeth to the Reckless Driving museum.

Two cars down – and counting.

I had pretty good fortune with my 1991 Saturn since moving to Oregon, but the little workhorse was no match for the boondocks or black ice and it was time to upgrade, like millions of Americans, to an SUV.

My neighbor Dave was getting rid of his '97 Ford Explorer and it seemed like a logical step to take during my adjustment period. I drove it around his driveway once in the dark and agreed to his slightly inflated price tag.

This "vintage" of Explorer was jokingly referred to as "The Exploder" because of rollover issues, but on July 23, 2003, it got my seal of approval. My boyhood pal Mike Ditz and his wife, Jennifer, and I were on our way back home from the local eatery around 9:00 p.m., so it wasn't daytime, but it wasn't night either. My lights were on, but they didn't have any effect. The road that connects to my driveway follows a beautiful winding river.

I was going around 40 in the Explorer. Mike was in the passenger seat and Jennifer was in the back. As I approached a tight left turn, a red Jeep rounded the corner – in our lane – moving faster than we were. Since he was taking up our entire lane, I decided to take his and swerved left. The driver of the Jeep, Drunky McGee, realizing that he might be in the wrong lane, corrected back to the right lane and we hit pretty much head-on.

The timing, from spotting the Jeep to the impact, took as long as it would to say: "Holy shit, that guy's in our lane – oh my God, we're gonna –"

Crash!

Neighbors reported later that they heard the loud impact from inside their homes.

My assailant was a classic shit kicker/redneck/asshole. This was to be his third DUI. His license had already been revoked and there was a warrant for his arrest for obnoxious littering. But wait, there's more! He had no car insurance, no health insurance, and he blew .23 on the alcohol Richter scale, which is almost three times the legal limit. All class.

To make Drunky's side of the crash far more destructive to his person, Drunky wasn't wearing a seat belt, didn't have a shirt on and the windshield on his sport Jeep was folded flat. When we hit, he was launched like a short-range ICBM and glanced our windshield. Drunky's downward trajectory included the passenger side mirror, which he ripped off just before face-planting on the asphalt. Granted, I didn't see any of this happen because the air bag was too busy deploying in my face, but Mike and I pieced it together after-the-fact.

On our end of things, we fared substantially better. I'm the product of a very aggressive ad campaign in the sixties to get people to buckle up and I've become increasingly thankful for that habit, so all three of us were seat-belted. The air bags deployed beautifully. In fact, I didn't even know they went off

Its exploring days are over.

until I got out of the car and looked back inside. We also got the benefit of out-sizing our opponent – my Ford Explorer simply was more Detroit steel than his Jeep.

As the Explorer braked, it dipped our nose down, just enough to get under the grille of Drunky's Jeep – which wasn't braking – so we basically popped him up and over. His Jeep smashed upside down on the opposite side of the road and immediately burst into flames. Mind you, this was July and the surrounding foliage hadn't seen a drop of water in four months, so the ensuing brushfire grew quickly.

Inside the Explorer, we did a three-way "you all right?," got a look at the fire directly in front of us and decided that it was time to flee. Mike had to step over Drunky's inert body to get out. I circled around to the back of the Explorer and we both converged on Jennifer, who was holding her chest and grimacing.

By that time Jason, a local contractor, had stopped his Dually truck to help. Because Drunky was so close to his burning vehicle, Jason and I dragged his limp body to the gravel on the opposite side of the road and backed off. Drunky's arm felt cold and clammy and flopped to his side when I let go. He could have been dead for all I knew – or for all I cared at that moment.

Like they say: "You should see the other guy."

Because summer keeps fire crews on high alert around here, the fine people of Fire District #9 were on the scene very quickly and all the rescue/ police/hospital stuff began.

Pacing incessantly from the adrenaline rush, I looked down to see that my right hand was bleeding. Apparently, in car crashes where the air bag deploys, inertia keeps your extremities moving forward. My right hand slipped off the steering wheel and punched the windshield, while my left hand ended up palming it. A circular bruise that formed on my palm an hour later confirmed my suspicion.

Mike got rattled. He wasn't bleeding, but he was wrenched something good. Sitting in the backseat during the crash, Jennifer was hurt the most. She didn't have the cushion of the air bag, so the seat belt – which certainly held her in place – fractured her sternum at the same time.

Jennifer spent a night at the hospital enduring tests. Mike stayed by her side and eventually slept in a residential section of the hospital. I got the glass picked out of my right hand and got back home around 3:00 in the morning – dazed and thoroughly creeped out by the whole encounter. The image of Drunky's Jeep coming around that corner replayed in my head like a bad loop for the rest of the night. The image still replays today but thankfully has been slowly fading like a retina burn.

Thinking back, I realized that this wasn't just a car crash between a Ford and Jeep; it was a collision of cultures, ideologies and traditions. Just ten years earlier, that accident would never have happened. Back roads have long been a haven for characters of all types – drifters, loners, explorers, sightseers and locals hoping to evade local authorities. Drunk drivers use back routes to avoid detection any time they can and I might not have collided with this joker had I not been part of a late-nineties exodus of people moving in from California.

Isolated roads that were only used by the occasional yahoo or logging truck are now as likely to sport BMWs and minivans. Drunky may not be happy with the change, but his days of doing whatever the hell he wants are over.

In the aftermath, there was much to be thankful for, but mostly I was glad that dear Ida missed the whole thing. She had been partying with a girlfriend in Seattle and never even knew about the accident until her presumably fun night was over.

I love making fun of idiots. Humiliating them is a veritable hobby of mine. Finding flaws in human nature is also a hearty pastime, so when the tables turned December 13, 2005, and I got a DUI, I became the subject of my own ridicule.

For those of you who have either narrowly avoided or are destined for a DUI, here are a couple reasons why not to do it:

1. For starters, it's fucking dangerous and irresponsible. Large

vehicles no longer drive like large vehicles, so it's easy to over-estimate the handling of an SUV, even when you're sober. I got off easy – I ran off my very rural road, wiped out part of a metal fence and collided with a majestic Douglas fir. Immobile trees tend to win most confrontations with flimsy SUVs, and this one totaled my 2003 Explorer.

2. Getting a DUI can be painful. Again, I got off easy – I only broke my collarbone, fractured the bridge of my nose, tweaked my wrist and generally rattled the living hell out of myself.

These injuries were not applied by a make-up artist.

3. Getting a DUI is really humiliating. Ever been arrested? Ever been arrested at your own house? Because I crashed in a rural area, there wasn't much traffic, but I soon got a ride back home from a very accommodating neighbor. Someone subsequently reported the wrecked vehicle and a local deputy paid a visit. I was administered a field sobriety test in my carport, handcuffed with my hands behind my back (even more fun with a broken collarbone) and driven to the station to be booked.

4. It's expensive. Between legal fees, municipal fines, higher insurance rates and the difference in value of paying off an old car loan and getting a new one (at almost twice the interest rate), I wound up forking over about $10,000.00. I don't know about you, but that was a completely unnecessary financial hot poker up the ass.

I can now say that I have been on both sides of the drunk driver issue and I can't recommend either one. I guess it's time to finally sit down and write that TV sitcom pilot, *DUI Guy*.

CALL OF DUTY

In a curious twist, I found myself back on the right side of the law. Most people cringe when they hear about doing Jury Duty. After going through the process, I encourage you not to avoid that official notice when it comes. Say yes and serve – it's a blast. Having said that, when the notice arrived my first thought was *not*: How can I get in on this?! Ultimately, it was a nagging sense that I needed some form of community involvement that led me to respond in the affirmative.

Jury Duty is like a box of chocolates – you don't know what kind of case you will be assigned to or how long it will last. You could be dismissed after twenty minutes, or you could wind up on the case of the century, lasting two years.

That was part of the thrill for me as I shuffled into an assembly room with about twenty-five other potential jurors. Apparently, that day they had two cases, so twenty-five people would be whittled down to two juries of six and six.

A basic questionnaire let the legal teams know critical things about us – whether we were felons, drug addicts, sex offenders, anything that would make us an immediately undesirable juror. Mathematics dictated that 50 percent of us had to be weeded out – and it turned out to be a good thing.

One of the lawyers asked if there was anyone affiliated with Law Enforcement. A few hands went up and a woman who was not a cop herself but came from a long line of police officers was excused.

Too biased, I assumed.

Another guy made a random crack about "disciplining" his wife and he got the boot in about nine seconds.

After collecting the information they needed, the lawyers disappeared, presumably to argue among themselves about which jurors were suitable or not. In a reasonably short period of time – as even criminal justice is on a schedule – the final lists came down and I was one of six chosen.

The courtroom we sat in was nothing dramatic or imposing. Most courtrooms aren't Gothic and oak paneled like you see on cable television. The defendant and the accuser were seated. I was shocked initially, because each of them had to have been at least seventy-five years old. The accuser was a woman, small and tentative, and the defendant was a robust man, who moved easily and sat erect in his seat.

The accuser got to go first and I have to say, she was one lousy-ass witness. Her words were slightly slurred and her sentences unformed. She admitted to taking three different medications – some of which were not meant to go with alcohol – and imbibing "at least" a bottle of wine a day. Not exactly a recipe for total recall.

"He grabbed me by the throat and choked me and threw me down and I got a concussion," she recounted ruefully.

As the accuser was testifying, the defendant was scoffing, snorting and grumbling after each statement out of her mouth. I've been called a ham actor, but this guy was over-the-top.

It was his turn next. Unfortunately for the accuser, this guy was sharp as a tack. He was totally dickish in his overall behavior, but his recall was complete and his refutes to the accusations were specific, thorough and without hesitation.

The thing that bugged me was that although accused of a serious crime, the defendant was treating this whole thing so offhandedly. I wanted to know why. Oregon law to the rescue. In court, it is one of only a handful of states that allow jurors to ask questions, indirectly, to someone on the witness stand. It's a great tool in the event that the lawyers aren't providing jurors with the answers they seek.

Having been briefed that we could do this, I submitted my

written question to the judge, which he evaluated, then read out loud: " 'Why was the accuser's testimony so amusing to you?' "

The defendant smirked. "Because she was making this all up. It didn't happen that way at all," and he very effectively reconstructed the events of that fateful night in his favor.

After his testimony was wrapped up, the trial took a recess for lunch. Jurors were instructed to not talk among themselves during the break. In a small town, it's hard not to bump into someone you know because it happens every day.

As I cut through the parking lot, I saw the defendant unloading his two dogs from his truck for a walk. I thought it was odd that here was this guy, doing an everyday task like nothing was wrong, yet his entire world could be turned upside down by the end of the day. I

A moment from the classic jury room drama, <u>1 Angry Man</u>.

gave him a wide berth and ducked into the closest local restaurant I could find.

As I sat down, the lawyer for the defendant stepped in. Our eyes met. He nodded and did an immediate U-turn. He didn't even want to be seen in the same place as a juror, which was appropriate.

After lunch, the six jurors began the deliberation process. Evidence was sketchy. Long before "body cams," the local police had no audio of the arrest. The only photo of the woman was a horribly illuminated close-up that didn't even show her neck – which would have potentially provided evidence of scrapes or bruising from being choked.

Because the accuser mentioned a concussion, you would think

that initial EMT reports, emergency room records or follow-up doctor visits could confirm that a concussion had in fact occurred. No such documents existed.

We even suggested a hung jury, so prosecution could take more time to "get its ducks in a row" and try this again. As jurors, we mostly thought this asshole did something unsavory, but we had to prove it. Word came back that we had seen all the evidence available.

There was nothing much else we could do as a jury. We didn't want to do the prosecution's job or let them off the hook. Collectively, we six strangers felt the genuine responsibility to make sure, since a person's liberty was involved, that the accusers had to convince us – and they did not.

We returned a verdict of Not Guilty and the guy walked. I felt bad for the accuser because she had to deal with that self-righteous jerk, but mostly I felt satisfied that as a jury we had performed exactly as directed to preserve the rights of our fellow citizens. Fear not, Small-Town America – justice was served that day.

GETTING HIGH

L ike a lot of American kids, I was exposed to high doses of
Disney movies and TV shows. *Walt Disney's Wonderful World
of Color* was a Sunday-night staple in our house for the better part
of a decade. I also went to every live-action Disney movie during
the sixties – anything from *That Darned Cat* to *Son of Flubber*. I
even bought the gooey Flubber gel sold in toy stores after the
movie came out.

I loved the way Disney movies in particular integrated special
effects with live action, creating something of a "hyperreal"
world, which was perfect viewing for a kid. When you watch an
animated movie you know it's all fake, but when I saw a football
player float over the goalpost in *Son of Flubber* it was *real*.

That string of movies made acting in Disney's *The Love Bug*
a huge thrill years later. It was part of a mid-nineties revamp
of the Disney Sunday night TV movie, and I was happy to be a
part of it. Working with the storied company was cool in and of
itself, but it was also refreshing as hell because *The Love Bug* was

as family-friendly as you could get. After I'd been appearing in unrated, mostly genre stuff for almost twenty years, it felt nice to broaden the ol' repertoire and act in something without a single drop of blood.

Not long after *The Love Bug*, I got a "development deal" with Disney – the sort of nebulous agreement that says you both want to do something together, but nothing is set in stone, so over the course of six months or a year you mutually look for projects. If nothing materializes, you often find yourself cast in shows produced by your partner – in this case, the ABC/Disney sitcom *Ellen*, as her uptight boss.

During the course of the development deal, I realized what a huge catalogue of material Disney had at its disposal, so I sifted through their catalogue. When I came across *Dick Tracy*, I perked up. That would make a *great* weekly TV show – very stylized, with fifty years' worth of stories already laid out in comic book form. I also thought I could have pulled off a convincing, if slightly snarky, Dick Tracy.

The notion was compelling enough for the TV mucky-mucks to kick it around, but eventually the idea was kyboshed by a Mr. Warren Beatty, who still had some control over the rights. The sands of time on my deal ran out and I returned to my exploitation-based career, remaining positively Disney-free for almost a decade.

My return to the House of Mouse came in the form of the kids' movie *Sky High*. Reading the script, I was immediately reminded of those Disney movies from my childhood – it had a fun premise (a high school for superheroes); it was fast-paced and had fanciful special effects. My character, Coach Boomer, determined who would be a Sidekick or a Hero at the school. It was an enjoyable, over-the-top part.

Being a decent budgeted studio movie, *Sky High* afforded

an interesting, appropriate cast, with more than a few nods to the past – chief among them was Kurt Russell, who head-lined Disney movies when he was a kid. Supporting Kurt was a great roster of veteran actors, like Kelly Preston, Lynda Carter and Cloris Leachman. *Kids in the Hall* comedians Dave Foley and Kevin McDonald added their own loopiness to the proceedings. But the anchor of the movie was a solid crew of young actors, led by Michael Angarano, Danielle Panabaker and Mary Elizabeth Winstead.

Disney bought Marvel, so how come this never happened?

One of the most unusual aspects of filming *Sky High* was that the young actors did a huge amount of their own stunts – and I'm not talking about general rough-housing; I'm talking about pulling kids through walls. It must have been something director Mike Mitchell was interested in pursuing, so all of the applicable actors went to a sort of "stunt school" to train for harnesses and flying rigs. The end result is very effective, with actors seamlessly blending into the stunts and special effects.

Overall, I enjoyed the movie and I think a lot of kids did too. I meet a lot of young adults who saw *Sky High* when they were little. One of the perks of my job is that I get to go from *watching* movies like that to *being in* movies like that.

LOVEMAKING

When the first editions of *If Chins Could Kill: Confessions of a B Movie Actor* came out, my publisher printed five thousand copies, which meant they didn't have a tremendous amount of confidence in sales. I hadn't appeared on the radar of St. Martin's Press yet. They weren't convinced I was actually a celebrity. No promotional calendar had been set up, so I had to finagle a tour schedule on my own.

Fortunately, the first edition sold out quickly and the publishers ordered additional printings. The book took off and became a *New York Times* bestseller within two months.

It turns out the publishing business is no different from the movie business. If you have a success, everyone scrambles quickly to get the next one out.

"You know, Bruce," my editor explained, "booksellers like writers who write. Writers who crank out book after book, year after year."

"Like a literary metronome," I added.

"Exactly. You gotta write another book."

When a career author cultivates that reliable rhythm, publishers, distributors and bookstores can plan ahead for next year's release. Relationships with retailers develop and they do their part to promote you. Along with all the love comes the pressure to deliver. Hilariously, for a guy who had never written a single book, I now was under pressure to write another – and fast.

Therein lay the rub. A book about my career as a B movie actor seemed like a one-off – and a "cultish" one at best. Like a slow-growing oak, it could take fifteen years for me to amass enough anecdotes for another autobiography.

FOREPLAY

Like Hollywood, publishing believes in formulas. If something worked before, it'll work again. My first book was non-fiction told from my point of view, so that formula should work again.

We started kicking around the idea of something called *The Manual* (aka *The Man Book*). It was intended to be a book of advice for men, a satirical vehicle for me to "play" a macho, know-it-all smart-ass, who felt entitled to dispense manly man advice.

My sketch for the cover.

Despite whipping up an outline and a few proofs for the cover, no one really got excited about the concept. The rapid development of my second book entered a glacial funk.

An editor named Barry Neville was brought in to reinvigorate the deal and guide me though the development. We spitballed concepts and bounced ideas off of each other in a very free-form way, still leaning heavily toward a guidebook for relationships. A few more outlines were hashed out about different aspects of relationships and we started thinking of some funny story lines. Finally, I said, "Wait, Barry, do you realize if we keep going in this direction, we're going to end up with a novel instead?"

What was once intended to be a sarcastic advice book was now being plotted as a novel called *Make Love the Bruce Campbell Way*, a silly Hollywood adventure with a schmo *named* Bruce Campbell at the core of it. The premise was a B movie actor finally gets into an A movie called *Let's Make Love* and it all goes to hell in a handcart – a completely self-referential romp behind the curtain of Hollywood.

The idea was to use real characters and place them in credible scenarios. In some parallel universe, for example, there could have been a movie called *Let's Make Love* directed by Mike Nichols, starring Richard Gere and Renée Zellweger. It could have happened.

Barry and I burned up a year and a half struggling with an angle, but once the story clicked I was able to wrap my head around it and take control. Now that I was dealing with fiction, it was easy to lay out this whacky tale in three acts, like a motion picture screenplay.

In any story, there is a main conflict. In a three-act structure, the first act is the introduction of the problem, the second act confronts the problem and the final act serves to resolve the problem. It's all about a character's journey to overcome a physical challenge, an emotional change or a cabin full of undead friends.

In the case of *Make Love the Bruce Campbell Way*, my character, Foyl, is a wisecracking doorman who doles out love advice to Richard Gere. Hoping to prove himself worthy in such an A-list environment, "Bruce" embarks on a fantastic journey of romantic discovery to prepare for his role.

Unfortunately for the fictitious production, my B movie, low-budget sensibilities infect the production and cause irreparable harm. A disgruntled studio executive, fired from *Army of Darkness* years before, is secretly behind the troubles, but he blames everything on Bruce. In a valiant Act Three, Bruce has to go undercover, infiltrate the studio, reveal the true culprit and clear his name – kind of like *Mission: Impossible* with cheap gags.

EXPLICIT IMAGES

With my first book, both a stylistic precedent and a personal preference were set by using a ton of photographs and images. For the autobiography, we could rely on actual archival photographs, clippings and memorabilia. For *Make Love,* we wanted the same density of images, but, because it was fiction, we had to make the images up from scratch – like *all of them.*

In the manuscript, I referenced fake movies and had scenarios of lunching with Elizabeth Taylor, getting in a fistfight with Richard Gere, hanging out with Mike Nichols, being a doorman, et cetera. But, since none of it really happened, I had to recruit my old photographer buddy Mike Ditz to undertake a massive photo shoot. Together, we created the poses for the fake photographs, screen captures, posters and character gags that appeared throughout the book.

I sent more than two hundred staged photos to my graphics guy and overall life coach, Craig "Kif" Sanborn (he added the life coach crap). Kif had been helping me with all my publishing projects over the years and this was his biggest test. A self-taught graphic designer, Kif had become much more advanced in the world of Photoshop, so he was able to take the reference photos and turn them into whatever we needed. Out of the 158 photographs, screenshots, posters, book covers and scans featured in

Make Love the Bruce Campbell Way, only four of them are images that actually existed.

Make Love also made it to the *New York Times* bestseller list, which was a relief, because as my first "fictional" book, these were uncharted waters.

For the audiobook, I decided to stick with the motion picture theme of the material and present the story in a radio play format – like a movie, without the picture. I love the controlled world of sound, so this was a fun, if epic, endeavor. I gathered up all the usual suspect actors, gave them each multiple roles and backed them up with movie-style sound effects to create a realistic environment.

Make Love the Bruce Campbell Way was released, incongruously, as a comedy album as opposed to an "audiobook." I made my deal with a record company, rather than an audiobook distributor, so it wound up in what I would consider a strange "catalogue." If you can find it, I hope you enjoy listening to the most expensive audiobook ever produced.

With two bestsellers, there was pressure for me to pump out a third book as soon as possible, but above all else, I was an actor and filmmaker. Like the salmon spawning, it was time to return to B movies and defend the world from alien termites and mad doctors!

THE BIG THAW

As a young man growing up in Michigan during the cold war, I was taught that the Soviet Union was the original "Evil Empire." I routinely participated in "duck and cover" nuclear attack drills during grade school. Even though I didn't sense the significance of what was happening outside my suburban cocoon, it was still scary stuff and it bothered me that someone I didn't even know might drop a big-ass bomb on me.

And because kids weren't allowed to fight in real combat yet, we held up our end with a mighty war of words, spouting ignorant, angry rhetoric at nobody in particular.

"Hey, Don, see any *commies* today?" I'd ask my brother, hanging out in the woods behind our house.

"Nope," Don replied with a rueful shake of his flattopped head. "But those *Russkies* are gonna get it if I catch 'em creepin' around."

Right or wrong, the only thing we allowed our midwestern selves to have in common with those vodka-swilling bastards

Tank Brothers: The Campbell boys prepare to defend against the Reds with our homemade tank.

was bad winters. Even by the time Don enlisted in the military, several decades after our wooded reconnaissance, Russia was still the number-one bad boy on the block. As a result, the big "thaw" didn't happen in my family until Russia imploded in the late eighties.

Through a fortuitous turn of events, I would live to face down my mortal enemy – not at a tense border standoff or as a result of some nuclear holocaust – but by making movies for the Sci-Fi Channel...

To clarify, the gig was in Sofia, Bulgaria, a former Soviet *satellite*. But to me, Bulgaria, part of the former "Soviet Bloc," was still a world apart, conjuring up medieval landscapes populated by stooped peasants, sporting hairy moles.

"Why Bulgaria?" I asked Jeff, the producer who packaged and financed the two movies I was supposed to make.

"Why?" he asked back in a tone one would use with a moron. "Do the math. Bulgarians make a hundred and ten dollars a month. Hard to compete with that. You want a Steadicam, don't you?"

To a producer in the low-budget movie business, that kind of cost savings is magic. To an actor, director or writer – you know, anyone who is actually *making* the movie – shooting a film in a strange land for the sole reason of saving money is a kind of madness that you either buy into or write about in a book because you can't believe what you've experienced.

For me, it was the latter.

"Okay, so have you noticed that there are virtually no people of color in Bulgaria?"

"Yeah. I noticed."

Jeff's responses were always like those of a Mafia don – short and matter-of-fact.

"Okay, and you noticed that my script is set in East L.A., where half of the characters are *people of color*? You did read the script, didn't you?"

"Yeah. So? Shoot around it."

You can't "shoot around" something that is *inherent* conceptually, but I wasn't done stating the obvious.

"Even if I could, have you noticed that all the street signs in Sofia [the city where we were to shoot] and all the giant billboards are in Cyrillic?"

"...Cyrillic?"

"Yeah, it's the upside-down and backwards lettering that looks like Russian only it isn't. It's all gobbledygook."

"So?"

I wish he would stop saying "So?"

"Can we afford to change all the signs?"

"No."

"And I'm assuming you're gonna say the same thing about the cars."

"What about them? They're a little weird looking. You slap on a U.S. license plate and away you go."

"Jeff, you've been around this city – to the clubs anyway. I don't know about you, but East L.A. doesn't have 1980s-era Soviet SUVs driving around next to those two-cylinder East German cars with a shell made out of pressed paper."

There was a long pause as Jeff, in his don-like state, pondered my logic. "Do you want to make this movie or not?"

At least he didn't say "So?"

The actual mission of going to Bulgaria was to make two

movies. One was *Man with the Screaming Brain*, which I would also direct. The other was *Humans in Chains* (the original, more compelling title), an idea almost as old, which my good friend Josh Becker was to write and direct.

I called Josh to explain the situation. "Hey, Josh, I've got good news and bad news."

"What's the good news?"

"Sci-Fi wants two flicks. I've got one, but I need a second script, so let's make *Humans in Chains*."

"Great, what's the bad news?"

"We're shooting in Bulgaria and you're going first."

ROAD WARRIORS

The flight to Bulgaria from Medford, Oregon, was uneventful, with a short, seven-hour layover in Frankfurt, Germany. Josh Becker and I knew what we were getting into. We cut our teeth together in New Zealand on *Hercules: The Legendary Journeys*, *Xena: Warrior Princess* and *Jack of All Trades* and were used to the assimilation process of working in faraway lands – or so we thought.

Bulgaria was something else. One of the most shocking things to experience once you get beyond the protective bilingual bubble of flight attendants and airport officials was the utter lack of English spoken in the country. Of the two hundred people claiming bags the rainy night Ida and I arrived, only one other person aside from us spoke English.

"Mr. Camp-Bell?" a voice inquired behind me.

I turned to face Ivan, the man who was appointed my driver/ translator/everyman. In time, I would regard Ivan as all that and more – he was my savior. Ivan wasn't the pasty, shaven-headed soccer hooligan type I assumed populated Eastern Europe. Ivan had black hair, half-hidden but intense green eyes and a dark complexion. There were few times when a cigarette didn't dangle from his mouth – or almost any other Bulgarian's.

I remember peeking through the window of a quaint little cafeteria. There were twenty-five neatly arranged tables, each adorned with an ashtray. Bulgaria in 2004 did not play the "smoking section" or "smoke-free" game

The official Bulgarian symbol of health and longevity.

– far from it. An indelible image at a popular restaurant was a father eating dinner with his wife and two small kids, keeping a lit cigarette at the table, taking puffs between bites as if it were a side dish of mashed peas.

I spent the first three days driving around Sofia, Bulgaria, with my mouth mostly hanging open in disbelief. I had read the history books about how Russia invaded so-and-so and it all kind of rolled off, but to see the aftermath of nearly forty years of Russian domination was a sociologically unpleasant adjustment.

In Sofia alone, it was impossible to count the number of partially completed building projects of every scope and variety. The halt in construction wasn't from a housing collapse – communism *itself* had collapsed. After 1989, state-owned property in Bulgaria lost its meaning, so nobody knew who owned anything anymore or who paid for what. Abandoned construction projects dotted the landscape, rife with anomalies – a brand-new, five-hundred-seat movie theater (stadium-style, with reclining seats), where I showed the cast and crew *Spider-Man II*, was constructed next door to a hulking shell of a building that had lain fallow for fifteen years.

Cultural oddities abounded. The use – or lack thereof – of seat belts confounded me. In a fifteen-person passenger van scouting locations, I was the only person who wore a seat belt. Maybe Driver's Education in Bulgaria didn't include screenings of the vomit-inducing *Signal 13* or *Death on the Highway*, where you could see in bloody, you-are-there detail, how seat belts save lives. Ivan chuckled to himself every time I fastened my seat belt – and each time, I would challenge his logic.

"Why do you wear seat belts?" Ivan asked.

"Because we're in a large, heavy object hurling down the road at twice the posted speed limit. I mean, you're a great driver, Ivan, but physics are physics."

"Oh yes?" he countered. "A friend of mine was in car accident. He did not wear his seat belt and was thrown free from car and lived. His friend, who wore seat belt, was killed."

"Okay," I said, shaking my head in disbelief. "I'll give you the one-in-fifteen-thousand chance of that happening, but statistics are on my side."

I enjoyed watching the elegance of Ivan spotting a police car, reaching over and buckling his seat belt until the car passed, then deftly unsnapping it.

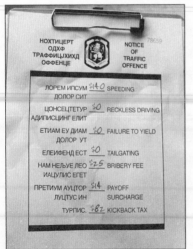

I guess it's a cliché to bemoan crooked cops in foreign countries, but I suppose if you look at the reasons behind it the reality becomes more sympathetic. Police in Bulgaria made scarcely more than Joe Blow citizen, which was Jack Shit, but they had a weapon the average citizen didn't possess: the ability to extort.

Ivan was pulled over one day by an officer waving a red stick with a flat round top, painted with a symbol. When we stopped, Ivan got out of the car and walked around the corner with the police officer to "deal with the situation." A few minutes later, I learned that Ivan had refused to play ball with the officer.

The claim was that Ivan was talking on his cell phone while driving, a transgression worth about ten bucks in cash – to the cop. If the "fine" was not paid and the cop had to write an actual ticket, the fee would become exorbitant. Normally, Bulgarians would roll their eyes, give the guy half of what he asked for and be on their way. Ivan was a different kind of guy who wasn't enamored with what he considered robbery. His conversation went something like this:

"I'm not paying it."

"Are you crazy?" the cop asked, incredulous. "Do you know how much the ticket is if you send it in?"

"It doesn't matter. I work for a company that will pay it. Write me the ticket. I'm not giving you anything."

The cop had no other choice than to write up the ticket and let us go. I have a sneaking suspicion that somehow, some way, Ivan made the ticket "go away."

BETTER THAN COMMUNISM

If you like to drink, stop by Bulgaria sometime. If you like cheap vodka, book your flight right now. It is no state secret that the Russians like their vodka. The Bulgarians, although rightfully separate beings, perhaps by way of almost half a century of influence, developed their own taste for it – and the stuff was readily available. Unlike the United States, where moral codes and doctor warnings keep us from drinking twenty-four hours a day, a culture without those restrictions sees the world through different cocktail glasses. As a result, it was no big deal to get your hands on a large bottle of vodka Sunday morning at 9:00 on almost any street corner for about seven U.S. dollars.

Personally, I enjoyed the Bulgarian beer. Most of it, even the crappy stuff, was better than our staples in the United States. My friend Josh and I particularly enjoyed the brand Kamenitza. It was so "off-brand," the restaurants wouldn't carry it, but the stuff was a premium lager by any standards. After three or four of them we coined the ad slogan: "Kamenitza – it's *better* than communism!"

Aside from the negative effects of alcohol, what I witnessed was a country in emergence. Under communism, you were not allowed to gather in groups and there were no such places as restaurants or cafés because, God forbid, original thoughts and ideas might get exchanged! Now, Sofia was a virtual explosion of places to eat, some of them first-rate, and it was exciting to witness.

One of the many pluses of Sofia was that Ida and I felt really safe. Ida walked home alone several times from events well after midnight and she never felt threatened or in danger. Under communism, if you got caught stealing, raping or killing you disappeared, so nobody dared to get away with anything.

With emerging capitalism came a demand for service-oriented, "quick grab" vocations – like driving a cab. In Sofia, it was easy to catch a cab but not so easy to get where you were going. After a few solid misfires, I realized that to get around town I had to adapt. Ivan translated the address of my apartment into Cyrillic and had it laminated on a little card. That way, languages be damned, I never even had to talk to a given cab driver – just hand over the card and that would be that.

It was nice to have a plan, but I wouldn't call it foolproof. After I confidently handed over my address card, the driver would rattle off a litany of questions in Bulgarian. My response would be in the form of a shrug, which would cause him to shrug back and we would begin the journey. If all seemed hopeless, I'd hop out, throw the guy a few leva (the official currency), jump in another cab, get closer, then repeat the process as many times as it took to either get home or recognize one of the many oversized monuments to Soviet glory near my apartment. The towering statue of a peasant woman clutching both a child and a rifle usually bailed me out.

Capitalism meant the arrival of goods previously unheard of in Bulgaria – like VCRs. Technopolis was a brand-new retailer for all things electronic. It was positively Best Buy in size and scope, but strolling the aisles for living-on-location gadgets I noticed a lack of high-tech consumers.

"Why is it so dead in this store, Ivan?" I asked.

"Simple. You have to pay cash. They don't take credit cards."

I wondered if American stores would be as empty if we only bought items we could afford and actually had the cash in our pockets. What a concept.

Tourism was beginning to pick up and Sofia was a hot spot for Eurotrash looking to have a cheap, good time. With the influx of foreigners, including American filmmakers, local panhandlers had new targets unfamiliar with their ways. The leading charity seekers were the Gypsies, or Roma. Personally, I have no issue with Roma or any other ethnic group, but getting the stump of a baby's missing arm shoved in my face took some getting used to.

The Roma were very persistent in their begging. A needy mother would hold her child aloft, stump prominently displayed a little too close for comfort. When I declined, the woman simply followed me down the street, refusing to take no for an answer. After a few of these disturbing encounters, I discovered the magic bullet: speak *French* to them. Americans are well known as suckers around the globe, but the French are much better at being detached and indifferent. The Roma must have known this, because as soon as I said, "Je ne sais pas si le Cameon pourra traverser le pont," in my best French (translation: "I don't know if the truck will be able to cross the bridge"), my stalker turned on a heel and never bothered me again.

WARNING: Eye contact with a Roma constitutes a binding marriage/adoption agreement.

The Roma were doing what they had to do, I suppose. Scorned for decades, mistrusted, they are still mostly ignored in Europe, and yet Roma are seemingly everywhere. I always wondered, *What does a Roma man or woman do all day?* Their main mode of transportation was a horse and buggy. The image of a Roma driving these carts around hasn't changed in centuries – like a snapshot from another time, only it still existed.

One sleepy Sunday morning, I heard *clip-clop, clip-clop, clip-clop* – the unmistakable sound of a horse's gait – from the street below my apartment. I shuffled over for a look. A Roma man pulled his cart, loaded with cardboard, to a halt in front of a Dumpster. After some motivated rummaging, he found a few pieces of cardboard, tossed them atop his pile and *clip-clop*ped away.

I made some morning tea, then heard another *clip-clop, clip-clop, clip-clop* sound approaching. This time, another Roma man pulled his cart full of metal scraps to a halt at the same Dumpster and added a few prize pieces to his collection. The construction site across the street was an added "supplier." Now I just waited, looking out the window, wondering who would come next and what they were looking for. It didn't take long. A few minutes later, a Roma woman arrived on foot, pulling a cart. She was looking for clothing and found several pairs of nylons. It was the ultimate form of recycling. Ida and I later noticed that clothing items, or broken appliances, were sometimes placed in the Dumpster neatly and purposefully by tenants, because they knew that the Roma were going to search for items anyway.

The Roma may be considered second-class citizens by some, but I almost lost my wife to one – at least in her heart. Ida was walking down a side street one sunny afternoon and a "stunningly beautiful" (her words) Roma man, driving a horse and buggy, turned the corner in her direction. Ida relishes telling the story, to *anyone* who will listen, about this mid-twenties demigod of a man with caramel, flawless skin, penetrating eyes and sinewy muscles, passing her in ultra-slow motion. Their eyes met for just a moment – but it was a *moment.*

At the end of Ida's story, I always have to wave my hand in front of her face to bring her back to reality.

DOG DAY AFTERNOON

I live in rural Oregon, so I've seen plenty of wildlife, but not the Bulgarian kind. As Americans, growing up on iconic animal TV programs and movies, like *Lassie* and even *Air Bud*, we get the naïve sense that, as "man's best friend," loyal canines are living the dream all over the world – fetching sticks or slobbery tennis balls for appreciative owners who feed them food that makes their coats shiny. Sadly, it's a very distorted and untrue picture of what our shaggy four-legged friends are really faced with beyond the local dog park.

It's a pretty basic situation: Whenever a country struggles just to put food on the table of its human citizens, everything else gets sloppy seconds. Dogs in Sofia, Bulgaria, ran in packs, partially out of instinct, but I would guess it was also for protection. Nobody really wanted to mess with nearly half a dozen hungry, mangy dogs. I had to make peace with this sad situation early on.

My first visit to the "production office" made it abundantly clear that I was not in the land of Lassie anymore. Upon my getting out of the production van, a pack of dogs peered out from scrubby fields and the relative safety of a crumbling building. Ornate concrete pots, once used to display large plantings in front of an abandoned office building, now served as uncomfortable beds for several canines.

Creeped out by this horrible situation, I returned the next day with the largest bag of dry dog food I could find. This time, I was ready for the mangy mutts and began the ritual of whistling as loud as I could – a skill honed at Tiger Stadium in Detroit as a kid – in an attempt to teach the dogs that the shrill sound was synonymous with eating food. It didn't take long for them to catch on, and soon I became the Pied Piper of homeless canines. One loud whistle brought out at least half a dozen dogs of all sizes and dispositions to see what was being served up.

But just because I provided food didn't mean we were going to become fast friends. To feed dogs in Bulgaria, you poured out a healthy glob of food and got the hell out of the way. You didn't pet these pooches, which had developed a latent mistrust of humans. I tried once and almost lost a finger, so I was content to provide a bright spot in their otherwise dismal lives.

THE UNTOUCHABLES

Bulgaria was racing toward the future (and has subsequently joined the volatile European Union), but remnants of communism were everywhere. When the central government lost control, many of the local power brokers simply stepped in and things got done "mafia-style." When I was prepping *Man with the Screaming Brain,* the local newspaper ran a story of two men dressed as priests who entered a restaurant, found their target, blew him away with automatic weapons and simply walked out – presumably to get back to the rectory for afternoon mass…

Bodyguards seemed to be everywhere. It was not unusual to see a sedan with black-tinted windows racing down the street with four ninja-like bodyguards flanking the car on motorcycles. These guys made no effort to hide their guns – they *wanted* you to know that armaments were part of the security detail.

Traveling back from set one day, we were on a road with a speed limit of 35 miles per hour. Traffic was thick and moving even slower than the posted limit. Out of nowhere, we heard the roar of engines as four black SUVs passed us in the opposite lane going around 70 miles an hour. Cars on both sides of the narrow street lurched to get out of the way. Ivan guessed that the cars were driven by mafia bodyguards who had little regard for anyone else.

A scene filmed at the Hotel Rankoff almost gave Ivan a heart attack. The sequence required a lot of vehicles coming and going in front of the swank hotel. The best way to accomplish this was to block the street and reroute civilian traffic. This was arranged, so we presumably "owned" the street for the shooting day.

You know what they say about *assuming*. No sooner had we gotten our first shot of the scene when a large SUV maneuvered around a guard blocking the street and proceeded to cut through the heart of our busy set. Joel, my dutiful assistant director, waved his arms and stepped directly in front of the SUV.

"Hey, hey, stop. Back off!" he shouted.

The SUV, driven by a little old woman who could barely see above the wheel, inched forward, undeterred. Joel became incensed and slammed his hands on the hood of the car.

"Hey, did you hear what I said? Get this car the *fuck* out of here!"

Joel was not going to lose another minute of shooting and forced the old woman to take the detour. Relieved that we could get back to work, I noticed that Ivan had a very different reaction to the event.

Translation: "Yet Another American Assistant Director Found Dead"

"Joel should be very careful for the rest of the day today," Ivan warned, nodding gravely to Joel, who was back to the business of running the set.

"Why?"

"Because the neighborhood she was driving to is very exclusive. How you say? *High-end*. There are only three types of people who live there: politicians, athletes and mafia. Joel better hope he didn't piss off the mother of a mob boss. They will come back and kill him – today."

Fortunately, Joel was not murdered in cold blood, but we did get our schedule severely messed with courtesy of Russia's Prime Minister Putin. It turned out his wife was coming to Sofia for a visit and she needed the entire hotel to herself.

PAIR ANNOYED

Learning to shrug off the daily twists and turns was just part of life in Bulgaria. Hell, I had nothing to complain about – I had a job and a third-floor apartment with no elevator! The place we chose in Sofia came at the recommendation of Ivan. He had grown up in the neighborhood and considered it "quiet."

Our neighbors were quiet, for sure – almost *too* quiet. Culturally, the passing of someone in the hallway of our building never required the friendly nod or "hello," because people didn't want to know anything – about anyone. Americans will spew their life story, physical ailments included, within ten minutes of meeting a complete stranger. In Bulgaria, there was more of a sense that information was "need to know."

The daily greeting in Bulgaria is usually "Doberden," loosely translated: "whazzup?" Whenever I offered it up while hauling sacks of groceries three flights up, the reaction was usually a surprised look, like "did that stranger just speak to me randomly?"

The privacy thing was evident in the number of locks on the average apartment door, which was around three. Our third-floor door had two locks, vertically aligned. The top one was a conventional dead-bolt deal-e-o and the bottom lock controlled a horizontal bar that secured the door side to side.

I got to use those locks one night, but not in a good way. In movies and on TV shows, I've played a lot of heroic characters, willing to put their butts on the line for the greater good. Sadly, in real life I'm mostly a coward. This became evident, yet again, one night after consuming a particular herb that grows naturally on God's green earth. One might assume that certain paranoiac tendencies are the result of such herbal consumption, and, sure enough, moments after partaking I heard excited shouting echo up from the street. I walked to the back of the apartment and looked out the window, just in time to hear a resident on the ground floor shout, "Americanski!"

Son of a bitch! They're on to me! I need to get word to brother Don right now and tell him that the commies finally got me! They've been spying on me and they must have smelled the herb and notified the authorities! I'm screwed!

To inflame my paranoia, I turned back to see flashing lights from the street in front of the building – the alternating, multi-colored kind that cops use. I ran to the front window, feeling a little bit like tough guy John Dillinger on the run. Sure enough – two uniformed police officers were approaching our building.

"Shit! Ida, what should we do?"

"Nothing. Stop freaking out."

It took a while for the cops to work their way up to us. It appeared that they were talking with residents on each floor. Then a dreaded sound: *boots on barren concrete steps.* Fueled by THC, the increasing sound became positively Edgar Allan Poe-like in its constant, growing intensity.

Desperate for a plan, I whirled to Ida. "Ida, as my wife, I *order* you to go out there and deal with them!"

"You *what?*"

KNOCK-KNOCK.

I half-pulled and half-pushed her to the door. "Talk to them *outside* the door, not *at* the door."

"What's the difference?" Ida asked, growing more annoyed.

"They might try and force their way in. If you take the conversation outside, it's harder for them to break the door down."

Ida didn't respond, just shot me a classic "I am so disappointed in you" look, opened the door and stepped outside.

My heart was sending so much blood through my veins that I became light-headed and experienced strange images of Russian gulags in Siberia and the dread of scurvy. It was all too much, so I *locked the door* – that's right: I locked my wife out of the apartment in front of two strange policemen who could have easily carted her away.

Ida and the cops were experiencing their own foibles. The

way the lighting works in Bulgarian apartment hallways is that you twist a timer, which turns on an overhead light for a given period of time – and it's never enough. This is to prevent costly waste, of course, but it's overkill. Another timer was at the base of the steps up to our apartment. You could turn it all you want, but nine out of ten times I'd have to dive for the timer on the landing of the third floor to avoid being plunged into total darkness.

The cops had turned the timer on, but it became forgotten in their ill-fated attempt to communicate. Ida knew three words of Bulgarian and the police knew exactly zero words of English. It made for a short, frustrating conversation. Ida was pretty much convinced that the cops

With local graffiti like this, it's hard for an American not to be paranoid.

were there to investigate a robbery, not perform a celebrity drug bust, but none of it mattered because the hall lights, with timer expired, turned off. In pitch-blackness, Ida screamed at the top of her lungs.

"It was a scream of innocence," she later recounted.

But as Ida turned and groped for the apartment doorknob, she realized that she was locked out and she screamed again, which made the cops freak out and argue while fumbling for the twisty timer. Eventually, the lights came back on, the shouting subsided and the cops, not wanting anything more to do with the situation, got the hell out of there.

Back in the apartment, Ida slammed the door behind her and delivered an impressive "what for" speech. I don't remember the particulars, but she used the words "incompetent" and "useless" more than once.

APOCALYPSE HOW

We've all heard the term "sweatshop." It conjures up images of overworked women packed into inhumane conditions. Bulgaria wasn't anywhere near as bad, but my costume fittings were in a second-floor sewing "factory" with a dozen small, chain-smoking women in white uniforms who stopped everything in unison as I stepped through the door. They looked at me like I wasn't supposed to be there. I stared back at them like I wasn't supposed to be there.

Turning to leave in embarrassment, I was stopped by, "It's okay, Mr. Camp-bell. You are in the right place."

I turned back to see a young, alert woman and her boss, an older, more traditional "battle-axe" of a woman.

"I am Raliza, assistant costumer," the young woman said, offering her hand in a businesslike fashion. "This is Katya, the costume designer."

"Hello, Katya, how are you doing? Nice to meet you."

I extended my hand and Katya smiled and nodded but did

not respond.

"She can't speak English, can she?"

Raliza shook her head. "Not a word."

"Okay, looks like it's you and me," I said, shrugging. "Shall we try some stuff on?"

In Josh's *Alien Apocalypse* (the new, "catchy" title), my character wears a space suit for the entire film, so it had to be versatile, durable, and not make me look like a dork. The first fitting didn't last long. I put on what was the equivalent of a scaled-down Michelin Man outfit – white and very puffy.

The prototype for my heroic space suit.

I turned to Raliza. "Have you ever heard of the Stay Puft Marshmallow Man?"

She smiled. "No, but I think I know what you mean. Too puffy?"

"Yeah, can we rip all the stuffing out of the legs and half of it out of the jacket?"

"Of course."

I looked to Katya for some form of approval. She smiled and nodded.

I looked in their full-length mirror again. Another issue was the shoulders.

"Hey, Raliza, I'm a good guy in this movie and he kind of saves the day, blah, blah, blah. Can we avoid the droopy shoulders and get some padding in there?"

"Of course. Come back tomorrow and we will fit again."

The next day I stopped by the sewing factory, the chain-smoking sewing women didn't look at me like I wasn't supposed to be there. In fact, they didn't even look up. Raliza was ready with a new version of my space suit. The "puffy" issue was solved and the shoulder issue was solved, but to a ridiculous degree. They not only padded the shoulders, they padded the shoulders so much that I looked like a superhero crossed with a Mexican wrestler.

"Well, that's certainly heroic, I'll give you that. Think we could get the padding to stop where my actual shoulder does?"

"Of course," Raliza assured me.

I looked to Katya. She smiled and nodded. That was the essence of our relationship for two films – lots of smiles, nods and shrugs.

When I was notified about a makeup test, I got very excited – tests weren't something that low-budget films normally do. I guessed they had their act together after all.

After feeding the dogs in the production office parking lot, I made my way into a dank room for my makeup test with Petia, the "key" of her department. She scrutinized my face for a moment, then asked very simply, "What would you like?"

"Makeup," I replied. "The good stuff."

Normally, that's about all that transpires between actor and makeup artist. Under most conditions, they exchange pleasantries or gossip, because the makeup artist already knows the color of base they want to use, the type of concealer, the blush, the powder – the whole routine. Bulgarian crews, I was starting to learn, were completely different in their approach. They have the tools and the skills readily available, but harkening back to the days of communism, thinking ahead wasn't part of the plan.

Make no mistake, Bulgarians are hardworking, generally pleasant people, but Petia wasn't going to "pitch" a pre-thought-out makeup plan like some artists do or have a long discussion of makeup theories or makeup brands. I simply had to tell Petia exactly what I wanted – item by item. There was a fine display of makeup in front of her, but I had to choose it. This was panic-inducing, because I honestly hadn't paid attention for so long, I didn't have a clue where to start.

"Uhhh, let's start with some…base?"

"Light or dark?"

"Well, I've been on a spaceship for fifty years, so I would really be pasty and tired looking, but I'm not gonna look like a vampire. Let's go for 'slightly tan.' "

Petia grabbed a container of base and applied it evenly. "Anything else?"

"Uh, yeah," I said, failing to recall the familiar pattern of application. "Let's cover up those bags under the eyes, uh, add some…blush on the highlights, like the bridge of my nose and cheeks, and, uh…skip the eyeliner."

Eventually, when Petia was done, I looked enough like my "movie self" to be satisfied, but I left the session terrified that I had omitted something elemental and would therefore wind up photographing like a rodeo clown.

My confidence was not boosted on the way out as I saw an early test of wigs and beards. In Josh Becker's post-apocalyptic story, everyone has long hair and beards. That sounds reasonable, but not if the end results looked like the beards were on the heads and the wigs were on the faces. It's safe to say that while *Man with the Screaming Brain* will never make anyone's Top Ten Best Ever list, *Alien Apocalypse* easily had the worst hair and beard work since our Super-8mm movies.

Making Josh shoot first was the smartest thing I ever did. From his torturous, pioneering labors I was able to cherry-pick all my actors from his cast. Acting across from them in *Alien Apocalypse,* I found out who knew their lines, hit their marks and did well under pressure.

I was glad for the local Bulgarian actors. The Sci-Fi Channel alone was responsible for employing former Eastern Bloc actors by the truckload. It's always amusing to hear actors from distant lands fake an American accent. The Kiwis did it pretty well for *Hercules* and *Xena*, but the Bulgarians had much less access to the English language and certainly no need to learn it, so it didn't really work. This reality prompted Josh to warn me that he was going to have to replace 99 percent of their voices back in the States and that I should be careful not to overlap any of my dialogue. If I talked over their lines, I'd have to replace mine, too.

The sudden rush to shoot English-targeted material in Bulgaria and Romania caused a huge need for actors who could actually speak like Americans. Producers, trying to fill the need, scoured embassies, military bases – you name it. Jonas Talkington was one such man. A year before I worked with him, he was humping water to small Bulgarian villages in the Peace Corps. Now the son of a bitch had been in six movies in eighteen months – about the same pace John Wayne cranked out cheapo Republic Westerns in the thirties – just because he was already in Bulgaria and he was American.

Among other roles, Jonas played a police officer in *Boogeyman 3*, a SWAT leader in *Mansquito* and a radar man in *Behind Enemy Lines II: Axis of Evil*. By the time Josh and I were finished shooting in Bulgaria, Jonas could add "bounty hunter" and "Larry the sleazy businessman" to his résumé.

From a business point of view, Bulgaria was pretty easy to deal with. You didn't need a work permit to ply your trade there – you just had to leave the country (crossing into, say, Serbia) and come back every thirty days. Known as the "Serbian U-Turn," this was a clever way for authorities to keep tabs on someone from another country.

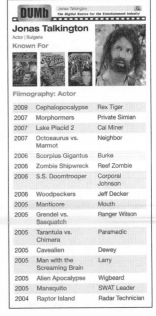

DUMb
Jonas Talkington
The Digital Source for the Entertainment Industry

Jonas Talkington
Actor | Bulgaria

Known For

Filmography: Actor

Year	Title	Role
2009	Cephalopocalypse	Rex Tiger
2007	Morphormers	Private Simian
2007	Lake Placid 2	Cal Miner
2007	Octosaurus vs. Marmot	Neighbor
2006	Scorpius Gigantus	Burke
2006	Zombie Shipwreck	Reef Zombie
2006	S.S. Doomtrooper	Corporal Johnson
2006	Woodpeckers	Jeff Decker
2005	Manticore	Mouth
2005	Grendel vs. Sasquatch	Ranger Wilson
2005	Tarantula vs. Chimera	Paramedic
2005	Cavealien	Dewey
2005	Man with the Screaming Brain	Larry
2005	Alien Apocalypse	Wigbeard
2005	Mansquito	SWAT Leader
2004	Raptor Island	Radar Technician

While I was able to skirt around the issues (since production took care of it for me), my poor wife, Ida, had to enter the demilitarized zone with scores of Gypsies and dodge angry Greek truck drivers to stay in the country past the initial thirty days. She gave me another "what for" speech when she got back that included words such as "reckless" more than once and phrases such as "never again" two or even three times.

The director of the Occupational Safety and Health Administration (OSHA) would have crapped their official pants if they saw some of the places we filmed. A long van ride to a rock quarry (good for simulating the surface of the moon) took us through what I dubbed "the Valley of Death." I had seen black pollution from coal in Arkansas and yellow pollution from an industrial complex in Detroit, but Bulgaria was the first *red* polluter. The offender was a brick factory. It makes sense, right? Red bricks, red pollution. The density of the noxious particulates was fog-like and filled up an entire valley. It was a good lesson in what life would be like stateside without the costly "scrubbers" we impose on dirty industries.

Yea, though we walk through the Valley of Death, we shall fear no sequels.

I had to get all cozy with co-star Renée O'Connor two stories *below* the production office.

By the way, if I am unable to promote this book because I have since grown an extra head you'll know why. The decision was to clear Soviet-era industrial equipment out of the way, throw dirt on the concrete floor, add some spindly pine trees, and voila – instant romantic forest.

If you survived the trip down the concrete steps to the set, everything else was cake. Railing was non-existent, and if you happened to slip your death would at least be quick because you would be impaled on a menacing tangle of rebar.

This large, underground "area" was creepy and weird. Now used to store oversized turbines, engines and God-knows-what in massive wooden crates, this was apparently the perfect place to stage a romantic forest getaway.

It might have been easier to accomplish this on the opposite side of the room, where the wall had crumbled away entirely, revealing a young forest growing directly out of a massive pile of rubble.

The interesting thing about filmmaking in Bulgaria was that they actually had a thriving film industry under communism. During pre-production, I saw the inside of a massive studio (unavailable to us – long story) that had been used for years. When communism crumbled, many key crew members left for work elsewhere and the whole thing sort of fell apart. As funky as our production was, it was nice to see a recently opened certi-fied Kodak film laboratory return to Sofia – a concrete sign of film production taking hold again after almost twenty years.

Sometimes, making films in foreign lands is more trouble than it's worth. To save money, you haul your ass halfway around the world to shoot in a place where English might as well be Mandarin Chinese – and yet we assume that a local crew would be hip to the type of film we're making or what would seem "normal" to Americans.

This became quite evident on the first take of the "great slave rebellion." Josh's story line provided for a group of slaves held captive by giant bugs to break free and fight back with primi-tive weapons. In this case, the weapon was a bow and arrow. I learned how to shoot an arrow at camp in northern Michigan when I was ten. My mom was a Western movie freak, so I saw

Thankfully, only actors with non-speaking roles were harmed during the volley of arrows.

plenty of "arrow action."

That's all well and good, but when my character, leader of the rebellion, stood up to shout, "Arrows!", the Bulgarian extras let their arrows fly – in every direction. I think the injuries sustained were mostly "same team." It turns out, the Bulgarian prop master, being Bulgarian, hadn't seen as many Westerns as the average American and the extras hadn't either, because nobody noticed that the key element – the notch in the back of the wooden arrow – was missing. Having an arrow firmly astride the bow is critical and it also explained why the arrows kept going willy-nilly until Josh discovered the glitch.

Alien Apocalypse, the first of my two-picture deal with the Sci-Fi Channel, ended after exactly eighteen days of shooting, and *Man with the Screaming Brain* began in earnest.

ATTACK OF THE SCREAMING BRAIN

Making B movies can be exhilarating. The pace is usually brisk and ideas, forced to the surface by a sheer lack of money, are kicked back and forth with the energy usually reserved for a World Cup soccer match.

Directors of these movies (referred to variously as genre, low-budget or schlock) are usually inexperienced, callow and unrealistic, but they are also enthusiastic, daring and indefatigable. The writers, typically working on their first screenplay, have something to prove, and while they revel in their awkward dialogue and stupid (or missing) plot, you'll occasionally find a spark of genius, fanned by simply not knowing what the rules are.

Fellow actors in these second-tier films are often very green with careers on the rise and it's fun to watch them deliver every line of dialogue like it's their last. Mostly, they'll suck, but there is a certain truth in early work that isn't always displayed by the other type of actor found in B movies (and I must insert myself into this category), who are very experienced, with careers more prone to gravity, and are excited just to remember dialogue. But, in the midst of the exhilaration, making B movies can also be a pain in the ass.

I was directing this second project for Sci-Fi and after witnessing the communication challenges while making *Alien Apocalpyse* I decided to go low tech. To improve clarity, I got my hands on a dry-erase board – that way, when words failed I could just draw the damn monkey wrench, or intersection or type of hat. It was a critical, battery-free, fallback device when translators hit an impasse.

The production office was a dead ringer for an abandoned building. In fact, the first floor was abandoned, so we worked on the second floor. The layout was essentially a long hallway with offices on either side, with a large room capping the end. I called this "the smoke pit." The bare, square room was home of the transportation department, the production accountant, the production manager and the production secretary and a steady stream of production assistants. Everyone smoked. Windows, which were plentiful, were never open. I would plan my time there carefully, since I put a premium on the ability to breathe, only venturing into the smog for a quick cup of tea or a question. My office was down the hall. You could tell it was mine because the window was open.

Much of *Man with the Screaming Brain* takes place in and around a large American city. I was able to convince the Sci-Fi Channel to let me change the script to set the story in Bulgaria rather than try to fake Los Angeles with no money. It saved money and innumerable hassles, allowing me to point the camera wherever I wanted and shoot what we saw.

Blocked streets were something of an oddity in Bulgaria and I was informed pretty quickly that they "didn't do that sort of thing." Faced with the prospects of almost constant noise and interruption, I was determined to find a way to fake it all – to do this on some sort of backlot.

What we found blew me away.

When communism fell in the Soviet Union, it fell hard. Building projects, numbering in the thousands, ended abruptly in Bulgaria and other Soviet satellite states. Completed buildings became orphans and stood fallow. One such complex was a creaky military base. It was sprawling, with rows of buildings, streets, parking lots and alleys. Of course, you couldn't see anything because nature had been reclaiming this urban environment for fifteen years. Trees, twenty feet tall, pierced the crumbling asphalt; parking lots and vines covered entire buildings.

Sensing the possibilities, we hired a team of Roma (my begging buddies) to "clean the place up." Every layer the workers peeled back was a joy to behold – a new alley here, an undiscovered sidewalk there. Eventually, the city within a city was revealed and it saved our low-budget asses. Now we had a base of operations, and you can be sure it was named Bruce's Backlot.

Finally, in a city that seemed chaotic, we had control – and we could tailor the production design around what we found. Bruce's Backlot provided a sackful of locations without going anywhere: a hospital exterior (adding a fresh coat of paint only to the parts the  camera saw), an operating room (a converted classroom), a chop shop (in a Quonset hut), the professor's laboratory (once a beautiful auditorium with excellent acoustics), a bridal shop exterior and interior and even a "Gypsy town."

And because we had keys to all the buildings, it was fun during prep to check out random rooms and artifact-hunt. Inside a dank storage facility, we found a pile of moldy Russian uniforms and the gifts of a lifetime for my army man brother, Don: a seemingly new gas mask and a chemical warfare book (in Russian), complete with a bullet hole through the middle of it. Don was delighted to get them, but I was a little nervous about getting those particular items through customs.

As much as I loved the control, Bruce's Backlot couldn't provide all of our locations. We had to venture into the actual city a couple of times and it was always amusing to do so. By this point in the story, my character has escaped from a laboratory after a massive brain operation and runs free in the city, scaring schoolchildren and trying to find out what the hell is going on.

Bear in mind, I have huge scars crossing my forehead and I'm running around in public sporting a disco shirt, Euro-fade blue jeans and white, clown-like shoes. And yet, in Bulgaria, nobody noticed. I would even hang out of the production van window at stoplights in full makeup, drooling and moaning to see what would happen. In the States, panicked mothers would be dialing 911 – in Bulgaria…nothing.

I concluded that under communism the average citizen simply didn't get involved. You did your job and that was it. The "State" would take care of anything weird.

RUST IN PIECES

What comes with shooting in countries with far greater needs than those of an American exploitation film is what I call the Bulgarian Box of Chocolates, whereby you never really know, day to day, what you are going to get.

A key scene in the film involved a Vespa. I'll spare you the narrative details of why it was critical, but the Vespa had to be pink, with streamers from the handlebars, and it had to be completely destroyed on film. At the time, I felt that my first meeting with the transportation department had gone well. Since only a small handful of crew members spoke English, my translator, Assia, was there as well. We discussed the alleged Vespa with Uri, the head of the transportation department.

"Now, look, Uri," I remember saying. "I'm assuming that when I say 'a Vespa' we're all talking about the same type of machine."

I brought this up because of the array of odd vehicles I had seen on the Bulgarian roads, and I drew a crude picture on my dry-erase board.

"Of course," Uri nodded in recognition. "No problem."

"And I can paint it pink, right?"

"Of course," Uri said, rolling his head from side to side in the Bulgarian way of expressing "understood."

About a week later, I passed Uri in the hallway of the production office and I couldn't help but follow up on the Vespa. Through Assia, who was continually at my side, I asked, "Hey, Uri, are we good on the Vespa?"

My wife still thinks this is the sexiest picture of me ever taken.

Uri thrust a thumb in the air and smiled confidently. "Of course."

"And we can paint it pink and wreck it, right?"

Uri responded simply by rolling his head in that "way."

A week after that, with no Vespa news, I began to get nervous – we were only a few days away from needing it. I insisted that Uri bring me an actual picture of the Vespa he intended to use. He did, in fact, produce a picture – of a blue Vespa.

"This is fine, Uri, but it's blue. You can paint it pink, right?"

Through translation, Uri assured me again that it was not a problem.

"Okay," I said, chewing on my lower lip. "We shoot with that in two days. Good luck."

Forty-eight hours later, the second unit was preparing for the shot of the Vespa careening out of control, sans rider, and smashing into the side of a parked car. I was filming in a laboratory set across the street but peeked out when I had a chance. I was relieved to see the crew prepping a perfectly pink Vespa with cute girlie tassels fluttering from the handlebars.

A few minutes later, the ill-fated machine was rolled to its doom. Bouncing off the parked car, it smashed to the ground and let out a final gasp, courtesy of a cheesy spark effect. The crew applauded politely, as is usually the case after a "stunt" is performed, but as I glanced at Assia I was shocked to see tears streaming down her face. This was very unusual, because Assia had always been calm and professional. I looked to Joel, the first assistant director.

"Joel, why is Assia crying?"

"Oh, that's because it's her Vespa," he said, glancing at the smoldering wreck. "It was a gift from her father on her birthday. I guess they never told her they were going to wreck it."

"But she is the fucking translator," I fumed. "She was there. How could she not know?"

Joel shrugged. "Welcome to Bulgaria." After an almost physical altercation with Uri, the sorry-ass "transportation" captain, I stepped away to cool down. The area I called Bruce's Backlot had plenty of room to ruminate about my lot in life.

For Chrissakes, I'm a middle-aged man. I shouldn't be dicking around Eastern Europe, wrecking the personal property of poor people just to make a movie about a jerk with a brain transplant! Grown men don't glue prosthetic appliances to their faces and run around in silly costumes, fighting digital creatures that aren't even there. Actors my age should be doing Shakespeare in the Park or at the very least head-lining some innocuous Neil Simon comedy in Branson, Missouri.

No, instead, I was halfway around the world, fighting off a nasty infection, courtesy of a rusty hunk of un-oxidized metal.

The incident happened simply enough. On a Saturday, we got special access to a large, formerly "State-run" studio in order to capitalize on its size and Byzantine catwalk system. Chasing after a crazy Roma woman in a wedding dress through Sofia's sewer system (it's a weird movie, okay?), I nicked my right elbow on a rusty piece of metal caging. I didn't think twice at the time and we shot everything else without incident.

A couple hours later, I couldn't stop paying attention to my right elbow, which was now reddish and slightly inflamed. I didn't "hit" the caging enough to make that kind of a lump, so I got the medic to look at it.

He wasn't very pleased. "It's infected, I think," was the prognosis.

"But this was just, like, two hours ago," I reasoned. "Wouldn't this be happening over a period of days?"

"Yes. Like I said – is bad."

"Jesus. Okay, get Bob on the phone."

Bob was our line producer – the nuts-and-bolts guy who gets stuff done. Bob would take this to the next level. The decision was to get the quick opinion of two doctors, just as a safeguard. By the time I saw the first doctor, about an hour later, my arm had continued to swell. He didn't like the looks of it either, especially considering how "young" the infection was and recommended an immediate regime of medicated wraps and thumb-sized anti-bacterial pills. The second doctor, found through the American

Embassy, confirmed the infection and assumed that I would take off work for the next week or so, just in case I need to go on drip medication.

"Are you crazy?" I asked. "This is an American low-budget exploitation film that I'm starring in and directing. They'll never give me that much time off. I gotta heal fast, Doc!"

Thankfully, the following Sunday was off, but it was still tense because the infection hadn't "broken" yet. That's the scary part – not knowing when the aggressive son of a bitch would stop invading my body. Ida was out of town that weekend, so aside from the occasional doctor visit, it was a lonely "I just wanna go home" twenty-four hours.

Monday delivered a good news/bad news scenario. The good news was that it appeared the infection had leveled off and was no longer on the march. The bad news was that because of the wraps and medication, my right hand had swollen to twice its normal size and had to be kept elevated in a sling. The good news was that we were able to adjust the shooting schedule so I was only a director that day and didn't have to appear on camera.

Man with the Septic Arm

By Tuesday, the jig was up – I had to be back in action. The infection was improving, but the swelling of my hand was only mildly diminished. Fortunately, my scenes that day were all in the back of a taxi, so I gestured mostly with my "good" hand.

When Wednesday rolled around, life was almost back to normal, but every night after shooting for the next week Ivan had to drive me to a clinic to get very annoying ultraviolet/electromagnetic treatment on my arm. I asked the doctor why I needed that treatment if the infection had receded.

"Because of the tissue."

"What has that got to do with it?" I asked.

"The infection might have killed tissue in your arm," he explained dryly. "This should help stimulate it."

Jesus, I thought to myself. *I'm going to be permanently maimed because of a movie called* Man with the Screaming Brain?

GAGGING GOODMAN

To lighten the load of a near-death experience, it was time to have some fun. My idea of fun is a practical joke – the more elaborate the better. Back in 1988, I tried to get my producing partner, David "Goody" Goodman, extradited from California to Wyoming to deal with a bogus car fiasco (see my original *Chins* book for details). I was able to execute the complicated joke over a three-month period, and it took Goodman completely by surprise. I assumed that he might smell something fishy if I tried to pull another stunt, but two decades had rolled by since, blunting even Goodman's usually keen recall, and he was ripe for the picking.

During *Alien Apocalypse*, I hung out with my director buddy Josh at his apartment in Sofia, drinking Kamenitza beer and bullshitting about the day's work. I learned that Goodman was going to take Josh's exact apartment when he vacated, which was great news because I already knew the location, the buzzer system – all the particulars. This would come into play later.

During Josh's film, I got to meet a number of really good Bulgarian actors. Among them, two stood out – Todor Nikolov and Vladimir Kolev. On screen, Todor played a hunchbacked gnome named Bill the Mountain Man and Vlad played Bob the fisherman. I enjoyed their acting but also their general sense of humor and command of the English language.

Since these fine fellows had both been in *Alien Apocalypse*, the wardrobe department knew their exact sizes, which would come in handy when it came time to rent police uniforms. Ivan managed to round up a pair of handcuffs and a magnetic police light. Todor completed the package with his nondescript white sedan, and the elements were in place.

The plan was for two Bulgarian "cops" to "interrupt" a "script session" that Goodman and I were having at his apartment, ransack the place, talking about "passport problems" and eventually take him away to "Serbia." The actors were instructed to do two things as soon as they could – get Goodman's passport and cell phone away from him.

Knowing that Goodman would want to make a call, we alerted Ivan that a panicked call might come, but he was not to help in any way. We also knew that Goodman would eventually offer up a bribe, as I had been regaling him with stories of the Sofia police and how everything worked a little better if you "greased the wheels." The actors were instructed to go ballistic if the subject ever came up.

Vladimir was tall and imposing. He would play the "bad" cop. Todor was short, and he would be the inquisitive one, or "good" cop. The important thing about the success or failure of this type of gag – getting someone arrested in a foreign country – all depends on timing. The trick with Bulgaria is to hit the victim within a couple days of arriving so they're reeling from both jet lag and culture shock – an unbeatable double whammy.

The timing was perfect. As planned, I arrived at Goodman's apartment around 6:00 p.m. for a "script conference." The basic premise of our story needed to be tweaked to accommodate a Bulgarian setting rather than East L.A., so there was actually a little bit of work to be done.

A half hour later, Goodman's door buzzer rang.

I shot my best "who the fuck?" look to Goodman, but he was already working on a priceless expression of his own. I had just showed him how to use his intercom. He approached it with apprehension and pushed the talk button.

"Yes?"

"Polizia."

Goodman whirled around to me. "The cops? Shit."

The buzzer rang again. It was not a polite sound. "Polizia."

"You better let 'em in, Goodman," I said, with building dread.

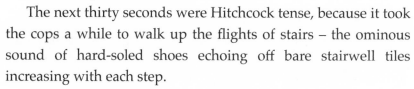

"Gentlemen, this is our target."

Reluctantly, Goodman buzzed them in.

The next thirty seconds were Hitchcock tense, because it took the cops a while to walk up the flights of stairs – the ominous sound of hard-soled shoes echoing off bare stairwell tiles increasing with each step.

The knock on the door was forceful, exactly what you would expect from cops in the former Eastern Bloc. "Polizia."

Goodman unlocked his door, revealing two cops. Unlike American officers of the law, who might, say, ask for permission to enter, our Bulgarian friends walked right in and began casing the joint. Looking directly at me, Vladimir asked phonetically, "Dav-id Good-man?"

Naturally, I pointed to Goodman. "There's your man."

The cops turned to Goodman and flanked him on both sides. "Pass-a-port?" Vlad asked, palm outstretched.

Goodman hesitated a second. "Passport? Why? What's wrong?"

Todor spoke up. "Problema pass-a-port."

Playing my own role of dutiful friend, I stood up to make my case. "Hey, do you guys even speak English?"

The cops ignored me and turned their attention back to Goodman, who by now had whipped out his cell phone and was nervously dialing. "I'm calling Ivan."

Ivan answered on the other end.

"Ivan, hey, there are some cops here," Goodman said, trying to sound calm and professional, but his trembling hands gave him away. "They say they want my passport. Can you talk to them?"

Goodman handed the phone over to Vlad, while Todor began a leisurely stroll around the apartment, opening drawers and cabinets.

The phone call with Vlad didn't go well. Bulgarian is an angry-sounding language to begin with, and when conversation gets heated it's a harsh sound. Goodman winced from the negative effect. Eventually, Vlad handed the phone back to Goodman.

"What did he say?" Goodman asked Ivan impatiently.

The answer didn't help. Ivan explained that there was nothing he could do and that Goodman would have to go with the policemen to Serbia to work this out.

"Serbia? You gotta be fuckin' kiddin' me," Goodman bemoaned.

Eventually, he hung up the phone, looking pale and distressed. Todor was getting a little nosy, so I stood up again and made a few threatening steps forward.

"Hey, pal, you got his passport; what else do you want? You got no right to go through his stuff without a warrant."

Vlad intercepted me with an arm out. "Problema? Problema?"

I stopped in my tracks. "No. No *problema*."

A pack of cigarettes on Goodman's desk caught my eye and I held them out as a peace offering. "Cigarette?"

Vlad took the pack, without comment, and shoved it into his pocket.

While Todor continued to case the joint, Goodman nodded at me to step aside for a quick sidebar conversation. "Look, I haven't had a good history with these Russian bastards," he said in a hushed, ultra-serious tone. "Last time I was in Moscow, I almost got arrested for throwing a shoe through a plate-glass window."

"Why the hell did you do that?"

"Long story. Look, do you have any per diem? I only have a few leva. I'm gonna give these commie bastards some cash and be done with it."

I dug into my pocket and pulled out the equivalent of $20. "This is all I have, but you're welcome to it, pal."

Goodman combined my money with his few leva and approached the two cops, who were starting to get impatient. He offered the cash with a smug look. "Here, guys, maybe you speak *this* language."

Todor's reaction to the proposed bribe was worth the entire gag. He exchanged an indignant look with Vlad

I would have used real police, but they were busy freaking out another paranoid actor and his wife.

and grabbed the money out of Goodman's hands. Crumpling it into a tight ball, he threw it on the floor and proceeded to lecture Goodman in his angry language while Vlad got handcuffs out and started to snap them on.

Again, I protested. "Hey, Jesus Christ, guys, this isn't necessary. He'll go with you, okay? He'll go, but no handcuffs," I implored, pointing to the restraints. "No cuffs."

By this point, Goodman had thrown in the towel. He looked at Todor like a lost little boy. "Can I at least put my shoes on?" Reluctantly, Todor relented.

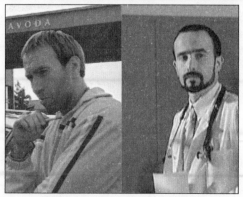

Vlad and Todor: My partners in crime.

"Goodman, don't sweat this," I said, trying to reassure him.

"Yeah, easy for you. You're not the one goin' to a fuckin' gulag."

"Look, I'll get Production on the phone. We'll get to the bottom of this."

Goodman laced up his second shoe and stood up, resigned to his fate. "Make it quick. I don't know how much time I got..."

Vlad took Goodman's cell phone and passport and they were out the door. I continued to make calls, which I knew would be answered by either Vlad or Todor, alternately demanding not only an immediate release but also an explanation for this outrage.

"No English, no English," came the response, and the phone would go dead.

Perfect, I thought to myself. *Those guys are giving the performance of a lifetime.*

In actuality, Vlad and Todor merely took Goodman around the city on a confusing joyride while I made my way to a very nice restaurant, where we would all rendezvous.

Goodman's expression changed dramatically when he entered the room and saw me sitting with Ivan and Ida at a lovely corner table. His grim look morphed into a rueful, tight smile. "Ooh, man, Campbell, you're gonna get it. You're gonna get it *bad*."

More than pissed, Goodman was relieved to know that he wasn't really going to a Siberian labor camp after all. What he didn't realize was that I had to talk Ivan out of dropping him at the local police station to spend time on the "trolley car" – an elevated, horizontal metal bar used to handcuff drunks with their hands over their heads, presumably to prevent fighting and general mayhem.

Goodman looked at Todor and Vlad, who by now had huge grins on their faces. "Fellas, I'm one of the producers of *Man with the Screaming Brain,* and you both got parts – you're fuckin' good actors!"

True to his word, when it came time to cast, Vladimir took a major secondary role as a sleazy cab driver and Todor did a great job as a solemn doctor.

This was the second time in twenty years that Goodman had been the butt of an elaborate, borderline mean-spirited gag. He's a sweet, mild-mannered guy most of the time, but I know I'm pushing my luck. He's going to get me back one of these days. I'm waiting for it, Goodman.

DOUBLE CHIN

In a post-script, it should be noted that the entertainment industry allows one to be a hero and a dog – both at the same time. *Alien Apocalypse* aired as a Saturday night original movie several months later on Sci-Fi and got the highest ratings of any original TV movie to date for them. Studio executives were delighted to share with me even the minute details of quarter-by-quarter demographics and how we kicked major cable TV ass.

Alien Apocalypse = Hero.

Man with the Screaming Brain aired in the same slot six months later and laid a massive Nielsen ratings egg. Studio executives were not so forthright with the ratings news, presumably because it was bad, and I never heard a thing. There was a brain screaming all right – mine.

Man with the Screaming Brain = Dog.

Thirty years from now *Brain* will no doubt be hailed as a "clearly ahead of its time classic," but for now it lies in a vegetative VHS state in a Van Nuys, California, warehouse. A recent *LA Times* article, touting "The Death of VHS," used *Man with the Screaming Brain* as the poster child for movies that videotape merchants simply couldn't "give away." The current backlog was "at least" five thousand copies.

Instead of being depressed, I used the opportunity to make the world a better place. I bought the entire lot off a group of Lebanese wholesalers for $1 per VHS and put them to good use – as insulation in an addition on my eco-friendly Oregon house, paid for by my fee on *Alien Apocalypse*.

In retrospect, would I say that the former Eastern Bloc is a good place to make a movie? Yes and no. Yes if you like a charming, hardworking society, struggling to emerge from communism. No if you are disturbed by roaming packs of wild dogs and a language that is spoken like the person is permanently annoyed. But after eighteen years of kissing everyone's ass in sight to direct my first feature film, Bulgaria was just fine by me.

LIFE ON THE WILD SIDE

Ida's best friend came to visit us in Oregon a few years ago. She had been working in Atlanta and hadn't spent much time in the Pacific Northwest. Upon arriving at the house, scanning the mountainous terrain, she was mortified. "This is where you live? Where are all the people?" she asked.

Ida's friend has never returned. All the more Oregon for me.

The farther out or away you get, the more interesting "civilization" becomes. I used to own a decommissioned Forest Service truck. You could see where the official decal had been scraped off. I bought it New Year's Day at a used car lot for $3,000.

Thinking I worked for the Forest Service, folks in town would wave and smile respectfully. In the outback, some people wouldn't acknowledge my truck or even wave back, because I was a "Fed." What was I up to? they wondered.

I enjoyed one particular drive into my "extended backyard" when I encountered a "tweaker." Meth is a huge problem where I live. My local town of Medford is known sarcastically as

"Meth-Ford." Billboards with the tagline "Meth: Not Even Once" dot the I-5 corridor through town.

Publicly owned land is not only a great place to make meth – as there are thousands of miles of unused Forest Service logging roads nearby – it's also a great place to take drugs and tweak your brains out. I spotted my guy, Tweaky Pants, deep into Forest Service territory, a good fifteen miles from civilization in any direction. As I got closer, Tweaky saw my Forest Service truck, assumed I was after him, panicked and raced across the dirt road to a wooded section. As my truck edged closer, I slowed down and scanned the foliage, immediately spotting Tweaky "hiding" behind a tree. I use quotations because the tree didn't really hide him – his belly stuck out one side of the tree and his ass stuck out the other.

As my official-looking truck passed by, I slowed to a tedious crawl and enjoyed watching Tweaky craftily counter-roll around the tree as I passed, now moving glacially. His wilderness ninja skills were impressive. I decided to stop the truck and just sit there for about five minutes, testing his resolve. Tweaky stood his ground, shivering uncontrollably. He wasn't going to budge. He was too good and this was life or death. Eventually, when my sadistic side had had enough, I gave the horn a friendly *toot-toot* and drove away.

I wouldn't exactly say I live in the howling wilderness, but I don't live in the suburbs either. Technically, it's called the Wildland Urban Interface, or WUI – life on the edge. While much of the forested land in southern Oregon, both public and private, is indeed fragmented, wildlife tends to be much less in retreat up here.

In Oregon, deer tend to be like dogs – you get used to seeing a lot of them. Over the years, we have always had no fewer than four deer on the property and sometimes as many as eight, both does and bucks. Our plan all along has been to basically ignore them. We don't feed them or adopt them as pets. We do our thing and they do theirs. Over time, we have learned to adapt to each other. Our first house had a curved grass roof that could be accessed from the ground. It was disconcerting as

Some folks have squirrels on their roof.

hell to walk out the front door and look up to see three deer casually eating on the roof. When the kids were younger, we had a trampoline, which made for great deer shade when summertime rolled around.

City people think they are being clever when they dump animals off in the boonies and drive away. "Clever" wouldn't be the word I would use. What an asshole thing to do! I got a taste of the consequences of animal abandonment one year when some jerk dropped off a cat at the bottom of our driveway. This black and white male cat was a beast. He wouldn't let anyone come near him and sightings eventually became as rare as Bigfoot. As a year or so rolled by, we weren't sure what had happened, but eventually we would spot the cat farther up our driveway, closer and closer to the house.

The time for action came when the feral feline started to get into epic fights with my domestic cats. That's when I drew the line. My number-one cat, Carpenter, had been messed up and I wouldn't stand for it. To motivate myself, I named the cat Perkis, after a jerky producer I worked with once and formulated a plan of attack. The cat was mostly just hungry, so I knew food would work. I put a fresh bowl of cat food at the ass end of a have-a-heart trap and caught the bastard in twenty minutes.

My trusty Forest Service truck was running and ready. I threw the trap in the bed of the truck, drove to the edge of my local city at dusk, found the nearest park and set Perkis free. Two can play *that* game, city folks!

Aside from annoying abandoned kitty cats, my property has been a crossroads for wild creatures great and small.

"Hey, there's that severed deer leg you were looking for," I said calmly to Ida one day while walking our driveway.

Ida skidded to a halt, staring at the severed leg in front of us. "You think a mountain lion did it?"

"Or a really pissed-off squirrel."

Ida and I pondered the image of death on our property and its implications. If a wild animal can rip the leg off a healthy, strong deer, surely they could mangle either of us unrecognizably.

"Hey, so, maybe we should pick up the pace," Ida offered cheerily, and marched off with one eye fixed over her shoulder.

Not long after this, I saw a mountain lion run in front of my car at dusk. When deer run, they're very stiff – they tend to jab into the ground as they run. This creature, roughly the same color and size as a deer, was very fluid as it crossed the driveway in one leap. Deer also don't have long tails.

According to Wilderness Survival 101, if you are attacked by a mountain lion you are supposed to fight back. As opposed to a grizzly bear protecting her cub, mountain lions have been known to cut and run if you make a serious effort to equally mangle them. So *they* say. Frankly, I don't want to test anybody's wildlife theory by fighting any large predator. I'm gonna do my best to stay out of their way and let my walking stick do the talking.

Living in the country, you do have your vandals. Smashing rural mailboxes with baseball bats has been a bored local teenager's favorite pastime for generations. Looking at the trash strewn about the bottom of my driveway one morning, I assumed that the local kids went crazy and had an impromptu party.

When I got closer, I realized that the damage wasn't caused by humans – this was done by a big ol' bear. My metal trash can had been upended like a Big Gulp and shaken empty for a hundred feet up the driveway. The bear had sampled a little bit of everything along the way – boxes were shredded and large bite marks ringed a smashed tuna can. I knew this was the work of a bear because when it got to the end of the garbage/food it promptly squatted and took an enormous, berry-dense crap in the middle of our driveway. Does a bear actually shit in the woods? This one sure did. You needed a high-clearance vehicle to get over this load.

As a kid, I watched all of the Walt Disney *Daniel Boone* outdoor-type TV shows. Invariably, no matter what the show, a cute skunk would waddle onto the scene and cause lighthearted mayhem until it was removed safely and set free back into the wild. You had to have it.

I guess it was time for our own skunk adventure. As I was watching television downstairs with Ida one night, we heard what sounded like an animal trying to force its way through our cat door upstairs. Most confrontational affairs, particularly ones involving animals, I leave to Ida – who rolled her eyes at me and began up the steps. Before she could get halfway, a skunk stopped at the landing above her. Both froze. Then the skunk spun around to tail-first mode and started to slowly retreat. Ida eventually grabbed a few pots and the ensuing clatter chased the skunk back outside.

When I was recounting this to a neighbor, he laughed but also felt that some schooling was needed.

"Son, funny story. Funny as a rubber crutch. But why didn't you just shoot the damn thing with your .22?"

I assumed he meant a .22-caliber gun, like the one I used for target practice at camp as a kid. "I don't have a .22," I said.

My neighbor looked at me, his smile quickly fading. "What guns ya got?"

"I don't have any guns."

"You don't have any guns?!" the man exclaimed. "Lord, son, you're four guns shy of a *plan*."

"What plan would that be?" I asked, genuinely curious.

"A *plan*. For *everything*. You need a .22 *for small critters* (like skunk), you need a rifle with a scope *for distance*, you need a shotgun for *'close work,'* and you need a handgun for *personal protection*."

I nodded my head as he sped up in pace and conviction. "Four guns shy of a plan," I muttered. "Four guns shy. Okay."

"Welcome to the country, son."

Before I could buy a .22 – or any gun – I handled the problem the Detroit way. Coming home one night during the ongoing Cat Door Wars, I was about to turn into the driveway when a skunk waddled right in front of my SUV. I made an honest effort to avoid impact, but it was too late – the skunk was destroyed.

My gun-toting neighbor collared me at a function a few months later. "Hey, Bruce, did that .22 solve yer skunk problem?" he asked, smiling assuredly.

"No, my Ford Explorer did. I haven't seen him since."

WALK THIS WAY

Whenever I tell people where I live, they tend to nod their heads and say, "Or-e-*gon*. Sure looks beautiful." Being a snotty person who doesn't want any more humans invading, my response is always the same: "Oh, you'd hate it up there. It rains *every day*."

Even though it does rain in Oregon, the amount varies greatly, depending on where you live. My area, unbeknownst to me when I moved here, is known as the "Sunny Applegate Valley." Geographically, it's in a "rain shadow," protected by the mighty Siskiyou Mountains, which run east and west – thereby blocking a ton of crappy weather coming north from California.

I always wondered why a retired airline pilot would live in my neighborhood. The answer came in what he saw from the air during the winter months: the entire Rogue Valley – including the airport – was fogged in solid, while the Applegate Valley, being elevated and protected, was clear as a bell. The bottom line was that we had a lot of clear days to get outside and I took full advantage.

A pleasant discovery was literally in my backyard. The Sterling Mine Ditch Trail, a little-used recreational gem dating back to 1877, runs across BLM land. Gold was discovered in nearby Sterling Creek in 1854. Hydraulic mining became all the rage, whereby you channel water downhill and force it into smaller and smaller tubes, until the subsequent pressure of water becomes powerful enough to rip entire creek beds and hillsides apart.

A very pleasant discovery.

For the Sterling Mine, water was diverted from the Little Applegate River along an earthen ditch, then diverted down to Sterling Creek, where the destruction began. The area is very lovely now, but twenty-foot-high piles of river rock, randomly stacked up during the mining process, are still evident.

The Sterling Ditch was in use until the thirties and now humans can enjoy the fruits of some very obvious labor. Around four hundred workers, mostly Chinese, dug a three-foot-deep ditch at a 1 percent grade (just enough to move the water) that weaves in and out of serpentine hills for about twenty-five miles. It was quite a feat and I thank the ghosts of the workers every time I take a pleasant jaunt on the almost level trail.

Exposure to the elements comes with inherent risk. You could fall off a cliff or be attacked by a wild animal. On a really bad day, you might be mistaken for a leaping deer and shot dead by a drunk hunter. Or – perhaps worst of all – you could get Poison Oak.

I grew up exposed to Poison Ivy, the Midwest version of this dreaded plant. Let me tell you, Poison Ivy can be annoying, but Poison Oak is nothing to scoff at. By some grace of the Almighty, I am barely susceptible to it, but I have seen my wife, daughter and brother suffer the tortures of the damned from the three-leafed menace. "Leaves of three, let them be," is what the almanacs say. No shit. If Ida even gets a small amount on her skin, it will boil and fester for weeks.

Brother Don and I finished an epic walk one day. Don, with no prior exposure to Poison Oak, proceeded to jump directly into the Jacuzzi. Poison Oak spreads through its oil, and if you want to avoid getting a bad case of it you need to lather up with a product like Techu before *and after* hikes to keep the oils from settling.

A Jacuzzi has just the opposite effect – it *spreads* the oils. Don was having the time of his life, unwittingly coating his entire body with Poison Oak – and getting it deep into every fleshy crevasse. I'm not sure if it was the positioning of the Jacuzzi jets or the poorly timed placement of his hands (only Don knows for sure), but for whatever reason the rash appeared to be worst around his groin. In years to come, whenever the subject arose, which was often, I referred to it as "the day Don got Ditch Dick."

Don would have much preferred looking for Bigfoot. There is a trail about forty-five minutes from my house, off of which the Forest Service built an enormous trap in the seven- ties to catch him. That's right,

some joker approved my dad's taxpayer dollars (hopefully not much) to catch the elusive Sasquatch. Today, it's nothing more than a tourist oddity off Collings Mountain Trail, near Applegate Lake.

The design, a wood and chicken wire "elevator" of sorts, was supposed to descend on a not-very-elaborate pulley system and trap the big fella inside – should he choose to enter the completely uninviting, undisguised device. To my knowledge, no Bigfoots were ever captured or killed in this trap. It was a fun, if slightly whimsical, idea, but the Forest Service was much more likely to catch a lawsuit from this rusting liability than a new species.

"WHAT'S A BLM?"

My introduction to the Bureau of Land Management came at about 9:00 one Saturday morning when a helicopter, hovering shockingly close to my house, began a heli-logging operation. I could have hit the thing with a rock it was so close.

This startling reality made me get acquainted with this heretofore-unknown government agency, lickety-split. Who was BLM and what were they up to?

The Bureau of Land Management administers 264 million acres – mostly in twelve western states. On land ownership maps, BLM areas are usually shaded in yellow. Look at a map of Nevada – it's about 75 percent yellow. Oregon is about 50 percent federal land. BLM tends to administer lower-elevation lands while the Forest Service assumes stewardship of higher elevations.

What can be done on BLM-administered land? Plenty. They oversee timber extraction, mining, grazing, fracking, road building, et cetera. About the only thing they don't currently allow is human habitation beyond two weeks of squatting.

BLM was my neighbor on three sides, so I started to attend meetings, symposiums and lectures on land stewardship, a subject that had always interested me. "How to use land" is also a divisive topic. Show ten people a landscape and you'll get ten different opinions about what to do with it. The answers will range from "do nothing" to "take it all."

Southern Oregon is an AMA, an Adaptive Management Area, something that was designated in the nineties with a revision of the Northwest Forest Plan. The AMAs recognized that not one size fits all with regard to land use, so eleven "adaptive" areas were designated to allow local and federal land managers more flexibility on approaches and decisions. The residents in our area have always been very vocal about land use issues, so our AMA focused on the ability of the public to give input and to influence decisions on the land around us.

I was thankful for this designation. It meant that locals could get on a list of proposed federal actions and we would then have ninety days to respond with what are called "Scoping Comments."

As citizens, we aren't scientists and we aren't hip to how many board feet can sustainably be removed from a given slope, but just fly over Northern California, Oregon and Washington and you'll see that some extraction policies should be revisited. Patchworks of clear cuts slash across the landscape – like a chainsaw was given to a kid with ADD and told to "go crazy." The West has wide-open spaces and vast vistas, but it also has wide-open strip mines and vast denuded landscapes.

I like to quote a neighbor of mine, Richard, who said, "I'm not against logging; I'm against *bad* logging." We all wipe our butts with toilet tissue. That redwood deck had to come from somewhere. Most of us still use an array of paper products every day. The trick is, how do you get the needed material out without wrecking everything for generations to come? We have tried a lot of different extraction methods over the years and most of those since the industrial age have been very destructive.

Back off, Mother Nature, we got this!

I decided to submit my first Scoping Comments about some upcoming actions the BLM proposed. I was loath to use any kind of "boilerplate" language offered up by local greenies and I knew that a long, bullet-listed, know-it-all letter might never be fully appreciated, so I upped the ante and submitted a short film called *Shed Talk.*

Most submissions about how to manage our watersheds and our wildlife are very solemn. I picture women with long, straight gray hair, tearfully drafting heartfelt suggestions on their grandfather's manual typewriter. *Shed Talk* had me, dressed as Joe Local in my shed doing gags – and plenty of them. Why shouldn't spit takes and double entendre be used to make a serious point? People can be very bitchy and preachy in the world of environmental protection – maybe a little sugar will help the Scoping Comments go down?

I was told after-the-fact that my Scoping Comments were

shown to a meeting of some seventy-odd land managers at the Medford BLM Headquarters. The gathering wasn't to honor how amazing my cheap jokes were – and they *were* amazing – but it was to exemplify to the managers that different people are living in the backcountry now: people with cameras and Web sites and Twitter accounts. Citizens are now armed – not with pitchforks or shotguns – but with the ability to communicate quickly, easily and effectively to the outside world.

Most people have never heard of the BLM. Local greenies here in Oregon call them the Bureau of Land *Mis*-management. Others dismissively wave them off as "Feds." Opinions vary wildly about whether the BLM folks are saints or sinners. I suppose they are a little bit of both.

In my personal experience, I find the BLM to be a decent bunch of local folks who are ultimately going to do what the bureaucrats in D.C. want them to do. If the current administration is very resource-extraction friendly, you can bet the BLM will be there to facilitate the removal of trees and they'll "frack" themselves blue.

Conversely, under the Clinton administration the North-west Forest Plan they introduced pretty much changed the way BLM had been doing business for decades – and it caused a stir in my community. The issue was and is that small hamlets in rural Oregon and elsewhere in the West are virtually landlocked – surrounded by federal land – and can't grow like traditional towns. Because they can't expand, they rely heavily on subsidies from timber and other extractive industries for schools, roads, fire/police.

The Northwest Forest Plan removed a large portion of "harvest-able" land from the chopping block and provided for a ten-year subsidy to replace lost timber revenue, thereby encouraging rural communities to adapt and diversify their local economy.

I'm not sure if it's human nature or not, but precious few of these towns used the decade to reimagine themselves and now they are in an even worse financial situation. The solution? Cut more trees, of course! Sheesh! As long as there is an overabundance of humans on this planet, we will not soon see the end of these use/conserve debates.

Shed Talk II is already in the works.

WHAT'S MY NAME?

After shooting out of the country for what seemed like a decade, I was desperate to work stateside again. I didn't want to travel for work ever again. B movie globe-trotting had almost cost me an arm and I was eager for a return to the tetanus-free valleys of southern Oregon.

Fortunately, state governments across the country had gotten sick and tired of American movies being shot in foreign warehouses and had instituted various incentive packages. My home state of Oregon was offering a 10 percent rebate incentive to entice prodigal productions to come back home. Better than a sharp stick in the eye.

Mike Richardson, the founder and president of Dark Horse Comics and Entertainment (*The Mask, Hellboy*), was another Oregon resident and had already taken advantage of the rebate package. We'd known each other since his company produced the first *Army of Darkness* comic books back in 1992 and we were eager to work together – particularly on a homegrown project.

Mike had been friends with a writer named Mark Verheiden since high school and the two collaborated on several projects going back to the very early days of Dark Horse. After the *Army of Darkness* comic, which Mark wrote, Dark Horse and Verheiden joined forces with Renaissance Pictures (i.e., Sam and Rob) to produce the movie *Timecop* in 1994. You see how Hollywood works? It's really just a big, tangled web of schmoes who keep running into each other over and over.

I hadn't been directly involved with Mike and Mark on a film project yet – until Mark remembered *The Adventures of Alan Ladd*.

Alan Ladd was a well-known radio and movie actor in the forties and fifties, best known for playing the hero in the classic Western *Shane*. He's not as well known for the nine-issue DC Comics series that featured Alan Ladd as himself in a variety of adventures.

The premise of gullible yokels enlisting an overblown actor to thwart evil had already seen the big screen with films such as *Three Amigos* and *Galaxy Quest,* but Mark's spin on it followed Alan Ladd's lead by having the actor play himself.

That actor turned out to be me.

In Mike Richardson's office, with Mark at his side, I recapped what I thought was their plot:

"Okay, let me get this straight – a small town is cursed with a monster, so they kidnap Bruce Campbell, thinking he would be an authority on monsters, but he turns out to be a worthless asshole and almost ruins everything."

"Exactly," Mark nodded.

"I'm in. Where do I sign?"

Mike Richardson had already made a deal with video distributor Image Entertainment. With Dark Horse holding all the creative cards, I would only have to deal with Mike and Mark, who were thoroughly rational human beings.

Now we're getting somewhere, I thought.

Bouncing ideas back and forth, we were all in sync that the film would be set and shot in Oregon. The monster, however, wasn't such an obvious decision. Bigfoot seemed like a good fit for the region but not necessarily for the story.

Since I was a resident of southern Oregon and familiar with the local history, I wanted to make the creature more relevant to the area. In the mid-1800s, the entire infrastructure of my region, including gold mines, was basically built by Chinese immigrants. I started investigating Chinese lore in hopes of finding a suitable candidate and a "Protector of the Dead" popped up – a former tofu salesman who went on to become immortalized as Guan Di, the Taoist god of war and protector of the dead. Seeing Guan Di as a vengeful spirit that haunted those who disturb the peace, I thought, *That's it. That's our guy!*

The elements came together, and the premise of the story – to be called *My Name Is Bruce* – was established: In the past, a mine collapsed, killing all the Chinese laborers inside. The mine and consequent graveyard has been protected by Guan Di until modern-day locals disturb the miners' resting place. Guan Di then materializes and systematically hunts down the local bumpkins. Described as a giant red-faced warrior wielding a halberd, Guan Di was not a character I had seen on-screen before – and even though our

Guan Di, savior of bean curd.

movie was bound to be campy, at least our monster wasn't going to be your run-of-the-mill vampire, zombie or demon.

WELCOME TO GOLD LICK

Generally speaking, there are a few fundamental rules of film-making:

1. Never start making a movie until you have a completed script.

2. Never start making a movie until you have the funding.

3. Never use your own money.

4. Never shoot on your own property.

Okay, so I blew all four and started before anything was ready. With a pending fall book tour solidly committed, I had to move forward on the project, or it would be delayed until the following year.

I needed help, so I brought in Craig "Kif" Sanborn, my "indentured artist" who had recently finished putting the finishing touches on my *Make Love* book and was begging me for money (I added that for effect). He also had some experience scouting and securing locations, not to mention the ability to do eight other jobs, so Kif was a mainstay during prep.

We scouted the nearby town of Jacksonville, Oregon, a historic mining town (the entire town is a National Historic Landmark) that had experienced a boom in the 1860s when gold was discovered. The actual history of this small town fit nicely within the backstory of *My Name Is Bruce* and its status meant that the buildings still had much of their bygone charm.

Kif to the Rescue!

Unfortunately, our rigid timeline meant we would need to film smack-dab in the middle of the local Britt Festival, a popular music jamboree that the town had absolutely no interest in interrupting. In fact, the city charter itself actually forbade issuing filming permits of any kind during the festival.

We were Britt out of luck.

I wasn't expecting this and had to quickly adjust what my vision for the movie was.

I finally said, "You know what? In *Man with the Screaming Brain* I took over a Russian military base and built a backlot on that. I've got property. I am going to damn well build a backlot."

Ignoring the numerous cardinal rules, I decided to fund the beginnings out of my own pocket until I could be reimbursed – after all, the deal was pending. What could go wrong?

When I told Mike of my executive decision to build the fictional town of Gold Lick on my own property, I was met with an ominous silence. Realizing that he had probably stopped breathing, I explained to him that Gold Lick was supposed to be a dilapidated small town – it wouldn't need new fixtures or four walls, and it could totally be ramshackle and funky.

After a noticeable gulp for air, Mike replied, "Well, I just hope it doesn't look like crap."

We had budgeted for location rentals and set decoration, but we hadn't planned on building an entire town square from the ground up. It was a crazy notion, but I was so desperate for a return to my roots that I wanted to literally make a movie in my backyard.

I got what I wanted, all right – I got it in spades. So did my wife. The ensuing chaos of excavation, construction and self-financing would become so stressful that the experience actually sent Ida to the hospital, fearing she was having a heart attack. Thankfully, she was not, but during the shoot that followed Ida could barely contain her chronic throbbing scorn for my ridiculous scheme.

Convincing Mike to go for it was one thing, convincing my ailing wife to allow it was another, but convincing the municipal government to let us do it was the most difficult of all. Towns without a history of filmmaking are a double-edged sword – on one side, you have an excited citizenry eager to give you the key to the city. On the other, you have a bureaucracy so unfamiliar with filmmaking that everything you say is completely alien.

Trying to convince the local planning commission to let us build a series of semi-modular, temporary structures that violated more building codes than an inspector could count was a crazy notion.

The commissioner's initial response was, "You want to build a *what*?"

Admittedly, there was no precedent for my outlandish request, so I took Oregon's film commissioner up on an offer he had made only a week earlier: "Bruce, if there is anything you ever need, just let me know…"

I called him up. "Do me a favor. Help this local commissioner guy out. He thinks we want to build Dollywood or something. He's just trying to do his job, but he needs to learn about the bogus nature of movies and sets. We're gonna dismantle the damn thing when we're done."

I never heard another word about it.

Crossing my fingers and concluding that we had been issued a "don't ask, don't tell" permit, I cut the ribbon and authorized the construction of Gold Lick immediately.

The task of building the three or four structures that we *weren't officially building* was another exercise in true "indie" resourcefulness. New, store-bought lumber was out of the question due to budget, so I put an old-fashioned ad in the local paper: "Got Wood? We'll haul away scrap lumber in trade (meaning for free)." The response was mind-boggling. Calls came in from all over the valley – one guy had sixteen feet of old fencing, another fellow had an old deck, and it went on like that until there was enough material to fill two twenty-four-foot trucks.

Brother Don came over from Michigan to help gather the lumber, mainly because Kif was sarcastic and irritable and I wanted someone else to talk to. For the next several days, the three of us drove around southern Oregon, loading up every old board, plank, beam, slat and toothpick we could get our splintered hands on.

My own land was not without its own share of useable wood. The lower part of the property had once housed the original homestead from the thirties. The decayed lumber salvaged from the site had great character and wound up being per fect for the ancient Chinese cemetery and mine shaft we also had to build.

Got Wood?

As if God Himself wanted to smite me for shooting a film on my own property, a lightning bolt shot down from the heavens one night and split a beautiful pine tree right down the middle. We were all in the house at the time and heard the massive explosion. Don swears he saw it happen. Within a week, that once stalwart pine was a dead skeleton of brown needles.

Rewind to a few years earlier. I met a group of local woodworkers who owned and operated a portable Swedish lumber mill that could have been a prop in a *Hellraiser* movie. To make a living, they would hook up this wonderfully efficient machine to the back of their pickup truck and take it wherever someone wanted raw timber milled.

I engaged the services of these portable millers and they dragged the carcass of the pine to a clearing.

"Nice piece of wood. Shame about the lightning. What size lumber would you like?" the miller asked.

We decided on Western-town-style slats. The beautiful ponderosa provided enough wood to face an entire building. To my surprise, the lightning strike altered the color of the wood itself and gave that batch of lumber a unique character we never would have gotten otherwise. Production Design by Mother Nature.

But the real gold strike came from down the road. I was driving home after scouting an area outside of Jacksonville and spotted a faded sign on the side of the road that read: "Items for Sale" and provided a local phone number. Upon closer inspection, the sign was leaning up against a motley assortment of old metal, which turned out to include a miniature train engine and a small-gauge rail track.

In *My Name Is Bruce*, the collapsed mine bookended the story. The mine should have a cart and track poking out from the rubble. Intrigued by the weird stuff on display, I called the number on the sign and spoke to a curmudgeon named Lowell.

"Yeah, what do you want?" he asked, not sounding happy about the call.

"Well, I saw your sign out front, sir, and I thought that you might have some stuff that I would be interested in using, or even buying."

"Hang on a minute."

Moments later, Lowell emerged, roaring on his ATV through a cloud of dust, asking again, "What do you want?"

"Well, I'm making a movie, and we need some cool old stuff to dress our sets."

Lowell grumbled a bit as he opened a couple of gates. "All right, follow me."

Up the driveway was a wonderland of vintage vehicles

and tarnished farming, construction and industrial equipment. Lowell used to mine on his own property, so he actually had old mining equipment in addition to the stacks of rail tracks.

Seeing the drool seeping from my mouth, he asked, "So, you're building some buildings, and it's supposed to look rustic. Is that what's happening here?"

"Um, yeah. Exactly."

"Well, come on over here. My wife made me buy this and I don't know what the hell to do with it."

Lowell opened up a shed and revealed a hoard of wood that had been taken off a barn. Weathered but still solid, it was exactly the type of stuff I was hoping to find.

"I want all of it," I told him.

I walked around agape at everything I wanted to buy and "loaded my cart" with corrugated steel, nine-by-twelve beams, roofing materials, metal signage, a 1930s Rambler and even a doggone windmill. In his seventies, Lowell was a hoarder who had  finally decided to sell off his collection to fund other aspects of his life. I needed a bunch of his stuff to build a town. The timing was perfect. Lowell, of course, had his own bulldozer, forklift and flatbed, so he was even able to deliver.

To ensure that nobody died from a rotting piece of wood causing a set to fall over, the key framing and everything sunk into the ground was purchased brand-new – but the siding, facades and picturesque charm all came from the collected resources. Finished off with some antiques, a wooden Indian and a large fountain, Gold Lick took shape.

All this out-of-pocket business was a bit over-the-top, as my wife will attest, but I was hoping to put enough pressure on the wallets to make sure this deal did not fall apart. It was definitely a white-knuckle situation, but the deal got signed and the official cash began to flow.

TOWNSFOLK

There was one final element necessary to complete the return to the salad days. There wasn't much of a point shooting a movie in my backyard if the cast and crew weren't full of the like-minded individuals and fun-loving Shemps I called friends.

Ted, "Wing-ing" it.

Naturally, I started with Ted Raimi. I like working with Ted because he makes my acting look subtle. He had already developed an elderly Chinese character who would be perfect for the caretaker of the mining graveyard and I knew he could add a certain amount of satirical sleaze to the role of my agent, Mills Toddner. Thankfully, I didn't have to pay him for each role.

The part of Bruce's ex-wife went to Ellen Sandweiss, who endured our shenanigans back in high school and suffered much, much worse as Ash's sister in the first *Evil Dead*. The roles of two "close" ranchers went to Tim Quill – a high school/*Army of Darkness* alum – and to Danny Hicks who played the infamous Jake in *Evil Dead II*.

The challenge in casting was to avoid members of the Screen Actors Guild. Five years earlier, Ted had changed his status in the guild to "Financial Core," a seemingly insane decision to become a fee-paying nonmember. A SAG card is considered critical to professional actors and I thought Ted had lost his mind by apparently turning his in!

The allure of Fi-Core is the option to work *both* union and non-union jobs. In return, you forfeit the right to vote and to get a SAG award – neither of which ever applied to me anyway. Interestingly, it was two conservative presidents of the Screen Actors Guild who championed this notion over the years – Charlton Heston and Ronald Reagan.

Unions aren't an option when you're counting pennies, so the only way to keep *My Name Is Bruce* on budget was for me to go Fi-Core and open the door for non-union actors. If I wasn't union, nobody else had to be union. This was to be the first completely non-union movie I had done in decades. I'm not saying it was good or bad, as I have been a union member for most of my professional life, but it was the only way we could have pulled it off monetarily.

Without union restrictions, we were able to fill the rest of our cast with Oregon actors. The quaint town of Ashland was nearby, so we had access to the many actors and resources utilized by that town's annual Shakespeare Festival, which is a full-blown operation. Grace Thorsen, our leading lady, was a trained Shakespearean actress and played our seemingly untamable shrew quite nicely. Taylor Sharpe, the movie geek who kidnaps Bruce, was plucked right out of high school theater.

Anybody who auditioned but didn't get a part was given the offer to be a silent resident of Gold Lick (i.e., an "extra"). Aspiring actors made eager extras and their enthusiasm helped give our fictitious town an additional layer of personality.

Now all the movie needed was its monster.

Our costume designer turned us on to Jamie Peck, a local prop maker and costumer for children's theater productions. His repertoire included crafting strange masks and animal costumes, then performing in them. Jamie was the perfect combination. Not only could he create the Guan Di mask, but he was also big enough to play the Tofu Titan himself! Win-win!

The fabrication of Guan Di was a joint effort between Jamie, the costume designer and Melanie Tooker. Mel specialized in special effects makeup and had transformed me into an elderly Elvis for *Bubba Ho-Tep*. When she wasn't turning Ted into the decrepit Chinese caretaker or building blood-spurting dummies, Mel was responsible for the monstrous elements of Guan Di's appearance, including the gruesome hands and neck.

All the pieces were finally in place. It was time to roll in Gold Lick.

HEARTS OF DORKNESS

The general public remains fascinated by the filmmaking process, so Hollywood continues to pump out behind-the-scenes documentaries and featurettes about the various tricks of the trade. I wanted to jam-pack the DVD edition of *My Name Is Bruce* with as much stuff as possible, so I brought Mike Kallio up to document the making of the film. Kallio was an independent filmmaker in his own right and very capable of spearheading the documentary.

Kallio edited all the behind-the-scenes footage together and presented it as if the MNIB experience was a descent into madness. Winking at *Hearts of Darkness: A Filmmaker's Apocalypse*, the documentary about the making of *Apocalypse Now*, Kallio called his featurette *Heart of Dorkness* – a testament to the trials and tribulations of low-budget filmmaking. His take on the production was prophetic.

If a production has money, shooting on location is not a problem. You can afford to "tame" a wild area to suit your needs. You create a way in and you create a way out. Tents and mobile toilets are set up and a massive base camp of trailers and equipment trucks create an ad hoc Gypsy camp. You make things happen.

If you don't have money, it's man versus nature – you're at the mercy of whatever irritable flora and fauna are lurking in the area.

My hobbit house became the VIP club for the actors and the extras claimed the area around the trampoline as their domain. A former garage became the makeshift production base camp and my office was defiled to become the greenroom/hair and makeup stations. A few odious trailers were brought in to line the perimeter of Gold Lick and serve as storage workshops for costumes and effects makeup.

In 2006, High Definition wasn't standard yet, but it was definitely up-and-coming. My director of photography, Kurt Rauf, was a veteran *Evil Dead* Shemp – and yet another old friend. We discussed the trending technology and decided to shoot in HD, mostly because it was all the rage.

Man Posing As Director Torments Local Actress

I wound up calling it HDelay. No matter which format you're shooting in, you're going to have to change lenses a lot. With traditional film cameras, it's an easy five-minute switchover and you're ready to go. With HDelay, it was a schedule-screwing hassle. You had to take the lens off and do some strange back-focusing BS. Okay, it isn't BS, but it sure seemed like it when my night was wasting away while some chart came out and you had to put a thing on another thing so some other things wouldn't expand and contract and make the first thing fall off. None of the above is an issue these days, but we were trying to be ahead of the curve and we paid the price.

Here's an interesting fact: Bees love lavender. Specifically, aggressive Oregon bees love the lavender growing on my property. Summer was the season to harvest lavender and the crops on the southern slope were almost bursting.

The catering truck was set up not far from the edge of the lavender, if only because the spot was flat and hidden from the camera. The bees were already swarming because of the lavender, but they love all kinds of herbs – and caterers tend to cook with lots of herbs. Parsley, sage, rosemary and thyme lured the insects toward the dining cast and crew.

The lavender managed to keep the bees relatively calm, but it wasn't long before they got the taste of flesh. I watched as one bee landed on a piece of chicken, carved off a hunk with its chainsaw of a mandible and flew away, struggling under the strain of the oversized chicken nugget in its grasp.

A plate with meat on it would get attacked by an entire platoon of bees, so it wasn't long before the crew abandoned the catering area and ate lunch in their cars.

The aggressive bees made lunch interesting, but their effect on production paled in comparison to the impact of plants. We filmed several scenes in the deeper woods – beyond the cleared safety of the Gold Lick backlot. Without money in the budget for proper greenskeeping, we were oblivious to the fact that we were dragging ourselves and our equipment through patches of heinous *Poison Oak*.

Some people reacted immediately with red rashes. Even the

ones with no reaction unwittingly brought the toxic oil back home, where it would spread to their allergic spouses and children. Poison Oak got all over the cables that snaked through the forest, which meant that the poor grips and electricians working on the equipment trucks got infected – even if they hadn't set foot in the woods.

As a result of the slowish production pace, I lobbied for an extra day of shooting. The general response from the bee-stung, oak-infected crew was, "Fuck that. We're not coming back to your goddamn property."

I conceded to the mutineers and our last night of filming was in a public park – about twenty yards from a massive interstate.

GET OFF MY LAND!

Production wrapped, and I headed straight to the airport to kick off my book tour. With no time to catch my breath afterward, I was off to Miami to film the pilot for *Burn Notice*. I returned to southern Oregon in time for the holidays and saw with fresh eyes how *My Name Is Bruce* had ravaged my property.

A shredded driveway and trampled yard were lingering evidence of the production, but those could be repaired or left to heal on their own. I still had a goddamned town to deal with. There was never any plan or budget to have production demolish the backlot.

For a while, the "general store" was left standing, if only because it was anchored to a storage container and could harbor my equipment that valued even a primitive shelter. The gas station facade attached to my office outbuilding was kept around so we could play cards and lollygag beneath the canopy.

Soon enough, the cost of *not* building something to code became very evident. Nothing was sealed. Nothing was caulked. Camera-ready coats of stain and paint had done little to keep the materials from becoming saturated by the ultimate enemy to structures: moisture. The windows were warping. One of the doors practically imploded and metal siding began to peel away in sheets, so I eventually got a contractor to take it down. The only really smart thing I did in building this dumb backlot was to ensure that everything was bolted together and that no concrete was poured. We could just take it apart.

The town of Gold Lick is a fading memory now and Ida is in good health. To make *My Name Is Bruce* I crossed a few lines, but at the end of the day there is only one true cardinal rule in filmmaking and it's simple: There are no cardinal rules.

The only business truth that continues to reveal itself in my everyday life is that I've never made money without spending some first. Don't be afraid to sow some seeds. The arts are always risky and if you want to be part of the process you have to accept risk and live with it.

Mercifully, the film gods smiled enough to sell about a hundred thousand DVD units of *My Name Is Bruce* – well enough to cover the roughly $2 million outlay. That's what it's all about – returning money to the investors, so you can get it back and do it all over again.

RISE OF THE MASTER CYLINDER

When I was a kid, I read *Sad Sack* comic books. I could relate to the main character: a down-on-his-luck schmo in the U.S. Army, just trying to make it through his day. The guy was nothing special, with no super-skill set – he was born on this planet and wore a plain, wool uniform.

Sam Raimi read *Spider-Man* comics and became well versed in that universe. His main guy was also an average schmo from Queens, New York, but he gets bitten by a radioactive spider and becomes a web-slinging superhero – a little different from my guy.

It's a good thing it wasn't the other way around, because Sam landed one of the primo directing gigs of his era – the motion picture adaptation of *Spider-Man*. Apparently, the project had been languishing for years, changing studios and directors.

I was impressed as hell when I found out that Sam got the gig. Hollywood gets this stuff wrong all the time, but it was a good fit – Sam was intimately familiar with Spidey's myth, he could

direct special effects all day long and his visual style was long influenced by comic books anyway. I was mostly pleased for Sam in that he's always had an epic sensibility. He loved things that were big and complicated and this movie could finally let the magician within Sam out of the box.

ENTERING THE RING

Selfishly, I informed Sam that there was no way in hell he was going to make this highly anticipated, epic movie without letting me play some kind of meaningless part.

For the first film, Sam threw me the role of Ring Announcer and I was off to my fitting on the Sony lot. My part was a little "Las Vegas-y," a little over-the-top, in both look and delivery. The wardrobe department gave me a flashy, heavily shoulder-padded gold jacket and put my look over-the-top with a Cadillac logo, dangling on a chain around my neck.

Scenes in big movies like this aren't really rehearsed, they're storyboarded and on any given day the workload is judged more by "shots" than "page count." The sequences involving my character all take place in an amateur wrestling ring. Between twelve hundred extras, stunts and choreography, there were a lot of moving parts.

In the van, on the way to set for my first day of work, I glanced inside an open soundstage and saw none other than Sam's self-proclaimed "Classic," attended by several serious-looking men in mechanic overalls.

"That's Sam Raimi's car, isn't it?" I asked knowingly.

Earl, the driver, looked back at me nervously. "Why do you ask?"

I then realized that Earl, a loyal teamster, wasn't going to spill the beans. For all I knew, Sam had issued a gag order about his beloved Delta, now playing the role of "Uncle Ben's Car."

"That's okay, Earl," I reassured him. "Just curious."

Earl dropped me at the corner of stages 32, 33 and 35. The backlot was a beehive of activity – really looking like it did in the movies with all kinds of crew members driving, pushing or pulling some ridiculously cumbersome piece of equipment in every direction. The only things missing to complete the cliché were a couple of Roman soldiers, casually walking by, smoking cigarettes and drinking coffee.

I collared the first person with a walkie-talkie who approached our van.

"Excuse me, which one is the *Spider-Man* stage?" I asked, oblivious to the actual scope of the production.

The assistant director smiled at me. "*Spider-Man* is on *ten* stages. You're the Ring guy, right?"

"That's me."

"I think you're in Thirty-three. Let me check."

She barked into her headset, then waited for the information to be passed along and up the ranks until she got a reliable answer. It took some doing. Productions like this are pretty much a military operation – very segmented and individually goal oriented, with a sometime Byzantine chain of command.

"Yep. You're in Thirty-three. Head over there. Someone will meet you."

Inside stage 33, which was ancient and enormous, the place was already loud and warm from twelve hundred wrestling fan extras shuffling and chitchatting. Bullhorn-wielding assistant directors were shouting orders and reminders to the anxious crowd.

Across the large ring set, I could see Sam behind a bank of

video monitors. He looked really busy and our handlers on set didn't want us wandering around, randomly bugging the director – even if he was an old pal.

Sam started the wrestling sequence by filming the wider, more establishing shots first. After a week of this, finding out whether I was even in a given shot became something of a game. Sam had five cameras among the throngs in the arena, so it was anybody's guess.

When in doubt, keep acting! I figured.

"Am I even in this shot? Oh, there I am..."

Eventually, I caught Sam during a break. He looked tired but excited. I asked him what it was like to take filmmaking up to the next level – to the A-list.

Sam smiled and shrugged. "I'm doing the same stuff we did in the Super-8 movie days, I just have a lot more money to play with."

Whatever Sam did, it worked. *Spider-Man* opened to a record $112 million. It's not as big as the oversized mega-openings of today, but it smashed a box office record or two at the time.

USHERING IN THE SEQUEL

With the massive success of *Spider-Man*, you could bet your Buster Browns there was going to be a sequel – this franchise was off and running. Naturally, the second film had to be bigger, better, with more villains, more stunts, more everything. Naturally, I had to invite myself into the cast.

The second time around, Peter Parker's romance to Mary Jane intensifies and he tries to see her in a play on Broadway, but since he's so busy saving the world, he's late to the show. That's where

I come in. My role as the Snooty Usher is to intervene and keep the tardy playgoer out of the theater.

Tobey Maguire was a nice chap. He was a little confused when he saw me back again, playing a different character, but he was happy to play along.

"Hey, Tobey, great to see you again!" I exclaimed, genuinely happy to be back. "Looks like it's time for me to play another pivotal role."

"Oh yeah? How so?" Tobey asked, trying not to be snotty.

"Well, as you recall in the first one, Peter Parker wanted to be called 'The Human Spider.' My character changed it, calling him 'The Amazing Spider-Man,' so, technically, I *named* your character."

Tobey's smile faded a bit and he arched an eyebrow. "Uh, yeah, I guess…"

"And I love how this new part is pivotal, too."

"Is it now?" Tobey asked, his expression back to smiling again, no doubt bemused by my audacity.

"Yeah. In this scene, Peter Parker *tries* to get into the theater to see Mary Jane perform, right?"

"Right. So?"

" '*Tries*.' That's the operative word. The Snooty Usher won't let Peter in late. Technically, he's the only character who ever *defeated* Spider-Man."

Tobey rolled his eyes.

The scene went fine and I got to see the finished film in, of all places, Sofia, Bulgaria. I was there filming the modern-day classic *Man with the Screaming Brain*. My partner and old Raimi family friend David Goodman was with me and we both lamented to Sam that we wouldn't be around to see the opening of his very anticipated sequel.

Somehow, Sam pulled a few strings – or a whole ton of strings

– and arranged for a screening of *Spider-Man 2* for our entire crew and their families in a brand-new, four-hundred-seat stadium-style multiplex in Sofia. This type of theater seems normal to most of us, but it was a rarity in economically burgeoning Bulgaria.

I am of the opinion that the second installment of the Spidey series really hit the nail on the head. It was just the right combination of myth, romance, action, huge set pieces and humor. Our private audience "oohed" and "aahhed" the whole way through. The only depressing thing about the entire affair was when the lights came back up and our humble crew had to get back to work on our crappy little movie.

DÉJÀ-VU

Back in high school, I had a French teacher named Elizabeth Tessem. She was *Le Grande Dame* of teachers. Mrs. Tessem had been teaching so long, my mother was also one of her students. Mrs. Tessem *lived* her teaching. She loved everything French, mostly speaking it during class, and she created a very fun learning environment. Who knew I would enjoy a French class?

It didn't hurt that Sam Raimi and old friend (even by high school age) Matt Dickson were also in the class. We were very happy to create and perform French skits, demonstrating our "amazing" grasp of the language but mostly overacting and doing cheap gags. When Sam tracked me down for my bit in *Spider-Man 3*, this was immediately what he referred to.

"Okay, listen – we're going to basically do one of those skits we did in Mrs. Tessem's old class, with the maître d', only it's Peter Parker trying to get a table, and –"

"Say no more, Sam. It's the perfect trilogy for my appearances in this franchise: I named him; I defeated him. Now Spider-Man, a superhero, comes to me, a mere mortal, for help. How often does that happen?"

"Not very often," Sam agreed, mostly just to end the conversation. "Okay, so –"

"So, it's pivotal. My role as the maître d' is pivotal."

"Look, pal, you can call it whatever you want. Show up Monday morning and do your job."

Click. Sam had hung up.

I pumped a fist in the air. "Nailed it!"

My scene in Spidey 3 was a personal fave, in that Tobey and I could actually let the scene play – it wasn't some quick bit, with extras and mayhem all around. Tobey was amused by seeing me on set for the third time, to play yet another annoying character.

"Of course he's back." Tobey grinned. "We can't make a Spider-Man movie without Bruce Campbell!"

"You're starting to understand how Hollywood works, Tobey."

Our scene played out as planned, with the usual additions, tweaks and changes that Sam makes all day long, every day that he shoots. I hope Madame Tessem would be proud of the end results.

Spider-Man 3 took a lot of flak. It was a bigger, more convoluted story with maybe one too many villains and it went a bit dark for some. Still, for me, it's hard to put in words how delighted I was to watch Sam – my boyhood buddy and filmmaking fraternal brother – direct one of the most successful movie franchises in history.

There were superhero movies before *Spider-Man*, but Sam's series truly set that particular genre in motion for decades to come. I'm not a film historian, but I sense that *Spider-Man* also represents a turning of the tide – or taste – where even A-list movies are now B movies, conceptually. Believe me, if your hero is bitten by a radioactive spider and starts web-swinging from buildings, that's not only a B movie; that's a *1950s* B movie.

I'm just happy that genre fare is no longer frowned upon in the world of entertainment – and that we're finally seeing how popular fantasy, horror and sci-fi stories really are.

ASHES TO AXES

I was no stranger to Miami, Florida. Thanks to both *Make Love the Bruce Campbell Way* and *Man with the Screaming Brain*, I spent a nice chunk of time touring the nation in the mid-00s. As an international outpost at the tip of a massive peninsula, Miami was an obvious destination for each tour.

As it turned out, attendance at both of these appearances consisted of merely a handful of fans and a fistful of empty seats. I have a great excuse for the *Screaming Brain* debacle – the Emmys were on, it was game seven of the baseball World Series and there was a hurricane watch in the area. That's a hell of a trifecta.

The *Make Love* event/bust in Miami had no such competition – the weather was great, it was a good store in a prime location, and nothing was on the tube. Still, folks just didn't show up. I was baffled, because in Orlando at a recent event fans were out the door and around the block. Perhaps it was Miami's incredible collision of cultures that blotted out the influence of Deadites upon the local consciousness. Whatever the reason, I concluded that

"Curse you, Miami!"

trying to promote or further my career there wasn't worth the time or effort, so a new rule went into effect: Never go back to Miami.

If you were watching a movie, this is where the screen would cut to black and a title card would slowly fade in:

"One Year Later…"

The phone rings.

"Hello."

"Hi, Bruce, Barry here. I have an offer for you to be a regular on a new, cool TV show pilot."

"Oh yeah? Where does it shoot?"

"Miami."

"Pass."

I explained – passionately – that I was not only done with episodic television, but I was also done with Miami and its "bad juju." I was really enjoying life in the boonies of Oregon, returning to my roots, making a couple of "homegrown" movies and doing cameos in the films of old colleagues like Sam Raimi and the Coen brothers.

"Ya gotta understand, Barry. *Jack of All Trades* left a bad taste in my mouth. Episodic TV is too much work for too much heartache."

"Let's just treat television on a case-by-case basis," Barry advised. "The script is really fresh. The role is perfect for you – and it's just a pilot."

A "pilot" is the first episode of a newly developed TV series. It's a "proof of concept" that helps a network gauge whether the premise has any marketable potential. As a rule, *most* TV programs never get past the first episode.

An actor's reaction to getting cast in a pilot changes over the course of their career. When an actor is young and eager, they react with: "Hooray, I booked a pilot! This could lead to years of steady, well-paid employment!" When an actor is old, bitter and jaded, they tend to react with: "Oh, dear God, not another pilot! This will never go *anywhere*!"

An actor has to grow a thick skin, keeping pilots at arm's length. It's best not to get too close to something that might get killed off. I had been burned by pilots before, so it was only fitting that this new project was called *Burn Notice*.

"Fine," I agreed. "You're right. It's only a pilot. It'll never get picked up anyway…"

AMERICA'S PENIS

Southern, Central and Northern Florida are like three different states – or even worlds – and it would take decades before I understood that.

My first real experience in Northern Florida came when I was scouting locations for *Evil Dead II* in 1986. Florida was a potential location for us because it was number three in film and TV production and they had a capable film commission established.

I had never before considered Florida to be a "redneck state," but some of my most disturbing brushes with racism happened when I was scouting the rural areas of Northern Florida.

As an example, passing a gas station one day, George, our location guide, gestured out the window to an African-American man pumping gas. "You see that fellow there? He's a *good* one."

It took me a moment to understand what George was insinuating, because I had never heard anyone – even in lily-white suburban Detroit where I was raised – say anything like that before about a person of color.

In the end, for a myriad of reasons, we didn't film there.

Thank God.

Central Florida was all about tourists, franchises and retirees. Orlando is one of the most franchise-infiltrated cities I've ever seen – not a mom-and-pop operation in sight. Orlando was all about things that were familiar, safe and fun. Theme parks on parade. It was like a midwestern town dropped into the middle of a swamp. I nicknamed it Borelando.

Miami wasn't even remotely close to a Midwest sensibility. It's one of the most culturally and racially diverse places I've ever been. The Latin culture had taken hold long ago and locals were very comfortable and proud of their heritage – whether it was Colombian, Cuban or Venezuelan. On any given day, you would encounter far more people speaking Spanish than English.

On more than one occasion, while struggling to communicate with someone who spoke no English, I was asked: "Why you no speak Spanish?" The explanation that five miles outside the city of Miami nobody speaks a word of Spanish would not compute.

After seven years there, on and off, my refrain became: "I love Miami because it's so close to the U.S."

CLIMATE CONTROL

I was born in Michigan and spent the first twenty-plus years of my life there. Maybe my body was hardwired for colder climates. Regardless, Miami was on the opposite corner of the nation from where I had chosen to live. Each year, for seven seasons, I had to transform from a pasty, rain-soaked Pacific Northwesterner into a tanned, semi-tropical beach bum.

When you exit the plane in Miami, you are immediately blasted with a fireball of humidity, a smothering heat that I had never experienced before – like a jungle outpost. Then I remembered I was only an hour's drive from the Everglades (1.5 million acres of tropical wetlands).

Miami *was* a jungle outpost.

At that level of mugginess and rainfall, the tropics were constantly decaying yet trying to reclaim civilization at the same time. Lush vines were steadily strangling everything, while foliage mocked landscapers as they vainly tried to keep everything tight and trim.

Avocados and bananas didn't stand a chance in Miami. Eat them immediately, or you were looking at a blackened mess forty-eight hours later. Not even a sealed freezer could stave off a moldy death.

The rapid decomposition was so impressive that Ida

Shedding a few layers in-between takes in order to beat the heat.

and I had to change how we ate. We couldn't assume that groceries bought on Sunday would be anything other than ooze by Thursday. Stockpiling wasn't an option, so we shopped like Europeans, only buying what we would actually eat within the next couple days.

Our bicycles were also under attack – from corrosion. Being so close to the ocean, the air itself was 30 percent salt. Taking your bike in to the shop to get "de-corroded" was just routine maintenance.

After a few years, I became an old pro at living in the Magic City and an expert in harnessing the power of the sun. When I first arrived in Miami, I was still just another ignorant tourist. The character Sam Axe needed to be a tan man, the result of years of being a relaxed, poolside lounger. How do you get tan quickly? A tanning salon, of course!

The first time I went, the attendant knew nothing about the

science of tanning or the mechanics of the beds. In retrospect, I shouldn't have been so willing to allow some babbling, orange-colored dipshit bombard me with ultraviolet radiation. But my naiveté didn't stop there. After being barbecued for way too long, at way too high of a setting, I casually headed out to the beach to catch some more rays.

It didn't take a dermatologist to help me understand why I couldn't sleep that night. Never again. Eventually, I would learn that fifteen minutes of sunbathing per side was all I needed to maintain a tan but not destroy my skin.

My costar, Gabrielle Anwar, absolutely loved the Miami climate. She was five-three and weighed only seven pounds, so she was immune to overheating. The Southern Florida climate was paradise to her. I think I only saw her sweat three times – and it's possible that the sweat was added by the makeup department. Conversely, Gabrielle couldn't tolerate air-conditioning. If a gust of cold, recycled air got too close, she'd start shivering, grab her set chair and drag it into the balmiest, sun-blasted spot she could find.

Gabrielle basking in the infernal Miami climate.

Adaptation is critical to survival. I needed to use every resource available to acclimate to the Sunshine State if I had any chance of making it through an entire season of shooting.

Over the course of the first couple seasons, we had to devise a wardrobe system that would allow me to stay as comfortable as possible or at least hide how uncomfortable I was. This was a challenge because Sam Axe was a covert operative, an infiltrator and imperson-ator. Sam couldn't wear short-sleeve floral shirts in every scene – he needed to be able to wear black, three-piece suits and look cool (both meanings apply) doing it.

When filming, I went through a lot of shirts. I'd sweat through a shirt after a few takes, so we'd swap it out for a fresh one. Over time, I researched lightweight undergarment fabric that whisked sweat away to another dimension, thereby giving my shirts "another take or two." Wool socks, counter-intuitively, kept my feel comfy and dry. SmartWool, the opposite of your father's "dumb, scratchy wool," was my new best friend. Try it sometime. Cotton is the Jose Cuervo of fabrics – we've been sold a shabby bill of goods for decades. Cotton, in sock form, lights a fire in your shoe through incessant friction. Wool, for whatever reason, came to my rescue and it's all I wear on my feet now, hot or cold.

Clothing control was only part of what I needed to endure the blazing climate. I had to lose some weight. My gut had expanded in the decade of living in rural Oregon. Playing Sam Axe was great because he didn't have to be fit and agile like the character Michael Westen – he was defined by his penchant for lounging around with a beer in hand. A gut was practically obligatory. Fat, however, is insulation intended to keep a warm-blooded body warm when it's cold. Gabrielle was comfortable on location because she had less fat than a rice cake and Jeffrey Donovan was a lean son of a gun as well. In seven seasons, I never saw him sweat.

I soon discovered how necessary a pool was to preserving my core temperature and my sanity. For the first season, I didn't have access to a swimming pool – only a small speck of rooftop upon which I could get my fifteen minutes per side of sunbathing. I'd end up drenched in sweat as I waddled through the house to the shower. After the first season, I refused to live in Miami without a pool.

It was possible to chart the change of seasons by the

temperature fluctuations in the pool. When I arrived at the beginning of a new season in March, water in the pool would be pretty much completely cold. A month later, the top inch of water would be warm, so I'd swim back and forth to swirl it all around. By early summer, the pool would be fifty-fifty cold and hot. Near the end of filming a season, by early fall, the pool would morph into a low-grade Jacuzzi and recused itself from providing relief – not a cool spot to be felt.

The house Ida and I rented was the same way. Everything was fine in March, but five months later the heat would become inexorably trapped in its bowels. I decided to adopt an admittedly strange ritual of "bleeding" the water pipes. Convinced that superheated water was trapped in the pipes because of sub-par wall insulation, I'd run the cold water until it actually got "cold" again.

The production schedule for *Burn Notice* had us shooting during the "low" tourist season which, ironically, was summer in Miami. Summer is usually associated with sun, fun and vacations, but the peak of Miami's tourism and tolerability was during the winter. Much like we did when we were kids, people head south for the winter. December, January and February are the perfect months to be in Miami. September and October are the perilous hurricane months and anything in between took place at its own peril.

Shooting is always easier when it's not crowded. Productions have a better chance of filming at popular restaurants, landmarks or recreation areas and you don't have as many gawkers coagulating around you.

Whenever I worked in New Zealand, the weather was flip-flopped because I'd cross the equator into the Southern Hemisphere. If I went down in June, the beginning of my summer, the New Zealand winter was just coming on full force. I would return home to fall weather, realizing that an entire season had passed me by. Some years, depending on when I went and how long I stayed, experiencing back-to-back summers or winters was not unusual – just completely discombobulating.

Spending my summer and fall in Miami meant that I only had about one good month of weather in Florida before the inferno began. By the time I got back to Oregon, I'd only have a few weeks until the weather turned into stereotypical Pacific Northwest – cold and wet.

For seven years, it seemed like I was never anywhere at the right time.

ON NOTICE

My role in *Burn Notice* was that of Sam Axe, a "former" Navy SEAL (I was informed to never use the term "ex" when referring to military service). After serving honorably, Sam was now devoted to a life of women, suds and sun. However, fate would deal him a different card when friend and

"You know spies…bunch of bitchy little girls."

spy Michael Westen gets "burned" by a mysterious organization and shows up in Miami with nothing.

Created by boyish, whip-smart Matt Nix, *Burn Notice* raced from pilot to production and became a seven-season hit for the USA Network, arguably influencing the network template for new shows over the next few years. It's also inarguably one of the most successful, challenging and rewarding projects I've ever been a part of.

I didn't know Jeffrey Donovan before *Burn Notice*. He was

almost exactly ten years younger than me but had fifteen years of experience under his belt in theater, movies and on television. Jeffrey and I bonded over the fact that I had been in his shoes before, starring in two previous TV shows or, as we would joke, "being number one on the call sheet."

Jeffrey was a very accomplished, dynamic actor and the show was a perfect vehicle for his unique gifts. Eventually, he became like a younger brother to me and our relationship remained strong throughout.

Gabrielle Anwar was an old pro by the time *Burn Notice* rolled around. Having acted since childhood, she was confident in her abilities and was wonderfully frank and direct on set in her dealings with directors and producers. I enjoyed her toughness and general fearlessness. Gabrielle had just finished a stint on *The Tudors*, a decidedly highbrow affair, and *Burn Notice* couldn't have been a bigger departure. She loved calling it a "silly boys' show" and seemed genuinely baffled by what made the show so popular.

Sharon Gless was a TV icon, having achieved deserved accolades on her groundbreaking show, *Cagney & Lacey*. I'm continually amused by actors who are, in reality, the opposite of the characters they portray. In the show, Madeline Westen (my character called her Maddy) was a life-hardened battle-axe with strong opinions. In real life, Sharon was a pussycat. I would even call her shy and slightly demure. Granted, she could laugh like a longshoreman and had a wonderful, bawdy sense of humor, but I was always dumb-founded how a multiple-Emmy

Celebrating a coveted TV milestone: 100 episodes.

winner could still be so questioning of her own abilities.

Coby Bell, my personal salvation in Miami, rolled in for season four and beyond as the character Jesse. Coby, although twenty years my junior, had done six seasons of *Third Watch* and a slew of other television. He was unfazed, or so it seemed, by coming into the show, late in the party, to take some heat off the rest of us.

Coby is a mensch. A father of four young children, he would dutifully fly back to Los Angeles every weekend without fail. I'll always be impressed by that. As a younger actor I never had that dedication and it damaged my first marriage. Coby and I became fast friends. I think the writers sensed this, because Sam and Jesse were often paired together in scenes apart from Michael or Fiona.

Aside from the regulars, we got terrific support seasonally from Seth Peterson as Michael's tormented brother, Stephen Martines as Fiona's ill-fated lover and the unsung work of journeyman actors Marc Macaulay and Brandon Morris, who played a couple of by-the-book FBI guys.

One of the great things about a hit TV show is that it attracts high-quality guest stars. Usually, actors will flock to a TV show for one of two reasons – either they're fans or it's popular. As seven seasons rolled out, *Burn Notice* benefited from both criteria and over five hundred actors passed through Miami.

Because this was an international spy show, this varied group of thespians fell into some of the obvious categories. For starters, you need an endless string of bad guys to defeat. Playing a "bad guy" appeals to many actors, mostly because they don't have to be "likable" and they can ham it up.

John Mahoney, who played the cryptic Management guy, was a fan of the show. Jay Karnes and Todd Stashwick were both good at being *smooth* bad guys. Jere Burns specialized in *creepy*. A handful of *Brisco* alumni even snuck in to play baddies – M. C.

Gainey, Andrew Divoff and John Pyper-Ferguson. Tricia Helfer, an early "badd-ess," was both beautiful and dangerous.

Certainly the "Most Colorful Bad Guy" award would have to go to Tim Matheson for his portrayal of Larry, the rogue operative. Tim was an old pro who had been in the business forever and I respected him a lot – hell, he did the voice for *Jonny Quest*, my favorite cartoon as a kid. Tim also returned in the director's chair to lead us through a number of our most epic season-ending episodes.

Aside from the "overtly bad," spy shows also need a layer of "not good, not bad" characters. We had plenty of very questionable CIA types who excelled at doublespeak. Richard Schiff, Alex Carter and the formidable John C. McGinley were all standouts. My favorite of the CIA jerks, though, were two numbskulls played by Brandon O'Malley and John Ales. These characters were imported from the Sam Axe TV movie and as actors we loved shouting at each other. Often, after the camera would cut, we'd all burst out laughing.

Eventually, you work your way into the "mostly good" guys. Barry the Money Launderer, a recurring character, was wonderfully played by Paul Tei. I always looked forward to scenes with him. Paul had a great sense of humor and the two of us came as close to ad-libbing as there was on the show, which wasn't a whole lot. Jack Coleman, Grant Show and Lauren Stamile capably headed up the more "serious" accomplices.

There was also quite an array of "maybe good, maybe bad" leading ladies for Jeffrey to play opposite, such as Moon Bloodgood, Dina Meyer and Alona Tal. I managed to spend screen time with Kristanna Loken in a couple episodes and I didn't complain one little bit.

If you stay on the air long enough, plenty of "random" casting will happen, too, where you get people who were perfectly fine for the role but who already had impressive careers of their own, like Warrior Princess Lucy Lawless, singer Gavin Rossdale, football great Michael Irvin, comedy freak Patton Oswalt, WWE legend Big Show and rapper Method Man.

Of all the guest stars on *Burn Notice*, the most awe-inspiring was the Bandit himself, Mr. Burt Reynolds. A lot of our Florida-based production team had worked with Burt on various movies and TV shows and they talked him into appearing in an episode.

Writing about a guy like Burt Reynolds, where do you even begin? Not only was he a fellow Michigander, but in addition Burt's acting career – well past the half-century mark now – encompassed the end of the studio system, early television and the Hollywood blockbuster.

Burt was the number-one box office star for five years running, which is unparalleled. At his peak, he declined the roles of James Bond and Han Solo.

His contributions to cinema and television really are iconic. In my profession, we would be lucky to have one *Deliverance* or *The Longest Yard* on our résumé. My contemporaries on the *small screen* would be thrilled to be associated with just one classic like *Gunsmoke* or *Evening Shade*.

The man's accomplishments are various and impressive. He founded a theater, posed naked in *Cosmopolitan* magazine and had a hit single called "Let's Do Something Cheap and Super-ficial." He's got an Emmy, some Golden Globes and a sack full of People's Choice Awards. From spaghetti Westerns to *Boogie Nights*, what hasn't this man done?

When I first met Burt, it was during a lunch break on set. We heard a rumor that the man himself was in the building for a visit. Jeffrey and I rode up on our set bikes and I executed a classic backpedal skid stop. I looked up to see Burt smiling and I decided to try my usual "Hey, buddy, this is a *closed* set..." routine, pretending not to recognize him. Thankfully, Burt ate it up and we quickly established an easy rapport.

During the run of Burt's episode, we got to socialize a couple times. One night at The Forge, a Miami institution, Burt explained one of the worst things about being a male sex symbol – encountering drunk female fans.

"You'd think it would be really fun," he explained. "Hot chicks throwing themselves at you. But not if they're drunk. Then it's really horrible. They'd wrap their legs around you and never let go."

Burt did a great job in the episode, his charm and charisma still evident, even after way-too-recent heart surgery knocked him for a loop.

Before the series ended, Ida and I wanted to see Burt one last time, so we scheduled a trip up to his home in Jupiter, Florida. Valhalla, Burt's name for his oceanfront estate, was befitting of the icon – masculine, sprawling, a little over-the-top. Burt was a gracious host, giving us the grand tour, which ended in his wonderful version of a man cave, which was even more masculine than the rest of the house with a giant bar, pool table, movie theater and enough dedicated movie star pictures to fill a museum.

As I scanned the photos, the inevitable questions popped up. "I see you have a picture of Errol Flynn. He was one of my favorites. You must have met him near the end of his career."

"Yeah, but he was still at it," Burt clarified. "I knocked on his dressing room door one day at Warner Brothers and he casually called me in. I stepped inside and he's being serviced by a young starlet. He carried on talking like it was nothing, like it happened all the time – which it did."

John Wayne used to invite Burt over all the time because "Duke" thought he was funny. Richard Pryor also thought Burt was funny – and this was coming from a funny guy. After a concert, Richard invited Burt to ride on his private jet. During the flight, Richard was more than a little amused by "the black man giving whitey a ride in a private jet!"

Burt could relate stories in a wonderful stream of consciousness from any decade you asked about. He was a great raconteur and I encouraged him to write a book.

"Hell, Burt, I've written a book and you've been around *twice* as long as I have. If anyone has a book in them, it's *you.*"

Burt did not disagree and in 2015 I was pleased to see his autobiography hit the shelves.

For the most part, the *Burn Notice* actors got along. Did we have shitty, pissy or even temperamental moments between us? Hell yes – on numerous occasions –

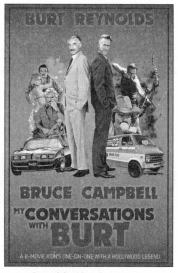

One of the ideas I was trying to pitch for Burt's book.

but compared to what I've witnessed on other sets, I'd give us a B+ for behavior.

What kept the cast grounded enough to grin and bear it through the heat and long hours was the fact that we all respected the end product – it also didn't hurt that the ratings were excellent right out of the gate.

NUMBER TWO ON THE CALL SHEET

Matt Nix shared a theory he had heard about baboons. The number-one baboon carried the most responsibility, along with the youngest. The top baboon, naturally, had a lot of stress to make decisions, defend the gang and lead by example. The youngest baboon also had a lot of stress because it was always being told to "keep up" and couldn't help being compared unfavorably to all the other baboons. The least stressed, according to Matt, was the number-two baboon – or me. Being second fiddle, or "number two on the call sheet," I didn't have to carry the load like Jeffrey Donovan, who was the face of the show. My character added humor and a wink, but *Burn Notice* did not live or die by me.

As a result, I had a pretty damn good time working on the show. Often, I would "open the store" by being in the first scene filmed to give Jeffrey or Gabrielle some time off, go home for some sun and a swim, return hours later to get made-up again and "close the shop" by being in the last scene of the day.

There were episodes where Sam was all over it ("Sam-tastic episodes") and there were those where he wasn't featured. On the "easy" episodes, I would make sure to tell the assistant directors to never announce my early departures over the radio because Donovan would most assuredly hear about it and give me the stink eye all the way to the production van.

The easiest workday I recall had Sam, in a single shot, walking to

A Sam-tastic wardrobe.

the end of a driveway, checking his watch and walking back – about fifteen minutes of work. I literally raced off the set that day, urging my driver, Olga, to "step on it, in case they change their mind!"

That's not to say that I didn't do my time or put in some gruelingly long hours. As we were shooting, on average, for fourteen hours a day, our call times would get pushed back day by day and come Friday, with an 11:00 a.m. crew call, we wouldn't wrap until well into Saturday morning – hence the term "Fraturday." There was no shortage of those.

LOCATION, LOCATION, LOCATION!

The diversity of Miami continued to enlighten me as production rolled on through the years. As covert do-gooders, we infiltrated virtually every upper-class venue in Dade County. But, for every extravagant nightclub, restaurant, marina and mansion we wormed our way into, we also got stuck in a host of abandoned sugar factories, chemical plants, storage containers and what I coined "shit-wipe" alleys. I'm pretty sure we filmed in every abandoned structure in the nearby town of Homestead.

I once shot an entire scene in a municipal garage stairwell with a homeless guy camped out on a landing directly beneath me. Like some sort of metropolitan troll, he had rooted himself and refused to move. A crew member assured me, "It's okay. He promised to stay quiet."

We even managed to find an abandoned four-story parking garage to shoot in. You'd think a city would always be able to find a use for a "vacant" parking structure, but this one in Miami was a ghost town – even the former homeless camps on each level had been vacated. Maybe the building had become unfit or too much of a health hazard to maintain – and if that was the case, why the hell were we filming there? The tricky part was getting up to set via stairwells choked with decomposing clothing, used syringes and makeshift toilets.

Jimbo was the father of all squatters. In 1954, Jimbo Luznar was evicted from his waterfront shrimp place in downtown Miami. In return, he got a lifetime free lease from the city if he moved to a place on Virginia Key, which was basically a swampy bog across from the sewage treatment plant. Jimbo took the deal and he kept the city to its word – much to their chagrin – for over fifty years. Jimbo and his two sons, Bubba and Bobby, changed their business model from shrimping to alcohol and maintained one of the funkiest down-and-out bars in the Northern Hemisphere.

Over the years, the place began to look like Gilligan's Island – if Gilligan were a drunken crackhead. The truly bohemian vibe attracted every weirdo, drifter, pirate, squatter and freak in the area. Jimbo's was a visual treat – if decrepit, dangerous island life was what you were after. When we filmed scenes there, the art department rarely had to add any dressing. Obviously, it was perfect and we weren't alone in our thinking – Jimbo's had been a film location since 1964 when *Flipper* was shot there and as recently as *The Fast and the Furious*.

A [trailer] room with a view.

Proximity to the sewage treatment plant gave Jimbo's a wonderful perfumed stench all day long. The treatment plant installed a line of sprayers, emitting some god-awful odor-neutralizing fragrance, but the combination of industrial-strength Febreze and human waste was a bit much on the olfactory senses. I would have preferred the pure smell of crap.

Ultimately, a family squabble ended the long run of Jimbo's Place. *Burn Notice* returned to the site one last time after it had been basically bulldozed and fenced. Oddly enough, as sleazy as

Jimbo's was, it was an original and I was sad to see it go.

Cities can be bipolar places, and the history of Miami explains a lot about its spectrum of glamour and grime. We filmed in an area called Coconut Grove, a touristy, ritzy little shopping neighborhood where a person could stroll from the beach to grab an iced latte or a Tommy Bahama shirt. However, if that same person were to walk a couple blocks farther, they'd stumble into Little Bahamia – an area that was noticeably poorer. A CVS drugstore on the corner of Grand Avenue and Margaret Street marked a harsh but invisible boundary between relative affluence and abject poverty.

I often wondered why there was such a distinct difference between two sides of the same street. After a little research, I found out that much of Coconut Grove was built in the late 1800s by laborers from the Bahamas. Apparently, Bahamians were the best of the best when it came to assembling and maintaining thatched structures. Starting with what was considered one of the first hotels in Florida, the Bahamians kept building. Many of the laborers decided to cut down their commute by literally building their own neighborhood next door.

Ironically, many of the Bahamian homes have proven more resilient than the wealthier ones built since. The Caribbean-seasoned Bahamians built their homes low to the ground so high winds just blew overhead and they chose yellow pine, a type of wood that termites avoided.

CAR CAPERS

While in Miami, I wasn't sure which car stunts were more spectacular – the ones on our TV show or the random reck-lessness I witnessed on the Southern Florida streets every day. Driving there was unsettling, since the diverse inhabitants all drove according to the laws of their home countries. On average, once per day, driving back and forth to set my driver Olga and I would experience what I called "holy shit moments," whereby a driver – usually a hopelessly lost tourist from another country – would do the most unexpected or unthinkable maneuver directly in front of us.

Whether it was the shirtless dude in flip-flops, flying down the freeway on his *Lawrence of Arabia* era motorcycle, weaving in and out of traffic with reckless abandon, or the two ninja motorcycle riders who whizzed past our car on either side – driving in Miami wasn't something you did casually. Add to that a flotilla of scooters (driven often by champagne-swilling out-of-towners), a mostly clueless pedestrian population and you've got yourself the Wild West of traffic scenarios. Driving to set every day was a great way to prep for our own shenanigans behind the wheel.

The character Michael Westen drove a bitchin' black Dodge Charger that became iconic over the life of the show. That car was good news and bad news, all wrapped up into one hot package – "hot" being the operative word. A black car being blasted with light on an asphalt parking lot in August in Miami is a combination that should never go together – but there we were, week after week, year after year, filming long dialogue-fests inside this 1973 motorized Easy-Bake Oven. Mercifully, right around season three, due to Mr. Donovan's insistence, the AC crisis in the Charger was solved. The transpo department installed a unit that would easily have cooled a tractor trailer.

I didn't get to drive the Charger much, but when I did I always had a blast. Nineteen-seventies American vehicles, for all of their shitty features, had balls. Any time I had to peel out after some bad dude, I'd slam that sucker into low gear and lay rubber all the way out of frame. I would routinely get applause from the crew after an action take because that car made it look so easy.

Unfortunately, my char-
acter, Sam, drove a different
car – a modern Cadillac. Not
to disparage a great American
brand (I grew up in a "Chevy
family"), but modern Caddies
suck raw eggs. Invariably, Sam
would have to stomp on the gas
and race out of a shot. Not in
the Cadillac. I'd bury that pedal

Charged up!

to the floor and the engine would heave before engaging – as if
thinking over what it was about to do before it did it.

"Bruce, we need you to give it some juice on this next one,"
the director would invariably radio to me.

"I'm juicing, believe me. This Caddy is shooting blanks, man!"

I tried every trick in the book – turning the AC off, pre-revving
and popping into gear, but nothing spun out like the ratty old
Charger.

Police escorts are a beautiful thing. You can't help but feel
presidential as you race down the street, cars parting like the Red
Sea before Moses. I got to participate in one such escort when
Sam was trying to catch up with some random scumbag. I pretty
much had two lanes to myself to race, skid and swerve, while
actual traffic zoomed past me on the opposite side of the road.
With cameras strategically placed, the end result looked like I
was driving like a maniac in the middle of traffic.

I consider *Burn Notice* to be a *contemporary* TV show, but in all
but one season our characters never wore seat belts. Nothing is
less sexy than a good guy sliding into his car in hot pursuit – then
stopping the action cold to buckle up.

I am aware of how completely irresponsible it was for us to
perpetuate the bad habit of not wearing protective harnesses in

large, fast-moving vehicles, but early on all the actors just jumped in the cars and took off. Realistically, we never had to do any driving that really required seat belts. When we squealed off in a car, it was only for about a hundred feet, or until we were out of the shot.

Season seven, the seat belt thing changed. Enter Hyundai – a sponsor! In Hyundai's cars, drivers had to be safe, so a nervous director approached Gabrielle and me before a scene, sitting in the new Hyundai, ready to do a bit of driving.

"Uh, hey, guys, when you get in the car, this time we really need you to buckle up. It's a Hyundai, sponsorship thing."

"Are you fucking kidding us?" Gabrielle asked, never one to hide her raw emotions. "Bugger off."

I was more diplomatic, perhaps, but I, too, declined the invitation to buckle up for the shot/sponsor. Neither of us saw any reason to change now. The director gulped and turned away. They filmed the scene "as is" but later digitally added seat belts in several interior shots. Thankfully, I only had to ride in that car once.

LAW AND DISORDER

A guy came up to me at a convention recently and said, "Bruce, I suppose for *Burn Notice* you have to go to the gun range regularly – just to stay on target, right?"

"Uh, no," I said, correcting him gently. "As actors, we never actually have to hit anything."

It's safe to say, being a spy/action show, guns were a big part of *Burn Notice* and guns on set, even if non-lethal, were something you had to pay attention to. Guns shooting fake rounds were still explosive and emitted wadding that was unsafe at close range. Tragically, a few actors have died because of sloppy, albeit "fake" gun handling.

Charlie, the prop master/gun wrangler and I forged a great relationship. He was always prepped, professional and chipper in executing his duties. Charlie and I got along well because he knew I wasn't cavalier about gunplay. I dick around on sets all day long, but not when it comes to cars, stunts or guns – any one of which can put a person out of commission.

Staging gunplay is like choreography. You duck out from behind a wall and fire three rounds, then dive back as ricochets pepper the area around you. It's a lot of back-and-forth. The problems arise when somebody loses count on either end. You don't want to be jumping into the line of fire when an effects guy is shooting "bullet hits" at your face. These tiny plastic balls are filled with a sparking agent and when they're shot out of the equivalent of a pellet gun they shatter into a million pieces. They look great exploding on a brick wall but aren't so fun when high-velocity sparkle dust and plastic shards are raining down on your moneymaker.

Squibs, or body bullet hits, are tricky as well. The mechanical effects guy rigs a thin protective metal plate on wherever an actor is going to get hit, straps a small explosive charge to that, then lays a sealed blood pouch on top of that. Wires are then run down the actor's leg to a power source. On cue, the effects guy hits a button, the charge blows and the blood is blown across the room, in a glorious, gory spectacle. When a person is shot in the front, the real mess is when the bullet comes out the back, but film-makers tend to ignore that and insist on blood spraying out the front as well.

In one scene, Jeffrey is facing an informant, who was to be killed, seconds before critical information is shared. It was the climax of an episode, so they milked the hell out of it. At the fateful moment, the actor is shot, the blood flies – and Donovan grabs his face, wincing in pain.

That was not part of the script. Needless to say, filming stopped immediately. Anxious crew members and stunt guys rushed to his aid. Jeffrey's upper lip was struck by the wadding blown out of the other actor's shirt and was now the size of a golf ball. I always get the most frightened after a close call like that. What if that was his eye, or gonad or whatever? That's the star of our show. If he went down, we were all unemployed. Donovan was a trouper and completed the scene – which required him to talk on the phone – by hiding his obvious wound with the prop.

By all accounts, gun ownership in Miami was very robust, which added to my general malaise. I soon drew the morose conclusion that I would be shot to death in Southern Florida – on the job no less! Why? Because I was Sam Axe, Michael Westen's gun-savvy buddy who was always watching his pal's back. That meant I'd routinely be filming scenes that had me carrying rifles and automatic weapons in plain sight. One scene called for me to dump half a dozen automatic weapons into the Miami River. In order to get a dramatic wide shot for the scene, the entire crew, everyone, had to be kept a certain distance away from me – preferably hidden or otherwise out of view. So, for all some local "hero" knew, I was just some creepo dumping illegal guns.

My sense of dread was much worse when Sam was actually firing weapons. Another scene had me *alone*, armed with a sniper rifle, situated on top of a four-story building downtown, firing "full-load" blanks, whose powerful report echoed off buildings like canyon walls in an old Western. Normally, I would be surrounded by camera equipment, lighting rigs and crew members, but this was also a wide angle. From street level, I was just

a lone psycho taking potshots at pedestrians. I was legitimately concerned that some espresso-fueled off-duty cop or a knee-jerk do-gooder would look up, spot the perpetrator, yell, "Shooter!" and unload his clip of real bullets into me.

The good news was that if I had inadvertently started a major shoot-out, the crew of *Burn Notice* wouldn't be outgunned. More than a few of them told me on the sly that they were packing heat "just in case."

We also had plenty of uniformed police assisting us with blocking roads and rerouting traffic when they were off duty. One of the officers we regularly had on set with us was a robust fellow I nicknamed Taser Ted – a likable guy with a perverse love of Tasering "perps." Over the course of seven seasons, Ted often invited me to do a late-night "ride along" with him when he was on duty. I never took him up on that offer, but I did enjoy playing certain "Tase the Perp" games with him in between camera setups.

"Okay, Ted," I would begin, "let's say you get a call that I'm in a Seven-Eleven and the pissed-off owner says I refuse to leave. What would you do?"

"I'd insist that you leave the store," he replied with an almost eerie tone of control.

"Would you give me a time limit or a countdown to leave?"

"No, I'd ask you to get out of the store now."

"Or what?"

"I'm going to ask you to get out of the store *now*," he repeated, this time resting his hand on his namesake Taser.

Apparently, by that point I had already disobeyed a direct order from a keeper of the peace and he could have Tased me – but Ted made an effort to remain calm and professional.

Pushing his buttons, I always wanted to see what would make him actually draw. "Hey, buddy," my play-acting character responded, "I just want to buy a peanut cluster. I'm a *customer*."

"Then buy it and get out."

"What about now? Would you Tase me now?"

"Well, I haven't *decided* yet… hmmm…which one…"

I loved to torment Ted because I knew he had to put up with jerks like that all day long, but this ad hoc training session was becoming all too real. Ted's face turned red, his hand twitching involuntarily on the Taser.

"Oh, you know what?" I would balk. "I loved Spree when I was a kid. Maybe I'll get some Spree instead…"

Zap! Ted had had enough of my bullshit. He didn't actually Tase me, but he often encouraged me to "experience" it – and I often declined.

WE BLEW IT – BIG-TIME

During the preparations to film *Burn Notice*, Matt Nix delivered an early and irrevocable edict: There will be no digital explosions on *Burn Notice* – they all have to be real.

Matt's explanation was along the lines of, "When a car blows up, you see these amazing fire funnels curling up underneath them in the aftermath. No digital guy is gonna do something freaky and random like that. Explosions have a mind of their own."

And so, it turned out, did the special effects guys! In the course of seven seasons, we saw and *felt* some doozies. Writers, directors and producers could not get enough of blowing the living shit out of everything around us. In the opening credits, one beautiful blast almost blows Jeffrey and me off our feet as we run away from an erupting boat.

And how do you really protect yourself from an explosion anyway? I didn't pack the charge. I don't know how much – or even *what* – material they used. Is the guy good with timing? Is he a trigger-happy son of a bitch? Honestly, as far as explosions went, I never knew if I was in any real danger or not.

With regard to the deafening noise of explosives, you can always protect your ears with wax plugs, but being part of the shot, I needed to hear all the cues distinctly, so I tended to put in just enough wax to dampen a loud blast but not enough to mask the voice of the stunt coordinator.

Of course, there wasn't much to stop a given explosion from launching errant shrapnel into your retreating ass. I guess overall, I was thankful to be running away from most explosions. But no matter how much you prep, there are always variables.

An explosion once launched a car hood fifty feet into the air, spinning like a giant metallic Frisbee of death. Crew members shaded their eyes to track its descent in the blinding sun.

One day, I heard they were going to set off a big one just before lunch, so I showed up early to take pictures from a "safe zone." When they called action I clicked away, but the first shot was tilted sideways from the concussion of the blast. It was only after I regained my balance and composure that I could finish the

Bruce vs. Shockwave.

series of shots – and I was half a football field away! I can't imagine the jolt those stunt folks felt, being so much closer to ground zero.

We maxed out, explosion-wise, at an office complex one day. Usually, when you film at a location where gunplay or explosions occur, you issue a memo to residents and nearby businesses, warning them about the noise so nobody becomes alarmed when chaos ensues. I'm sure the leaflets were distributed, but sometimes it's hard to reach every last person.

In this case, a massive explosion was to be set off on the second floor of an office building – and it was a whopper. Crew members filming on top of the building reported later that the building actually shook from the impact. Office workers inside hadn't expected the size of the blast and the people who never even got the memo were convinced that an airplane had struck the building, terrorist-style. I'm not exaggerating when I say mayhem ensued.

In a classic example of "timing is everything," one muggy afternoon we blew off a Big Bertha of an explosion just as Air Force One was departing Miami International Airport. I wondered if more than a few Secret Service guys on board didn't spit out their black coffee when that sucker blew directly beneath their ascending craft.

Welcome to *Burn Notice*, Mr. President, I hope you like the show!

SEND IN MR. PARKER, PLEASE

Stunt guys are mostly anonymous. You couldn't pick the average one out of a police lineup. That's kind of the idea. Stunt performers do their thing in painful silence and the actors take most of the credit. It's all part of the movie magic. I'm very happy, however, to shine an appreciative light on my longtime *Burn Notice* stuntman, Chris Parker.

When stunt coordinator Artie introduced us, Chris was a studly, polite man about twenty years my junior. That's just how I like my stunt guys – young and limber. Chris had solid facial features and he was game for anything. After clearly busting his ass on a fall or some kind of impact, he'd always crack a boyish smile and shoot a thumbs-up – no matter how shaky he really felt.

I'm very thankful for all the running, jumping, swimming, fighting and legitimate crazy-ass driving Chris did for me over the course of the show. Chris and the rest of the stunt team all got busier after the cast members refused to be part of any future explosions. We'd had enough. Let the stunt folks handle it, we reasoned. That's what they do.

So, thanks, Chris, for sweating your nads off and making me look badass for seven seasons. I hope I can be your "dialogue double" again someday!

MOON OVER MY HAMMY

If you're not chasing international drug-runners in a car or shooting at them, you're going to use your fists. With a bunch of action-based entertainment under my belt, I was no stranger to performing fight scenes, but my body wasn't so sure anymore.

For my fiftieth birthday, Ida and I enjoyed a leisurely weekend at Islamorada, a swanky spot in the Florida Keys where middle-aged, slightly paunchy guys like me go to relax. I relaxed all right. I showed up on set the following Monday loose as a goose.

But not loose enough.

The scene called for me to fight two henchmen. It was all

planned – and while we never really fight, actors and stunt guys like to at least show "exertion" when they go at it. One of my moves was to knee a guy in the face – a sharp, short movement. We did it several different times from several different angles. We basically had it in the can, but they wanted one more take.

It always seems to work that way.

The additional take rolled, we fought and as my knee extended to "hit" the stunt guy's face I heard a distinct "pop," followed by a sharp pain in my right thigh. Before I could react, the second stunt guy was upon me from behind – all part of the routine. Without thinking, being the good little soldier, I continued with the fight for another beat, flipped the baddie over my right shoulder and collapsed to the pavement on my back. There was an agonizing beat as the stunt guys halted their routine and looked back at me to see what the problem was.

"Should we call cut?" Jeremiah, the director, asked.

"Yeah," I responded. "And get a van around to take me to the hospital because I can't walk."

Getting an MRI done to see the extent of the damage was a comedy of terrors. The nurse saw me lying on my back in front of the Tube of Doom, right leg bent in the air.

"You'll have to flatten your leg for the MRI."

"I can't straighten my leg."

"You'll have to. Otherwise we can't do the MRI."

"What do you suggest? I'm all ears."

"We'll have to strap it down flat."

Beautiful.

The MRI proceeded and the prognosis was not great. I fully tore two out of three connecting hamstring tendons. In all of my random roughhousing I had never hurt myself this badly before and it was as alarming as it was disabling. I literally could not walk or even straighten my right leg.

Through the production office, I was referred to a specialist – who was also a surgeon.

"So, Doc, as you can see, I have a torn hamstring. What are my options here?"

"The options are physical therapy or surgery. I recommend surgery. You have a bad tear."

Coming from a surgeon, his opinion wasn't a shocker. "Okay, Doc," I asked casually, "if I went down that road, what's involved in reattaching my hamstring?"

"Well, first, we'd have to *move the sciatic nerve...*"

"You can stop right there, Doc. I saw my dad go through that. No deal. Let me ask you, have you ever torn a hammy?"

"I have, actually, windsurfing."

"Did you get surgery?"

"No. I was young and foolish back then."

"Did you go to physical therapy?"

"No. I was young and foolish."

"I'm starting to get that. Without doing any of that, what percentage would you say you are back now?"

Due to my hamstring injury, the scripts needed a few "tweaks."

"About eighty percent."

"Then, Doc, sign me up for physical therapy!"

For the next ten weeks, I got to know the world of physical therapy, going multiple times a week, grinding it out, whenever the shooting schedule would allow.

The news that I was released on set was sometimes embarrassing by way of the words used. Oscar, our intrepid first assistant director, would bark over the walkie-talkie, "Bruce Campbell is released. He's going to rehab."

I'd always jump in immediately to correct him. "No, Oscar! It's *'physical therapy,'* not *'rehab.'* "

Whatever you called it, the *Burn Notice* production marched on unabated. Since I could still sit and talk without impediment and all the signs of injury were disguised under my pant leg, I was back on set thirty-six hours later, sitting in a car talking with Gabrielle.

For the rest of that episode, I leaned, or had a foot up or was sitting every time you saw me. By the end of shooting, our director, Jeremiah, could have subsequently published a *Filming Actors with Disabilities* manual, from what he learned about faking the shots with me.

As I slowly got better, I could stand in scenes again and do simple, smaller movements. The next episode was directed by Tim Matheson and he fully adapted to my lessened abilities. There was a big moment during his episode when I had to walk across the set, imploring Michael Westen to listen to reason. The entire take, as I gingerly made my way forward, all I could think was, *C'mon, hamstring, don't fail me now.*

As the weeks went by, I gradually got limited strength, stability and flexibility back. It was a huge relief and I give my Miami pool a lot of credit. I had always loved swimming, but now the pool was a necessity. Floating in water took most of the weight off my leg – it also slowed down and smoothed out my movements, which was very appealing. The chances of getting reinjured in the pool were practically nil, apart from getting in and out on slick tile.

The real test came about four weeks later when my character had to fight Jeffrey's. Donovan was great about it all, being careful to avoid certain danger zones and we broke the fight into enough pieces to avoid any real strain. For my part, it was a relief to be able to complete enough moves to at least be convincing in the scene – it meant that I was on the mend.

In retrospect, I feel that doing ten weeks of intensive physical therapy was enough to do the trick and I highly recommend the process if you ever bash yourself or tear something bad. Thankfully, ten years later, I can still do most anything now that I could do before the injury and the ol' sciatic nerve remains intact.

OFF SET

Time, weather and schedule permitting, Coby and I would hang out after hours, watching some of the thirty-seven *Lawrence Welk* episodes I had recorded on PBS – *yes, Lawrence Welk*. People ask me, "Bruce, why the hell do you watch Lawrence Welk? Isn't that show for people over eighty-five?" My answer is long and circuitous, but "Lars" is entertaining on multiple levels.

The show ran on U.S. television from 1952 to 1982 and became a staple of "wholesome" American entertainment on Saturday nights. Lawrence himself was an accomplished bandleader and his cartoonish accent was a broad imitation of the immigrants he grew up with in North Dakota. The weekly *Lawrence Welk Show*, considered "embarrassing and grueling" by Ida – who was forced to watch it as an unruly teenager – was so relentlessly square it was hip, so tragically unfunny it was hilarious. You get my meaning? When Coby and I laughed ourselves senseless, it wasn't because of a scripted joke. With hokey dance numbers, costumes from Planet Polyester and old-timey musical themes, the *whole show* was

Bruce: "Hi, I'd like to order the Lawrence Welk box set."
Coby: "Make it two."

kind of a joke.

Because *Lawrence Welk* ran for so many decades, fashion historians everywhere can rejoice that thirty years' worth of skinny ties, bouffant hairdos, long sideburns and bell-bottoms are preserved forever for our viewing pleasure.

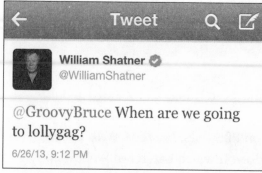

@GroovyBruce When are we going to lollygag?

6/26/13, 9:12 PM

This graphic is actually real.

To round out our after-hours viewing, we added the occasional *Soul Train* episode, which was the funk version of *Lawrence Welk,* or a *T.J. Hooker* rerun.

As an actor in his mid-fifties doing *Burn Notice,* I couldn't take my eyes off of William Shatner, also in his mid-fifties, on *T.J. Hooker.* What was he up to when he was that age? What did he look like? Did he do his own stunts? It turned out that he did. In fact, Bill repeatedly executed what I have since called The Shatner Power Slide.

Any time Bill's character had to arrive at a crime scene on *T.J. Hooker,* his squad car would race up and screech to a smoky halt. The shot would continue and, without editing, Bill would step out of the car – which meant that he had done it without the aid of a stuntman or an editor. I was always impressed by that and mentioned it the first time I met him in the greenroom at a Wizard World Comic Con convention a few years ago.

"You know, the producer didn't want me to do that," Bill added, with obvious delight at the recollection. "Too dangerous, they said."

"I wouldn't have let you do those either," I said. "How does one actually pull that kind of a slide off?"

Shatner looked over his shoulder quickly, like he was still keeping this a secret. "I got with the stunt guys and they feathered the emergency brake, so it wouldn't catch. It's a four-part maneuver as you come to your mark: foot off the gas; pull the emergency brake; steer; foot on the actual brake to stop."

Counter-intuitively, you can still steer when the emergency brake is on. If you follow the first three steps, by the time you hit the actual brake the car will come to a dead stop. I was particularly thankful to Bill for that little tidbit, as I was asked to perform just such a maneuver in the pilot of *Ash vs. Evil Dead*. Ash was supposed to pull his hulking Delta up to a dive bar and skid sideways. I smiled at Sam as he explained the scene.

"Don't worry, pal. I got this."

I recently won a Saturn Award for *Ash vs. Evil Dead* and ran into William Shatner at the event. It was the first time I had seen him since his advice and I was able to dedicate my award to him and The Shatner Power Slide.

WHEELING AND DEALING

When I was a kid, my universe wasn't divided into nations or continents – it was divided into neighborhoods, the largest geographical division I could imagine. The expansion of my universe was only made possible by the advent of the bicycle.

Once *Burn Notice* was picked up as a series, I knew I had to plan for what could be a long haul. Production had taken over a massive former performance center on Dinner Key – the one where Jim Morrison infamously attempted to "free Willy" in concert – so the place had some history, albeit questionable.

This leaking, molding million-square-foot building became our makeshift studio for seven years. A handful of permanent sets were erected – Michael Westen's loft, Fiona's apartment and Madeline's house among them. A small fleet of Dodge Chargers, fake cop cars and burned-out wrecks packed the place to the gills.

Based on the way everything was laid out, cast trailers

positioned outside were actually quite a "schlep" from the interior sets. Considering the debilitating heat, I looked for a quick, easy way to crisscross the "campus."

On official studio backlots, bicycles are everywhere, driven by maintenance folks, delivery people and even security guards. They are emission-free, make no noise and don't clog tight roadways. I decided to get bicycles for the cast, so I bought four single-gear beach cruisers, each with old-school backpedal brakes.

At first, the crew chuckled derisively whenever the thespians rode to set. They stopped laughing after a couple weeks of sixteen-hour days as we pedaled past, breeze in our hair, while they trudged along on concrete-impacted feet.

Gabrielle and I played our own version of Marco Polo with our bike bells. Whenever the mood hit me, I'd flick the bell with my thumb: *shing-shing*. If Gabrielle was within earshot, she'd return the call with a *dink-donk*.

For years, riding back and forth to various sets and locations, we played this silly game:

Shing-shing.

Dink-donk.

Shing-shing.

Dink-donk.

And that silly game made us laugh every time.

Overall, I bought something like fourteen different bikes during the run of *Burn Notice*. Most of them were part of my ever-growing home fleet for visiting dignitaries, but a few got stolen and had to be replaced. Donovan's bike didn't even last a year before it went missing in a daring daylight raid. Some schmo strolled right through our base camp, spotted the bike propped up against his trailer and simply rode off with it.

Over the course of the show, two of my own bikes were also stolen, so it was a bit of a revolving door at the Coral Gables Bike

Shop. They smiled each time I came in – not because of the TV show, but because they knew I was going to buy another bike. Some random advice: Ditch the cable lock. U-shaped locks are the only way to go. I haven't had any bikes stolen since.

Cycling started out as an on-set utility, but it was really a pleasant reintroduction to something I loved as a child. Even though Oregon is an incredible place for outdoor recreation, I never really did much cycling back home. Living in the foothills of the Siskiyou Mountains, I was always going up a hill or down a hill, pedaling too hard or not at all.

Florida, however, was *f-l-a-t*. While you're riding leisurely, the man-made breeze was a great way to inadvertently mitigate the humidity. Cycling became a rekindled hobby. To my delight, I discovered extensive, car-free bike paths nearby, so epic, Zen-like rides were planned often with the likes of Ida, Coby, guest stars or random writers and directors. Producers got to join in, too, but only if they paid for lunch.

How we "rolled" in Miami.

It was amazing how many of these participants hadn't been on a bicycle in years because they still considered them toys, associated strictly with childhood. I guess I was one of those people, but thanks to *Burn Notice* and the wonderful flatness of Florida, I still jump on my bike to explore new sections of my expanding universe whenever I can.

ODE TO FOX'S

I love dive bars. I always have. Fancy bars are all well and cool, but I'm not an attitude guy or a hipster, so I tend to avoid anything with too much chrome or too little atmosphere.

I'm not sure how I first stumbled across Fox's. Likely it was during a local bicycle outing. The exterior was very nondescript, as the best places are, except for the outline of a fox and martini glass. I immediately knew it would be my kind of place because it was almost pitch-black inside. For the first ten minutes after entering, you have to let your eyes adjust from the bright Florida sun.

Fox's Sharron Inn, right on the edge of Dixie Highway, had been around since 1946 and sported a well-worn, S-curved bar. The bar stools were raised captain's chairs that swiveled and I'm sure all the old nautical types who frequented the place felt at home. Fox's was a prime rib kind of place with decent grub and a larger-than-you-would-imagine menu.

But Fox's was all about the atmosphere and the hooch. My favorite libation was/is a Patrón silver tequila martini. My favorite bartender in the world, Margo, served the martinis with a "sidecar" – a minicarafe of extra pourings, kept cold in its own miniature bucket. After a long day shooting bad guys, nothing was more enjoyable than to ride the two-wheeler to Fox's and listen to the regulars bullshit. Fox's was all about regulars – Larry and Terry and Ken and about half a dozen others who would make their way over at 4:00, the beginning of happy hour. Sociologically speaking, it was interesting to see the same group of guys sit in the same chairs at the same time, for years on end. I learned quickly about the territory of old-time bars and their patrons. I made the mistake of invading their space one day

– albeit unwittingly – and got the stink eye from Margo.

"Better not sit there, hon."

"Oh?" I said innocently.

"That's where Larry sits. He likes his seat."

"Got it. Where's safe?"

Margo directed me a few stools down, outside of the "regular zone."

I got to know the regulars fairly quick and they were nice enough, but they didn't really open up or fully acknowledge my existence until I had been going there for about six months.

"You're not a tourist, are you?" Larry asked one day, squinting at me in the dark.

"No, sir. I'm here working on a TV show."

"Oh."

That's all Larry had to say about it. He wasn't impressed with Hollywood or anything else. Larry and the gang pretty much made fun of everything all the time. Everyone was an idiot. The world was going to hell. The difference was that these guys always had a smile on their faces. They never got too grim. I never knew what half of them did or what their personal lives were like, but I also didn't care. That's what I like about local dive joints. Nobody cares about any of that – all they care about is getting away from whatever it is they do, sitting with like-minded folks and forgetting about life for a while.

Margo was the captain of Fox's ship. She was the day bartender and she looked the part. A longtime Florida resident, she had shaggy blondish hair, "a little too much sun" complexion and the rasp of a smoker. She had a great sense of humor, which helped modulate the sometime mercurial moods of the regulars. Margo also poured a mean drink. Her trick was never to measure. These days, the second I see a bartender fish out the one-ounce stainless cup to measure my drink I already know it'll be a crappy pour.

Margo was also the type who would slip you a little extra if you and the boys were having an *extra* fun afternoon. Some would call that pushing the envelope, but I call it customer service.

Over the years, with some degree of practice, I have broken down the various types of "pours" one gets at various establishments.

The Piss Pour   The Corporate Pour

The Presidential Pour   The Dictatorial Pour

A generally crappy pour is called a Piss Pour or Pauper's Pour. Bowling alleys pour a lot of these.

A pour that you would get at, say, Applebee's would be a Corporate Pour.

A substantial pour is a Presidential Pour.

A Dictatorial Pour is where the bartender is serving a dictator – with a gun to his head – so he just keeps pouring.

I caught Fox's at the ass-end of a long run. The standards-only jukebox gave up about a year after I started going there and management changed hands a couple times. When the Southern Florida college crowd started seeping in for the "kitsch" factor, I knew the end was near.

Fox's is officially closed now. I don't miss it because I was part of it and – as Margo knows – I certainly had my fill.

TO IRAQ AND BAQ

Not to be dismissive, but I didn't know Iraq from a hole in the ground. As a young adult, I remember the long gasoline lines and something about an oil embargo and Iran, but that's as close as Iraq got to my consciousness. It was a vague, distant land. We've all heard the "cradle of civilization" thing, but what does that mean?

About a quarter century later, my brother Don got a little closer to that neck of the woods. He served in the first Gulf War of '91 and, because of his military police background, guarded Iraqi prisoners in Kuwait. This was just after Saddam's troops were pushed out and all the oil wells were torched. A new soldier to the environmentally disastrous area asked Don when the sun was going to "come up." Don reminded him that it was one o'clock in the afternoon.

I knocked on the back door of Iraq in 2004. The location for my undisputed American classic *Man with the Screaming Brain* was Bulgaria, just two countries away. But it wasn't like after shooting

I could hop a puddle jumper to Baghdad and see what was going on. You didn't just "go" there.

Five years later, as I was sitting on the *Burn Notice* set with star Jeffrey Donovan, the subject of Iraq came up again. Two active-duty servicemen had visited that day and informed us that the show was very popular with the armed forces. "Mr. Donovan" (I called him that on set to keep him calm) and I began to engage in slightly more than idle chitchat. We talked about "the wars" all the time and were both up on current events, but the conversation was now more like: "Okay, so what can we actually do to help? We're just actors. Should we go over there and visit the troops? You think? That would be crazy!"

We agreed that we would go if they would have us and put the feelers out through Brad, the PR guy at USA studios. Life moved on; Donovan and I went back to work. It's easy to forget about things when your brain is boiling in its own tropical stew.

About a week later, word came down from Armed Forces Entertainment that they would be delighted to have us. Donovan and I shared the same immediate reaction: "Shit!"

"We really have to go now, don't we –" I said, half-asking.

"Yeah. We *do*." Jeffrey nodded, with an inexplicable look on his face.

Channeling one of my heroes: Bob Hope.

This isn't to imply that we dreaded the idea of *actually* going to Iraq. It was just a lot to take in: traveling across the country, then the Atlantic Ocean, then into a war zone via Black Hawk helicopters, going to outer bases around Baghdad, et cetera, et cetera. It was all enough to give us whiplash, but we were in – we were actually going to *go*. This was an opportunity to finally put a face on the endless news cycles about Iraq and put it all in proper context.

UNCLE SAM

It was fun spreading the news. It's not every day you tell people that you're going into a war zone. A lot of friends and relatives were taken aback. Reactions starting with "Oh my God" were common. But, ultimately, regardless of their views on any given war, they were mostly happy to see the troops get a little sunshine.

My mother was pretty casual about the whole thing. I asked if it concerned her that her little "Booey" was going to a war zone.

"Not really."

That's Mom. She'll suffer quietly after I hang up. She wouldn't want to concern me with her concern.

My brother Don never really gets excited. He's a mostly close-to-the-vest kind of guy, but when I told him Donovan and I were going to visit the troops his glee was unabashed.

"That is so cool!" he practically shouted over the phone.

In some way, I had just become legit in Don's eyes. He always felt that as an actor I never experienced the reality of the world and that being a soldier (now active thirty years) gave him a leg up in that department. Perhaps now, I was becoming a person of substance.

"Hey, see if you can get me some orders," Don asked out of the blue. "I'm military police; I have security clearance. I could be your escort over there."

"Really? C'mon, Don, it's the military. Wouldn't it cause a 'disturbance in the force'?"

"Hey, try it. I'll get you my info."

The idea was too absurd not to pursue, so I passed the

request through my agent, Barry, along with Don's "official" info: SFC class. Seventy-fifth Division, Third Brigade. Stationed in Southfield, MI. Been "downrange" three times. Currently intel with a Top Secret clearance but also spent over twenty years as an MP.

Life rolled along and I engaged in the usual post–*Burn Notice* season ritual back in Oregon: fix the place back up, reconnect with local friends, hike, swim, take cool road trips, hang out and generally do as little as possible!

That worked pretty well for a couple weeks; then Don shot me an e-mail. His orders came through.

"Holy crap, Don – you're in!" I exclaimed.

"Yep. I haven't told anyone until I actually got my orders. Now I'm good to go!"

Don made for the third stooge on this bizarre entertainment tour of duty.

My orders arrived via e-mail as well – official ones – from the Department of the Air Force Headquarters. The funniest part was that it was technically an invite from the secretary of defense.

Technically, we were Distinguished Visitors (DV Code 6). We therefore ranked up there with a two-star general with regard to travel, accommodation and security. That translated into being very safe and well looked after. It wouldn't be good military publicity to lose half the cast of the number-one-rated show on cable.

I joked with Jeffrey that if we didn't show up now we'd be AWOL (Absent Without Leave) and they would send Don to pick us up! There was no turning back now.

The general elation of getting our orders faded a bit when it came time to slog through a sea of military paperwork. Lest we forget, Uncle Sam is the biggest bureaucracy in the world. Along with orders, we had to either sign or fill out a U.S. Air Force contract, bank transfer forms, provide a copy of our passport, bank routing numbers, federal ID numbers – and I'm sure they needed my mother's maiden name for some reason. Thankfully, the military is part of the twenty-first century and almost all of it could be done electronically.

It was time to gear up. There is a travel store in my local town of Ashland, Oregon, and I love to poke around in there, searching for some new innovation that would make my life easier while trapped in a giant aluminum tube.

Appropriate gear is nothing new to those of us in the film business. We work under any and all weather conditions when making films in different climates. This trip was cake in comparison. In Iraq, the weather was a downright chilly eighty-five degrees during the day – positively L.A.

It was enjoyable to engage in a semi-political discussion at a local outfitter store. I was in search of new wool socks for the journey and I found myself explaining the upcoming trip. People become acutely interested in every minor detail of actors they recognize. But this fellow was more than curious. He was a bit put off that I would visit the troops if I was against the war.

"It ain't about the war, pal – it's about the flesh," I argued.

"You want to support that mentality?" he shot back.

"I want to support the schmoes who risk their lives."

"Needlessly."

"Whatever. Look, how much are the socks?"

Did I mention that Ashland, Oregon, is a *very* liberal place? Neighboring Medford, a mere fourteen miles away, is very conservative and I find my world straddling the two. The reaction to my trip in Medford was completely different. Universally, I'd get a big smile and an immediate, bone-crushing handshake. Vive la difference.

In bidding adieu, Ida and I chatted about safety issues. She wasn't worried about my physical safety; she was worried I might see something that would break my heart.

Fair enough, I thought. But it's not enough of a reason to stay home.

MIDWESTERNER MEETS MIDDLE EAST

I try not to be a political guy, but what bugs me bugs me and wars are pretty high up on the list of infuriating human activities. War represents a failure of every other policy – a tragic loss of civility, a coup for barbarism. War is way too primal for me, too savage of a concept to wrap my head around.

It's safe to say that I disagreed with the invasion of Iraq (as opposed to Gulf War I) from the get-go. I'll spare the world another actor's dissertation on achieving peace, but I do support the amazing idea that citizens are willing to take up arms and defend their country – it strikes me as a bizarre and mythical ritual.

So, aside from plain old curiosity, I wanted to give thanks to the young men and women who were willing to fight – not necessarily the old men who sent them there.

From my small town of Medford, Oregon, Iraq wasn't exactly around the corner. The journey was as follows:

- Nov. 9, 2009, 10:05, Medford to San Francisco
- San Fran to Washington Dulles airport
- D.C. to Kuwait
- Kuwait to outlying U.S. military Forward Operating Bases (FOBs – the beginning of an endless stream of military anachronisms) – destination: unknown

Jeffrey Donovan and I were going to travel on our own dime regardless, but we contacted the studio higher-ups to see if they felt like "kicking in" – in a "support the troops" kind of way. It was interesting to watch the various reactions of the USA Network (who aired *Burn Notice*) and Fox (who produced it). Given the fact that two of the three leading actors of their show were going into a war zone, the reaction wasn't great. In fact, we were asked not to go.

There was technically nothing in our contract that prohibited us from visiting so-and-so country or doing such-and-such – we were on hiatus and could ultimately do what we wanted. That's why so many actors get in trouble during the hiatus of a given TV show. If they just kept working all the time they wouldn't have time to do foolish things!

It turned into a fingers-in-the-ears sort of thing, so Jeffrey and I made our own plans directly with the military. This tour was different anyway. Unlike a press junket, where everyone kisses your ass up one side and down the other, this time around we couldn't be picky. There was to be no "Oh, I don't eat that" or "Sorry, my bed isn't comfortable" crap. The word "no" would not be welcome. We were there to offer our thanks. This trip wasn't about us and it was actually kind of liberating – not to mention humbling.

I was oddly at peace as I boarded the plane for the first leg of the trip. The decades of international travel may have influenced my mood, as I have certainly flown farther to "work." A twelve-hour commute from Los Angeles and Auckland, New Zealand, during my *Hercules* and *Xena* days set the bar.

But the idea of going to a war zone was a whole new ball game. I was used to playing war, but to see it for real – that was the great unknown.

I met up with Jeffrey in the Red Carpet Club in Washington, D.C. We both had the same reaction upon seeing each other: *Yikes! We really are going!*

It hit me when I walked up to Gate 14. The schlumpy businessmen normally associated with air travel were now scruffy PSDs (Personal Security Details) and unshaven middle-aged contractors spitting tobacco into Styrofoam cups. We were not going to Kansas.

Brother Don arrived at the gate and by the time we exchanged hugs all around it was time to board.

My seatmate on the twelve-hour flight to Kuwait was Hilary, who worked with the State Department. She was a fount of information regarding what we were about to encounter.

Hilary specialized in infrastructure projects in small villages in Iraq and Afghanistan – ironically, putting back together what the military takes apart – and both factions were well represented on the plane. Jeffrey was seated next to an ex-Blackwater security guard back from leave, so he got a twelve-hour earful about the other side of the tracks.

I'm not an airplane sleeper, so I got well into my Buster Keaton biography. Reading about a silent movie era comedian seemed the perfect antidote for the current reality.

Kuwait City from the air at night was pretty similar to most – a mix of ancient mercury vapor lights and the new halogen. Oil well burn off, which seemed to be happening in all directions, resulted in a very science-fiction movie effect in the atmosphere – and not the healthy kind.

Touchdown was 6:15 p.m. There were no visuals to report. We left in the dark and arrived in the dark. I always get slightly claustrophobic when I can't see a new city skyline or geographical feature. We could have been anywhere.

Visas were had for three dinars. The currency of choice in the TV shows *Hercules* and *Xena* were dinars and my character Autolycus stole many sacks of them, but now I was using dinars for real in the place where it all began. A case of art imitating life meeting real life.

On the other side of Customs, which wasn't any more intimidating than usual, we met up with our team – security guys Dave and Dave and our driver/local expert/ ex-military guy, Brody. Our mode of transport was a perfectly cushy SUV. Brody explained that since a lot of

To ensure the safety of the valiant soldiers I met in Iraq, their identites have been obscured.

SUVs are used to ferry brass and contractors around, much had been learned about which U.S. brands sucked in 130-degree heat and which ones did the trick. Brody was a big fan of the Chevy Tahoe.

On the road, we assumed "the formation." Our car was in the lead and Dave and Dave stayed consistently two car lengths behind. They were certainly low-key in their dress and attitude, but they didn't dick around either. If Brody had to dodge around a bobbling Chevy Impala from the seventies (and I was astounded at the number of them on the road), the boys always kept right behind.

As is the case in many foreign countries, driving in Kuwait is all over the map. We were passed on both sides by every kind of SUV, luxury and sports car available – some driven by women. Kuwait is a tad more relaxed in that department. It was a stark reminder that something considered "unique," in this region, like allowing women to drive, is so mundane back home.

TANKS FOR STOPPING BY

Our destination was the sprawling Camp Arifjan. Used as a Forward Logistics Base (or FLB), anything that comes and goes to the Southwest Asian Theater passes through this crazy-big place. Word on the street was that the Kuwaitis covered the cost of Arifjan and still supply all the oil/gas needed to operate it – free of charge. You could say it's a holdover gift to us for stepping in during the first Gulf War.

Camp Arifjan hosted all the "comforts" of home.

Kuwait has a lot of oil and would very much like to keep it. With them sitting on top of 104 billion barrels of proven reserves, with oil accounting for 90 percent of their yearly revenue, you can understand their edginess that Saddam Hussein, their aggressive neighbor to the north, was gonna march in and grab it.

Their intuitions proved correct – so much so that this rich country was hesitant to flaunt its wealth for fear that something as grand as a palace was an easy target. Brody, who makes his home in Kuwait, explained that all the new construction was unique in that now they weren't afraid to strut their stuff a little.

It was also significant that Arifjan was permanent, with multi-story administrative buildings, living quarters for nine thousand, three buffet-style mess halls serving four meals a day and four base exchanges (stores) that would dwarf your local Walgreens. Recreationally, a massive weight room, an outdoor pool and a full-sized basketball court were available – some twenty-four hours a day.

Not that it was necessarily good for them, but apart from the base chow, the modern-day soldier had access to an astounding array – fifteen to be exact – of brand-name fast-food outlets.

The basic plan was to crash for the night in our dorm-like rooms (Building 162), get to know the base a little better and do some signings the next day.

Because my sense of time was whacked, I was up at 5:30 in the a.m. doing e-mail and changing my return flight. The base really did make it seem like you were just in a different state, albeit a hot, dusty one, rather than a different country. I guess that was the idea.

Most everything is planned in the military, so grub was in order at 7:15 a.m. Chow was at the Oasis, a bright, superclean facility where we dined on made-to-order omelets. I know that many soldiers have it rough, but not here.

We did a walk-around after breakfast, trying to take in the scope of the base. It started to dawn on us what it takes to stage a military operation. I swear to God, half the soldiers we met at our 11:30 signing were in some form of logistics. It makes a hell of a lot of sense when you have hundreds of tons of gear and thousands of humans coming and going from sea, land and air.

A pattern soon developed at signings. Soldiers stepping up to our table would invariably blurt, "Hey, where's the chick?" We were *okay* was the insinuation, but Gabrielle Anwar would have been way better. This became such a regular refrain from soldiers that Donovan eventually insisted that I give him a dollar every time a soldier made that reference. I'm not exactly sure why I agreed to the payout. It was really a losing bet and you never want to bet with Donovan. He's a wicked gambler who actually understands what he's doing at casinos.

To combat an ever-dwindling pile of single dollar bills, I therefore insisted that he fork over a dollar every time a soldier came up to the table with, "Hey, Ash, where's your chainsaw?" The *Evil Dead* films are very popular with the armed forces – I knew that from meeting servicemen and women at "civilian" signings over the years and it turned out to be the perfect antidote to this stupid bet. For the next week, Donovan and I silently exchanged dollar bills whenever the appropriate references came up. Soldiers wondered what the hell was happening, but it amused us to no end.

The afternoon was free and we readily accepted an invitation to drive an Abrams tank. It wasn't an offer you get every day and it wasn't something Donovan – a motor sports guy – and my crazy brother Don were going to pass up. Hey, what the USA Network didn't know wouldn't hurt them.

Donovan was up first. The controls of an Abrams tank are kind of like a motorcycle, but the grips are much closer together. You steered and revved with the same controls. Donovan was off like a shot around the dusty oval track and he tore the place up, taking turns that made even the tank guys shudder. A quick reminder: The Abrams tank is powered by a gas turbine engine. It's a freaking jet turned sideways – and it sounds like one.

After three or four laps, I was up next. As I maneuvered all sixty-two metric tons of this beast onto the track, I gunned it. Nothing happened.

"You got to give it some gas, sir," the commander urged me from his perch in the turret.

"I'm gassing, I'm gassing," I said, twisting the throttle toward me as much as possible.

Then – *poof!* Dark smoke billowed from the back of the tank. I'm not a mechanic, but I knew that wasn't a great thing.

"Uh, we should go ahead and hop out," the commander said

calmly, but he wasted no time putting distance between himself and what was soon to become a fire.

Brother Don and Donovan reacted with unmasked glee.

"Way to break the tank," Don said, smiling. "It's only six million and change."

In about five minutes, a fire truck showed up with an assortment of men on ATVs, fire rescue equipment at the ready.

"Thanks for giving us something to do today," one soldier offered as he drove past.

Arifjan was also a RAD (Repair Activity Depot), so they had what they needed to repair just about anything. Minutes later, another fire truck arrived and a group of men stood around watching a couple guys do the actual work.

Just like home, I thought.

Eventually, a giant vehicle arrived to tow the disabled war machine away. If you've ever wondered what kind of machine is needed to tow an Abrams tank, the answer is: a *really big one.*

This was just a glitch in the road to our gracious hosts and they simply brought over a different piece of equipment to drive around – this time an M2 Bradley IFV (Infantry Fighting Vehicle), which was also a troop carrier and a tank killer.

Don was all over this thing like a cheap suit and he cut a pretty macho rug over a large, dirt training area. Driving a Bradley was kind of like driving a giant go-cart. The controls were primitive, with an oversized gas pedal. As with driving anything large, nothing could be done "on a dime." You always had to give extra room and time to any maneuver.

If you have claustrophobia, tanks aren't for you. If you're heavier than two hundred pounds or taller than six feet, give up your dreams of staging epic battles in the desert. Manning a tank is a job for short, wiry guys who don't have an issue with baking in their own little Kuwaiti desert oven. Luckily for us, the temperature was a chilly eighty-three degrees.

Tank Brothers II. (Tonight the role of Mike Campbell will be played by Jeffrey Donovan.)

Cliff the tank guy ran us through our paces. Cliff was a throwback from another war. But this wasn't a Vietnam or even a WW II throwback – this guy was positively WW I. He had "a pinch between his cheek and gum," but he may as well have chomped on cigars. His teeth were yellow, veering into brown because he chewed tobacco, and like most scary people you meet, there was a coldness in his eyes. He had a warm smile, but it evaporated quickly, depending on the subject at hand.

Cliff's current goal was to get to Afghanistan.

"Why would you want to go there?" I asked.

"That's where the action is. They won't let us do nothin' in Iraq anymore. We're just babysittin' here."

"But isn't the idea for the soldier to get his ass back home as soon as possible?"

Cliff shrugged. "I got everything I need here."

"Everything?" I asked, pushing him a little. "I thought this was a dry kingdom?"

Cliff looked at me without blinking or smiling, but his voice reeked with sarcasm. "Yeah...okay, sure it is."

When pressed about his personal life, he explained that his

last leave was mostly wasted finishing up a messy divorce from his second wife.

"Tell you what – I'm done with that shit," he said, shaking his head slightly, letting a brown streak of goo dribble out. "Ain't worth the aggravation."

"That shit" I assumed meant dating, or wives or women in general.

"Sometimes war makes a lot more sense," Cliff said, scanning the horizon. "I can fix a tank in my sleep, but I can't fix a damn woman."

I could have talked with a guy like Cliff all day. He was a zero BS-er who also acknowledged, as a soldier, that not all of it was good.

"I done some bad things," he confessed. "But I seen some bad shit they done and it was way worse."

A rigid military schedule pulled me away from Sergeant Rock and we were off to a different part of the base and another signing. En route, we saw remnants of the Gulf War. A series of concrete bunkers had been destroyed by what was clearly precision bombing – and who's gonna clean that crap up?

In an interesting twist, the bunkers weren't destroyed by Saddam; they were destroyed by the United States once Saddam took the airfield over. This caused an uncomfortable situation, as the bunkers, built by the French, were supposed to be bomb proof. The French position in the dispute was simple: "We did not say the bunkers would withstand *American* bombs."

Signings for military folks half a world away always came with their own curiosities. Although we traveled with our own miniposter to sign, this was, after all, the information age and these people had access to the Internet.

This produced freshly printed obscure photos of my past or present and some very interesting DVDs. Some bases allowed third-country nationals to sell wares to the soldiers at small bazaars, or "haji shops" as they were known on base. For starters, most of these DVDs were bootlegs and in places such as Kuwait and Iraq the cover art has to pass a different set of codes.

Showing bare skin is a Bozo No-No in this culture, so it was very amusing to compare the cover of a legitimate *Burn Notice* DVD brought from home and the "photoshopped" cover of a bootleg, where Gabrielle Anwar now mysteriously wore leggings and long sleeves. With a couple clicks, she went from Hollywood to Bollywood. Either way, I was just glad that *Burn Notice* was popular enough in Kuwait to drive such a need, albeit under-the-table.

Not a Globemaster, but a Super Hercules, another big ass aircraft

While waiting for our "ride" – a C-17 Globemaster III – we took in a concert by Hip Kitty, a really fun band that did upbeat, familiar music. With music still ringing in our ears, we loaded our gear into the massive C-17. With just five civilians and a couple white SUVs in the hold, we were comfortably shy of their 170,000-pound payload limit.

There was room for Donovan and me in the cockpit and we jumped at the chance. I was continually astounded at how young the soldiers were – or airmen in this case. The three-man team seemed barely out of college, but this was no frat house. They were focused, coolheaded and generally pretty cheery. It was a kick to listen in on the chatter (which may as well have been a different language) as these guys methodically checked and cross-checked in preparation to get this hog up in the air.

THE GLASS PALACE

Along the route (which is only an hour by car from Kuwait City to the border), we were invited to check out a local oddity, courtesy of night-vision goggles. As I scanned the desert below, the goggles revealed about two dozen flickering lights, with a pronounced haze around them.

"That's eerie looking," I said to the pilot. "What the hell is it?"

"Those are the oil fires that Saddam lit on fire."

"The ones back in '91?" I asked, incredulous. "I thought they were put out."

"Not all of them," the pilot said casually. "I guess the Kuwaitis figure it's not worth it."

"That's disturbing," I said, handing the goggles to Donovan.

Around 11:00 p.m., we touched down at the "Glass Palace" – Saddam's personal airfield in its heyday. On the ground, we got acquainted with our new guides – J.J., an ex-military guy who spent some time at Disney Studios, and his soon-to-be replacement, Judd.

It was dark again, so there wasn't much to see on the way in, but we were again going to another sprawling complex – Camp Victory. In the morning, wandering outside before 7:30 chow, I took in the layout. When Saddam ran the show, this area was a series of palaces. He had sixty-some around Iraq. In order to hunt and fish at will, Saddam dredged a massive lake and built a series of palaces, large and small, around it. The lake is stocked with enormous "Saddam Bass," which aren't even bass – they're a species of asp fish that grows upwards of six feet and weighs over a hundred pounds.

When coalition troops rolled into this area, a number of soldiers were assigned to round up the odd assortment of wild animals that were roaming free. Sharpshooter Saddam couldn't get enough of randomly gunning down exotic animals on his "back forty."

The base provided plenty of incongruity. Roadways named Missouri Street leading to an Iraq despot's vacation palace. On the base, when soldiers didn't have to wear uniforms they wore black shorts, a gray T-shirt and an M4 slung over their shoulder – like a crossing guard with an attitude.

Our hotel rooms at Camp Victory were in one of Saddam's smaller palaces, but "small" would not be the way you'd describe my suite. The ceiling was easily twenty feet high and pretty much everything was covered in a marble veneer. These rooms, used mostly for military personnel now, have gone from not-so-shabby chic to upscale multi-purpose. Don's room had bunk beds and mine had an eight-seat conference table. Hey, if you're going to have a boring logistics meeting it might as well be in an ornate hall.

Furnishings provided by Home Despot.

But looks weren't everything. You didn't want to drink the tap water in our palace under any circumstances. Cases of bottled water in the bathroom told the whole story. My shower was positively *Green Acres*. The hot water was a long time coming and when it arrived you never knew how long it was going to last. Either way, it was odd to take a military shower in a dictator's palace.

ODD FOBS

The plan for the next three days was to base out of this camp and visit a series of FOBs of varying size. Troops were informed about our arrival and it was all pretty casual – we'd find a folding table, set up a couple chairs, take pictures and sign stuff that we brought with us, Sharpies included. We didn't want the troops to think about anything.

On our list were bases Nasir Wa Salam, Aqur Quf, Sheik Amir, COS Meade, Mahmudiyah, JSS Yusifiya – none of them even *close* to Wichita, Kansas.

Departure the next morning, via Black Hawk helicopter, was at 0800 from a small but very busy airfield. It was really just a place for choppers to come and go, as there was no actual landing strip. This field was populated by an interesting cross section of folks involved in the war effort – National Guardsmen (you could tell those guys by the twenty extra pounds they carried around on average), contractors (older, not in uniform), Special Forces (young, bearded, also not in uniform) and diplomats (looking as out of place at the airfield as we did).

Waiting for our ride, Donovan and I made our way up to the control tower to sign a few things for guys who couldn't leave their post and we got a great overview of the field. A large hill in the distance had every imaginable kind of radio or cell tower on it.

"That's an odd-looking hill in the middle of nowhere," I mentioned to a young controller.

"Yeah," he agreed. "That's where they put the dirt from Saddam's lake. Now it's the best place for towers."

Our tandem Black Hawks landed right around 0800. They travel in pairs as an official policy now, since the very ugly "Black Hawk down" incident happened in Mogadishu years before. Armed with what seemed like vintage flak jackets and helmets, we were ready to roll.

The UH-60 Black Hawks are amazing to watch in action. They are both fast and powerful and armed with dual .50-caliber machine guns. We wanted to watch one land in front of us, but after the first wave of dust and rocks hits you in the teeth it dawns on you why everyone turns away from a helicopter landing.

We raced to the chopper and ducked inside. These were "open" models, no glass in the windows – we were flapping in the wind. The two gunners who helped us buckle into fabric seats were all business – there wasn't any small talk. After a few of these rides, a pattern emerged. If the pilot knew who we were, the gunners would hand us headsets as we boarded and we'd chat up the captain or co-pilot along the way. If they didn't, we just kept our helmets on.

As we rapidly ascended, the gunners snapped up the barrels of their guns and swept the horizon for bogeys. Down below, we got a better sense of geography and landscape. Because two major rivers converge around Baghdad, the place is remarkably irrigated and it would have been a good double for Phoenix, Arizona, or San Bernardino, California.

Each of our chopper rides was ten minutes or under, as these bases were mostly on the outskirts of Baghdad. Our first landing was Nasir Wa Salam, a Stryker division. The captain who ran the base was a really cool guy – reserved, tough and smart. We found out later he got a Silver Star in a tank battle a few years before. He was the old man now, but it was clear that his guys respected the hell out of him.

Most commanders started us off with a tour, which always gave us a quick idea of the size and focus of the base. The perimeter was essentially concrete blast wall panels, fifteen feet high. The grounds were covered with four inches of river rock, so there was a maddening step forward, slide half a step back sort of thing going on. I was assured that this was far preferable to the "moon dust" on the desert floor, which permeated clothes, equipment and every personal "nook and cranny." The rock itself was from the Euphrates River and implemented by Iraqi engineers.

Each base had a way to keep an eye on itself – literally. A

tall tower at the edge of the compound provided radio and cell communications but also hosted a high-powered video camera that could zoom in to amazing detail, night or day. The young soldiers manning the cameras looked very much at home with their joystick/video game style controllers.

At JSS Yusifiya, we were asked to participate in a reenlistment ceremony. One of the recruits was reupping and the base commander was making a big deal of it in the mess hall where all the soldiers congregated. The ceremony was very sincere and straightforward. The soldier in question received a patch on his shoulder – something to add to the other patches. This was a very Boy Scout approach, where you hold ceremonies to laud the accomplishments of young men. These patches are so prolific that soldiers now have Velcro on their sleeves to more easily rearrange or change their layout.

As visiting dignitaries, we started to build our own collections of swag – not only patches but coins, too. I wasn't hip to the whole "coin thing" when it first happened to me and I bungled it right off the bat. The idea is that a base commander or higher-up reaches his hand out to shake yours, usually accompanied by a "thank you for your support of the troops" type of thing and then he surreptitiously transfers a commemorative coin into your hand.

When it first happened to me – when my hand touched a strange, cold object – I impulsively yanked my hand away, thinking it was a joy buzzer and launched the sacred coin into the air. Every war-hardened soldier in the room winced at the gaffe and you can bet your bottom dollar that I never dropped another coin. The trick, upon shaking, is to turn the officer's hand horizontal and let the coin simply drop into your hand.

Sure, I know that *now*...

Food on these forward bases was all over the map, quality-wise. Nasir Wa Salam had easily the worst food I've ever eaten – certainly top five. It was a buffet layout of brown, deep-fried food. Some visiting soldiers knew better and went straight for the "meal replacement" drinks instead. A smaller base we visited a few days later was ten times better because their food wasn't provided by outside contractors – they had their own cook. There we dined on prime rib, mashed potatoes and green beans.

Each base did what it could to create a sense of normalcy. The smallest base, Aqur Quf, kept three dogs. One of them was white but was so covered in dust they called it Dirt Bag. Another pooch, who slept all day, was aptly nicknamed Duty. The third dog, Courage, ran away anytime you tried to pet it. The familiar sight of these friendly canines really did have a positive impact. It made your mind jump out of a concrete and river rock encampment in a generally hostile foreign country to a sleepy fishing hole in rural Georgia, where you and your mutt, Blue, are angling for catfish on a lazy summer afternoon.

Sprawl of Duty.

In a war zone, there are a lot of fully automatic weapons. FOBs were no exception – these men and women were armed to the teeth. Donovan, Don and I were invited numerous times to "pump a few rounds" and we never turned them down.

Shooting live ammo isn't that much different from shooting

blanks on a film set – both are extremely loud. The difference is that when firing fake bullets you don't inhale a steady stream of gunpowder residue and you never see the effects of your weaponry, like the side of a dirt hill being shredded in front of you.

Each FOB had a history. Some of them were chosen for strategic placement (there were dozens around Baghdad alone) and others were selected because the owners of the land were willing to cooperate. One base had previously been a farm, but with several tall structures and a two-story farmhouse the place was ideal for a base. The Pakistani farmer agreed to a $70,000-a-year deal and only stopped by a few times a year to get paid and check on the place.

Greeting soldiers on duty posed slightly different problems because sometimes you had to figure out how to get to them. The young recruits on lookout duty at this former farm were stationed at the top of a concrete grain silo. To reach them, we had to make our way up a jury-rigged series of wooden ladders and platforms – not unlike a tree fort.

Our visit to Sheik Amir culminated in a pickup game of basketball. I can't personally recommend this activity – at least not for an out-of-shape middle-aged guy playing against war-hardened twentysomething studs in the desert. It was a fast track to humiliation. When a soldier yelled, "C'mon, Ash, suck it up!" it was the one time I couldn't tell him to shove it up his ass – mostly because I didn't have enough wind to speak.

It was always fun rounding out our FOB visits with a trip to the communications area, where scores of soldiers on these remote bases could Skype live with family members or shoot off an e-mail – on a daily basis. God bless technology. This type of direct communication has got to be better for the families and troops than during the Vietnam war, as an example, when soldiers still relied on excruciatingly slow "snail mail."

Jeffrey and I enjoyed interrupting sometimes "romantic" calls between a soldier and his significant other on the other end of the line. These remote wives or girlfriends were often wearing very "relaxed" clothing and some of them weren't wearing much at all.

The morning after our six FOB visits, I awoke feeling like hammered dog shit. I felt extremely hungover and there wasn't an ounce of alcohol involved. I assumed that it was a combination of shockingly bad air quality, dust inhalation, stress and the fact that a thunderstorm in the middle of the night sounded like we were under direct attack.

Jeffrey felt like crap, too, while Don, Mr. War Torn, chuckled at our state. "It's a war zone, guys – it's natural to feel like shit."

COMMAND AND CONQUER

Our next stop, after mingling with the troops, was to visit the administrative/support side of the war, which was a huge part of the equation. In our random sampling of troops at signings, we were amazed that about two-thirds of the folks we polled were not actively in combat. Their support came in the form of transportation, communication, information technology, logistics, medical and engineering. It's the lopsided nature of modern conflict – the roots of the warfare tree run deep and broad.

I finally got to see for my own eyes that big-budget action movies aren't all full of shit. Giant command centers in auditoriums the size of a top-ten college lecture hall, boasting easily two hundred HD monitors, do exist. The setup provided Operation Iraqi Freedom with its eyes and ears. In addition to the myriad of small screens, averaging five to a person at smaller stations, a screen worthy of a high-end movie theater anchored the room, where desired images could be magnified for all to see in incredible detail.

This made me recall the white blimps we saw floating above

the city of Baghdad. Initially, I thought it was odd that they were not moving around or advertising anything – until I was informed that *those* blimps were wired with digital cameras and audio sensors. From their multiple fixed positions around the city, the blimps could triangulate the location of, say, a random gunshot. Scary cool.

I've always found it amusing that invading or conquering troops always base out of the former headquarters of their opponents, as a way of saying "fuck you" to the vanquished. I guess that's why German and American troops alternated use of the finest European chateaus and castles during WW II.

The notable thing about Saddam's palaces was the smoke and mirrors aspect: They *looked* impressive as hell from a distance, but upon closer inspection most of them would be condemned

Brother Don about to say "fuck you" to the vanquished.

for shoddy construction. A sweeping second-story balcony overlooking the "lake" Saddam constructed was breathtaking until you inspected the many elaborate columns, which were crumbling and packed with dirt. There was no "solid" granite or marble anywhere. Even the world's largest chandelier, hanging in the grand entrance hall, was made out of plastic, not crystal. I couldn't help likening Saddam's palaces to Las Vegas casinos.

That was mostly the topic of conversation when we dropped in to meet the military brass – in this case, two-star general Joe Anderson. General Anderson was very gracious as he welcomed us into his expansive office, which was part of a huge administrative complex based out of Saddam Hussein's largest, most impressive "hunting" palace.

"This is my army-issue boomstick!"

I'd been in the world of make-believe as long as General Anderson had been in the ultrareal world of waging war, so I wouldn't say we shared the "tons in common" award. Mostly, Donovan and I marveled at the size and scope of the operations General Anderson and his troops had put into place and how impressed we were with the quality of the personnel along the way.

In turn, while General Anderson most likely will never see *Evil Dead II,* he certainly appreciated that actors help entertain and/or distract his soldiers when they are not on the battlefield, bringing a little cheer into their overstressed lives.

The next morning, our last in the war zone, I sat down outside the palace and jotted some Baghdad musings:

> Hard to believe I'm in a war zone. Sunrise over Saddam's palace is, dare I say, bucolic. Cool breeze, lovely cloud patterns – all the more deceptive.
>
> In reality, after only four days in this city, I'm very ready to leave. I believe I'll be kissing the ground upon return. The air sucks and there is a faint gloom slathered over everything. The soldiers seem as well adjusted as possible, but "happy" is not a word to describe their mood.
>
> Wars blow. The idea of a "good" war or a "just" war sounds great in speeches and on talk radio, but it halts the march of civilization, kills and maims humans and disrupts families – not to mention the god-awful cost. It

*really hit me that if you're going to go to this much effort
and expenditure, it had better be for a damn good reason.*

RETURNING HOME

The return plan included a stop at the fabled war hospital Walter Reed (now defunct), in Washington, D.C., to visit the wounded. It didn't seem like our troop visit would be complete unless we stopped in on the folks who really sacrificed.

Approaching the physical therapy gym, Donovan and I exchanged a wary glance. What was this going to be like? What would we say to these kids that would have any positive impact whatsoever? We decided that these kids were tough and that we shouldn't tiptoe around what had happened. If a guy was missing his legs – there must be a story behind it and we wanted him to talk freely about it.

Most of the fresh patients were soldiers from Afghanistan. The casualties were from roadside bombs (the dreaded I.E.D.) or RPG (Rocket-Propelled Grenade). The damage to their physical bodies ran the gamut from mild to grotesque, but you couldn't look away.

The first soldier I met told the story of how he lost his right arm.

"RPG tore the thing right off," he said matter-of-factly.

"So, it blew up nearby?" I asked ignorantly.

"No, man, the rocket itself did this – just the force alone. I'm not sure where it blew up."

Behind me, a gravelly voice called out: "Hey, Ash..."

I turned to see a soldier holding up the stump of his arm. "I could use that chainsaw right about now," he said ruefully.

I couldn't help but smile at the *Evil Dead* reference, but there was nothing funny about his wounds. You could see, from his injuries, where a bomb had impacted the entire left side of his body. His left eye was glass (which he cheerfully popped out to show me), his left arm was half-gone and his leg was a nightmare of reconstructive titanium pins.

"So, do you at least have some good days?" I asked tentatively.

"Hell yes," he said with a smile. "I got drunk and laid this past weekend, so I'm good."

Another soldier, who was also missing a leg, explained that everything was fine with his girlfriend, even though his leg was mangled badly – as long as he still had it. The doctors had explained that all of his complications would end if they just removed the leg. In excruciating pain, he reluctantly agreed. The good news: His complications ended. The bad news: So did his relationship, because his girlfriend couldn't handle the new reality.

One young kid, maybe eighteen, was fresh from an Afghanistan battlefield, sprawled out in bed, tubes connecting him to a half-dozen machines. This kid literally didn't know what hit him.

"Where were you when it went down?" I asked.

"I don't know," he said, after some hesitation.

"What happened to you?"

"…I…don't know…"

The soldier began to tear up, attempting to reconstruct the recent events and his young mother gave us a nod like "It's time" and we moved along.

One of the striking things about meeting these young soldiers was that their number-one concern and driving motivation was to return to their unit and resume active combat. A legless soldier was utterly convinced that he could rejoin his unit before it came home in a couple months.

Like all wars, casualties are unpredictable and the ripple effect is wide. We visited a female reporter who was imbedded with troops when her Stryker vehicle hit a roadside bomb.

"Fucking death traps." She scowled, looking down at her badly shattered leg. In order to get the care the reporter needed, her schoolteacher sister had to take a leave of absence and travel from another state to help out.

The saddest case Donovan and I encountered that day was the soldier who refused to see us. Every other soldier, no matter how bad off, seemed surprised and pleased to see us, but this soldier had been shot through the face and was in no mood for glad-handing. Not everything works out all neat and scripted – not even the warm and fuzzy "visit the troops" part.

Jeffrey and I left the hospital humbled and quiet. In our line of work, nobody is really in danger, our food service and workplace accommodations are off-the-charts in comparison to the average military grunt – and they're the ones getting shot at! It's safe to say that neither of us will complain about hot summers in Miami ever again.

LEGENDS OF THE FALL

When a TV series approaches its third season, entertainment lawyers and studio accountants brace themselves for a showdown. The speculative freshman first season is over and season two has helped create a momentum that both audiences and networks can respect. A third season of a TV show – or even a second season – was unfamiliar territory for me, but I had been around long enough to know that season three was when actors renegotiated their contracts.

The momentum of *Burn Notice* was undeniable and the cast knew it was going to be around for a while. Renegotiating my contract was practically obligatory.

ILLICIT AFFAIRS

With tradition on my side, I brazenly approached the Business Affairs team, through my trusty representatives, and said, "Hey, guys, this is a great show we're all making. Remember that moldy old contract we signed a couple years ago? Waddya say we just throw that silly thing away?"

"Suck it," was *essentially* the reply.

"Business Affairs" – aka lawyers for studios and networks – are tough, ruthless negotiators who don't know the meaning of the word "compromise." End of the year bonuses are not calculated by "compromise."

In the midst of renegotiations, I ran into one of those cheery fellows at some unrelated event. Even out of the context of our deliberations, he was distant and resolute.

"Bruce," he sneered, "I know it seems like I don't care about your problems. The truth is, I don't even care about my *wife's* problems, so there's no way I'm going to care about *yours*."

It's risky to ask a network or studio for a better deal when you've already agreed to a worse one. Characters get killed off all the time. Regardless, we approached the powers that be and asked for a better contract.

When a show becomes a hit, there's a strong argument for the possibility that it's a hit because of the cast. Story lines and production value aside, the interaction of the characters and the chemistry established by the actors are undeniable factors when it comes to whether a show works or not. Writers, producers and directors will all flip me the bird for saying this, but they can write their own memoirs and state their own cases.

Actors don't typically make a percentage of profit, so if a show starts making more money the only entities that benefit are the studios, networks and other stakeholders. It may seem greedy, but when you're one of the forefront faces of the franchise it's only natural to want a bigger piece of the pie when the pie starts getting bigger. That's why, around season three, so many lead actors become "producers" and so many supporting characters become dead.

"What money!?" barked the defensive line of negotiators.

"You don't understand. We haven't gotten the foreign sales back yet. We're still hemorrhaging money. It's not in syndication. The license fee doesn't cover the production cost and we haven't recouped the DVD money back yet because season one only just came out. So, what are you looking for? You're looking for nothing."

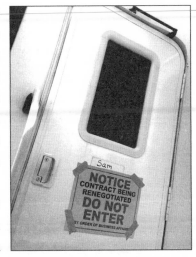

Let's do some math: *Burn Notice* was made by 20th Century Fox for X million dollars an episode. The USA Network paid a license fee of Y million dollars per episode (approximately half of what the show cost) to air it – and made its money back through advertising revenue. Fox still had to finance the remaining Z million out of its own pocket. Hence the term, "deficit financing."

Accounting-wise, until Fox made back more than X million dollars per episode from the remaining sources of income (foreign sales, syndication licensing and DVDs) it was in the red – as each production is its own accountable entity.

Therefore, tonally, Business Affairs took our request as something of an affront – a big "ask" at an inappropriate time.

They reminded me, "Bruce, you forgot you signed something that you were perfectly happy with once. Your contract is for seven years."

After the obligatory pushback of their pushback, they agreed to give me a nominal raise. It wasn't what I was hoping for, but I signed the updated agreement – thereby accepting their economic sob story at face value.

Literally the next week, I was in London promoting *My Name Is Bruce* when the trade magazines reported that Jeffrey Donovan had successfully renegotiated his *Burn Notice* deal – to earn *more than twice* his original contract.

What the fuck!?

The official Business Affairs recruitment manual.

I had no problem with Donovan. He deserved it. If I were him, I would have said, "You're killing me with this workload. I'm the stem-to-stern star of this huge show. I do voice-over for the entire episode. I'm in almost every frame, every scene."

Business Affairs knew, fiscally, that Michael Westen was the one character who couldn't be replaced. That part I understood. My beef was that instead of being straight up about it, they led me to believe that *nobody* was getting a raise.

Kicking at the air in my London hotel room, I felt swindled and mentally prepared myself to walk away from *Burn Notice*. Dialing my lawyer's number, I paraphrased my complaint: This was an unwarranted decrease in comparative value.

When we started *Burn Notice*, the rates for each role were X and Y – establishing, in my mind at least, a "pay ratio." The new math threw everything out of whack. Sam's role in the series hadn't diminished – in fact, it had been increasing in screen time.

Business Affairs may have been insulted that I asked for a raise at all, but I was offended that they saw such little relative value in me – and so *emphatically.*

Normally, I have a good handle on my temper, but this situation pushed my big red button. "I don't want to play in their sandbox anymore!" I screamed to my lawyer, Bill. "Ask them to release me from my contract. I would like to go elsewhere with my services."

To keep actors from leaping across corporate tables, we have representatives. They take our knee-jerk rants and physical threats and translate them into rational corporate speak for Business Affairs.

The Fox response was not unexpected in the least. They stated formally, "We are not releasing you from your contract. You have an obligation." That was rational corporate speak for "Don't fuck with us."

The first day of shooting season three was fast approaching and a standoff had created scuttlebutt among the key people of *Burn Notice*. The e-mails flew: "Dude, are you really gonna bail?"; "Are you serious?"; "What's your plan?"

I explained to a few folks (Nix and Donovan included) that this wasn't "about them." This was about "the suits and my deal."

Before it got officially ugly, with delayed shooting schedules and lawsuits served, Matt Nix offered a brilliant solution: make a Sam Axe backstory TV movie and pay Bruce out of the Fox TV movie fund, not the *Burn Notice* account. I thought it was a great idea and agreed to do it.

Nix was able to convince Fox to finance it, but the kicker was: as long as USA agreed to air it. The corporate versions of a snake and a mongoose had to come to their own terms on top of everything else. Eventually, they worked it out and my contractual squabbles were over.

It was a great solution, not only because it resolved the dispute, but it also gave me an opportunity to explore the depths of Sam Axe. Creating a spin-off based on your character is something an actor always hopes a TV show will do.

Burn Notice started production up again for season three with a happy Bruce Campbell, but two years would pass before production started on the untitled Sam Axe movie.

My reps would gently remind Fox of their commitment.

"I thought we shut you up!" they'd cry.

"When are we making the Sam Axe movie?"

"Maybe next year. Go away!"

"Then give us some money. We get paid whether you make the movie or not."

"Here. Go away!"

Cut to one year later.

"What!? You again!?"

"When are we making the Sam Axe movie?"

"You tell that son of a bitch Campbell to go away!"

"Give us some more money. We got it coming."

"What!? The audacity!? We just –"

Fox suddenly realized they were paying me without making a movie. Giving money away and getting nothing in return is not part of the Modern Business School syllabus. "Okay, we'll make your damn movie!"

COLOMBIA PICTURES

It didn't make any sense. The story of *The Fall of Sam Axe* was actually set in Colombia, so it couldn't possibly be filmed in Colombia, right? In my experience, you shot Michigan in Tennessee, Chicago in Portland and Metropolis in Burbank.

The shoot was set for Bogota, Colombia – all of it, not just a few random exterior scenes where you "sell" the fact that you were really there. Bogota was not known for being a particularly hospitable city, so why spend the entire schedule there? The answer was pretty simple: Fox was owned by NewsCorp. In 2007, NewsCorp acquired a majority of Telecolombia, a full-service studio that mainly produced soap operas, affectionately known as telenovelas.

Corporate Mantra: Use the resources you have.

I met with Samuel, the managing president of the Colombian

studio and he showed me the research he did when his business became part of this multinational corporation. On the wall of his office was a hierarchy chart of NewsCorp. With all of its branching bronchioles and subsidiary connectors, it could have been an anatomical diagram of the lungs.

Samuel pointed down to the lower right at Fox Telecolombia. Almost as far from the top as one could get, he understood his company's place on the international totem pole and had learned to accept it.

In the general worldview, Colombia was widely known for its coffee, its cocaine and its neckties. Bogota, its capital, had a reputation for being the Detroit of Colombia, a violent place where people got stabbed, shot or kidnapped.

Ironically, locals rarely talked or joked about or used cocaine. The citizens of Bogota held great disdain for the drug because they equated it with all of their problems. Cocaine hurt them not only individually but also socially.

The citizens wanted to end the drug wars, so they worked out an arrangement with the Fuerzas Armadas Revolucionarias de Colombia. FARC was essentially given a playground near the coast and everyone else looked the other way.

Colombia was shockingly close to Miami – only a two-hour direct flight. Flying in, you could instantly see that a reputation for vice and violence wasn't the only thing choking Bogota – a thick, terrible smog hung over the city in a way that made the L.A. sky seem pristine.

Beyond the typical urban pollution, the air was cursed by an

There's a massive city down there somewhere...

abundance of traffic with no emission safeguards. Catalytic converters weren't installed as a rule, so even brand-new Colombian cars and trucks farted out exhaust in an endless standstill of gridlock.

The city is nestled along the foothills of the Andes Mountains and it was common for me to traverse from eighty three hundred to eleven thousand feet in altitude for a day's work. The roads going over the mountains weren't just steep – they were narrow. Going uphill, I felt sorry for the cyclists navigating the gridlock. By "felt sorry for" I mean that I was amazed these idiots thought turbo training during rush hour at exhaust-pipe height was a good idea.

Going back downhill after shooting, we appreciated that the smell of exhaust was at least replaced with a new one: brake pads working overtime to stop lumbering vehicles from plunging off the mountain roads.

LOCKED AND LOADED

Bogota, because of what was mostly in its past, had a "thing" about security. Personally, I've never seen things so locked down in my life. An armed man often stood in front of any packed restaurant – gun on full display. Policemen were on many random corners and fully-armed military troops stood atop numerous bridges and walkways.

Ida and I only had a key to our actual apartment, not the outside door. We couldn't get in – or out – without the help of the lobby attendant. Ida was mildly claustrophobic and hated the idea that she was involuntarily sealed into the building.

For the first time while on location, I was assigned a body-guard. His name was Jose – and yes, he was packing heat. A real pro, he was clever enough to keep a distance as he shadowed me. Being seen as "needing a bodyguard" was just another way of saying you were "probably worth kidnapping."

Honestly, I didn't have a single problem while in Bogota – not even dirty looks from the locals. Other crew members, who actually lived there, weren't so fortunate.

I put my foot in my mouth while working with Malena, a young woman from the wardrobe department. She was doing her best to make my scarf look exactly the way the director wanted.

"You better get this right, Malena," I quipped, "or Donovan's gonna cut you."

Malena practically staggered backwards, her face stricken and pale. "W-w-why –" she stammered, "why would you say something like that to me?"

"What do you mean?" I replied, oblivious to what I might have done. "I was just making a joke."

"I was stabbed a month ago."

Oh, shit.

The redness of embarrassment shone through my movie makeup. "I am *so* sorry," I apologized earnestly. "I never would have been such a jackass if I knew that."

Malena's story was chilling. She had been casually walking through her neighborhood, which was not far from where Ida and I were staying, when she rounded a corner and saw four loitering hooligans.

"Give me your purse! Give me your wallet!" they demanded.

"Screw you," she boldly defied them. "I'm not giving you anything!"

The thugs attacked, but Malena was tough and managed to keep them at bay. Before they scampered away, she felt a sharp pain in her arm. Looking down at the fresh blood pouring out, she knew she had been stabbed.

To her amazement, a police officer was directly across the street. He had seen it all unfold and had done nothing to intervene.

"What the hell!?" Malena shouted at the cop, crossing the street toward him. "They're right there – you *saw* them!"

The cop's expression didn't change as Malena gestured to her injury.

"What about this? They *stabbed* me!"

The cop looked at her fresh wound and said, "You're a rich girl. You can afford to go to the clinic."

In this case – and I have found it true whenever the police force of a given country is woefully underpaid – the officer gets to make a judgment call, instead of enforcing a fixed set of laws. The "assailants," in his view, were more contemporaries than anything and because Malena clearly had more money she wasn't really a victim.

I promised myself that as soon as I got home I would thank the first police officer I saw.

THE RISE OF MICHAEL WESTEN

Earlier in the year, while we were in the middle of shooting *Burn Notice*, Jeffrey Donovan sauntered over between setups. My contract issues had been resolved and it was public knowledge that I was getting a spin-off TV movie.

"Hey, uh," Donovan said somewhat sheepishly (which made me immediately suspicious), "so, I guess I should say congratulations on your TV movie."

"Oh yeah. Thanks," I replied.

[Awkward pause]

Finally, Donovan broke the silence. "So, uh, who's going to direct it?"

"Oh, you know, we got a handful of guys in mind."

"Oh, like, some of the *Burn Notice* guys?"

Show runner Matt Nix and I had assembled a short list of directors who had done impressive work on the series and could handle a larger-scale endeavor.

Donovan nodded and offered, "Well, uh, hey, if you wouldn't mind, I sure would love to put my name in the hat."

"Oh. Yeah. Sure. I'll mention it to Matt," I replied, being careful not to sound too excited or concerned.

Actually, Donovan had directed his first episode of *Burn Notice* early on in season four and we were all really pleased with how it went down. During the shoot, Jeffrey had a completely different vibe. He skipped around set like a little kid and had a great time directing.

As an actor, I love directors who actually care about the mechanics of acting. Sometimes you get stuck with folks who don't think twice about character progression or performance. Donovan knew how to talk to actors and that mattered to me.

I fired off an e-mail to Nix: "Hey, JD just expressed an interest in directing this thing. What do you think about putting him on the list?"

"Sure. Why not?" Nix replied.

So, Donovan entered the list – at around number four. At the time, Matt Nix had another

Donovan miming how to eat a huge hamburger.

show in production called *The Good Guys* and a recurring director on that show was the top candidate for helming *The Fall of Sam Axe*. Unfortunately, he did *something* and ended up on Matt's *other* list.

Donovan was up to number three.

Now, I may not remember this correctly, but rumor had it that the other two candidates became unavailable due to a "series of mysterious accidents" shortly after Donovan entered the list. Long story short: Due to a freak lead pipe/kneecap accident and a faulty brake line, Donovan became our one and only choice.

The more I thought about it, the more I realized that getting Donovan to direct was an elegant solution. It was almost a form of paying tribute to the headliner of the show and it gave him a connection to it. If *The Fall of Sam Axe* was a success, he and I could celebrate together. If it failed, we'd have some war stories to chuckle about.

Ultimately, Matt Nix and I were right to put our faith in Donovan – he directed *The Fall of Sam Axe* with the confidence and skill of a veteran. Having a professional cohort I could trust down in Bogota didn't hurt either.

THE PREQUEL DIET

When the audience first met Sam Axe in *Burn Notice,* they met a lounging lothario, a lager-swilling retiree with love handles and liver damage. He was a character who created an entire lifestyle around the notion of not giving a shit anymore – the beer gut and muscular atrophy were just part of the package.

To be the Sam Axe in *The Fall of Sam Axe,* I would have to transform into the "younger, still on duty" version. I needed to lose at least fifteen pounds and regain some degree of muscle tone. The goal in presenting this character, as I attempted to turn back the hands of time, was to not embarrass myself.

To lose the weight, working out wasn't going to be enough. I had to stop ingesting everything that I had ever enjoyed – booze, meat, oil, sugar, flavor and happiness – until I reached my goal. I could have absolutely no fun at all or any of the things that I desired, craved or enjoyed. I thought all that leading man, over-exertion and sacrifice crap was behind me when *Jack of All Trades* was canceled.

I did successfully drop from around 225 down to 210 in time for production. What was surprising, though, was that the workload caused me to lose an additional ten pounds over the course of the four-week shoot.

When I left Colombia, I was 200 pounds – the allegedly "perfect" weight according to my height and build. Stepping off the plane in the States, I immediately stuffed my face with as much meat, oil, sugar and flavor as I could find and washed it all down with the finest hooch. That ideal weight lasted about an hour and a half.

BATTLE-AXE

The Fall of Sam Axe was scheduled for a four-week shoot. With six days of filming a week, it was an aggressive workload. The upside was that I wouldn't have to endure the smog or stabbings for too long. The downside was that it was the toughest shoot I'd experienced since the 108 days of filming *Army of Darkness*. I remember sending texts to friends, grumbling: "You can take this leading man shit and shove it!"

Sam Axe was a character whose every other line on *Burn Notice* was: "Hey, buddy, hand me one of those beers." Now front and center, Sam was suddenly expected to make impassioned speeches and carry every scene. As the primary focus of the plot, my character had more dialogue than I'd seen since my days in *The Adventures of Brisco County, Jr.*

Despite having access to a portfolio of cheat sheets developed for *Burn Notice*, I didn't want to go down that road on *The Fall of Sam Axe.* The courtroom scenes had epic amounts of dialogue and I wanted to be ready. I respected Donovan as a director and I didn't want to piecemeal our way through the material. Long scenes need to get into a groove to work. Thankfully, we were able to do that and by wrap time Donovan and I had established a mutual record – shooting 17 pages in one day.

"You want another take?"

The Fall of Sam Axe was born out of an internal, corporate conflict, but despite all the hassles, negotiations, Business Affairs, disputes and obstacles, I'm happy to report that the spin-off was a success. If this TV movie had been an actual pilot, the ratings and reviews would have merited its own episodic series.

Happy endings are always the best kind.

THE TURN OF THE BURN

As always, TV ratings run their course. *Burn Notice* started strong, jumping to the head of the cable TV pack and staying there for roughly four of its seven seasons. The USA Network was a great partner at the right time and they treated us like the network tent pole that we were.

Eventually, whether it was viewer fatigue, an increasingly serious and complicated story line, or USA's repetitive "blue sky" TV show model, viewers began to tune out. I got better insight, anecdotally, a year or so after the show ended when folks would ask, "That ran for six seasons, right?" After correcting them that it was, in fact, seven, I realized that some people thought *Burn*

Notice ran for as many seasons *as they watched.*

After committing to seasons five and six concurrently – which was a thrilling vote of confidence – USA decided that season seven would be our last. Mercifully, because everyone was warned in advance, we could all prepare for the end. The story could be wrapped up cleanly and production could plan ahead for the big shutdown.

It's a big deal getting rid of seven years of accumulated sets, props, destroyed vehicles and racks of wardrobe that ranged from pimp outfits to SWAT gear. Bob, the head of production for Fox, let us know that we could get first dibs on our wardrobe – but not for free. Fox was running a business and studios are not known for their sentimentality. Basically, everything that could be sold off was – from the bar stools at Carlito's Restaurant to Michael Westen's trusty Charger.

For my part, I took first dibs on the best Hawaiian shirts (patterns matter), some sunglasses, watches, Sam Axe's jewelry and the most prized possession of all – a prop spiral binder that contained roughly five years of "in-scene" note-taking. It was fun to flip through after-the-fact and review all the diagrams, random notes and actual lines of dialogue scribbled within.

All in all, *Burn Notice* had a great run. Seven years on television is nothing to sneeze at. Ultimately we shot 111 episodes – exactly the same as *Miami Vice,* the first iconic show to put Miami on the map.

AFTERBURN

When *Burn Notice* ended in 2013, Ida and I rented a place in
Los Angeles. It was time to find a new gig. We hadn't lived
in southern California for almost twenty years, so it was exciting
to reconnect with old friends and business acquaintances and to
see what opportunities lay ahead.

When you live outside of Los Angeles, you can drop in for
extended meetings and a few follow-ups, but it's hard to keep
things moving week after week to get a project in gear, like you
can do when you actually live in the city.

After being back in Los Angeles for about six months, with
dozens of exciting meetings and business opportunities, I began
to realize a bit of what I had left behind – the wheeling and dealing
– and I missed it. Bullshitting with producers and networks can
get tiresome after a while, but in just a couple of focused weeks
in the same city as dozens of production entities it's amazing
what can happen. The following is a smattering of projects that
unfolded – or didn't – immediately after *Burn Notice.*

LAST CALL

With the completion of *Burn Notice* I wasn't interested in "working for the man" – I wanted to "be" the man and have my own show. The opportunity arose when Jeff Wachtel from the USA Network collared me at a promotional event.

"Let's take a walk," he said with an inscrutable smile.

Jeff explained that he had a show in mind – a fun, late-night genre-centric show where you view a culty, kitschy movie and do skits during the breaks with funny guests. The name they had was *Night Cap.*

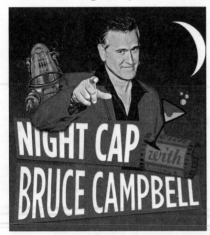

I was all over it like a cheap suit. In my formative years, I religiously watched local Detroit goofball Ron Swede, aka The Ghoul, host a late-night show on Saturdays that was very similar in concept. Another local wacko was Sir Graves Ghastly. His show was during the day on Saturdays, so I definitely had early influencers in that department.

I had always wanted to host something, but in reality it's a bit of an odd gig. Part of it falls on your shoulders to be accessible, charming and able to think fast. The other part – like acting – is scripted and you're often reading off a teleprompter.

A host saying, "We'll be right back after this," is indicative of the structure of almost anything on television, due to the necessity of commercial interruptions. Skits within a late-night show can be ad-lib-y and freewheeling, but they are still timed and trimmed for length and as witty as a host may be, his or her show is still well plotted.

A pilot episode for *Night Cap* was written by Brad Stevens and

Boyd Vico ("Brad and Boyd"). I thought the end product, taped very quickly and painlessly, was very "sellable" while knowing that there was always room for improvement.

USA ended up rejecting it for their late-night – or any – slot. Thankfully, NBC Universal, the parent company of USA, had a large collection of networks under their corporate umbrella, so we pitched *Night Cap* to them all – including the newly renamed Syfy Channel.

Still no takers.

We pitched the show "beyond the corporate veil," to anyone who would watch it but, like many pilots before it, *Night Cap* found no suitors. I was surprised and bummed that we laid an egg. I figured the idea was light and funny enough to find a home. Failure is never thrilling to experience, but *Night Cap* remains a happy memory because at least I got a little "host practice" out of the deal.

"BAD" SESSION

Now that I was living in the actual city of Los Angeles, I could follow up on opportunities much more quickly than when I was hiding in the boonies of Oregon. It was also a funny thing with my representatives – I suddenly became more "real" to them, more "tangible." I could take *actual* meetings. Whatever the case, it seemed to make a difference and things continued to line up.

Next on the hit parade was a TV pilot called *Good Session,* starring James Roday from *Psych.* I got on his radar guest-starring on his long-running show and he tapped me to play his hippy-dippy father in this "dramedy" about a young couple in therapy.

A "table read" is a funny thing. It happens before you shoot a given show and it can be a nervous affair because all the mucky-mucks are present – as well as a sea of flunkies and assistants to provide the sometimes-needed laughter.

A good table read crackles with energy and the room beams with possibility. The read-through for *Good Session* did not crackle – it just kind of sat there. In this case, it was hard to place the blame. The actors were all trying hard, the writing seemed okay, but the magic somehow passed them by. After a good read, participants will often linger about, congratulating one another and making small talk – after this one, the room emptied like someone ripped a nasty fart.

The pilot episode was shot without incident. It was fun to step back into "whacky supporting mode" type acting, after head-lining *Night Cap*.

The fate of a project lingers as long as a studio or network needs it to. Legitimately, some networks need to wait for a slot in their lineup to open and they'd rather wait until the last minute, contractually, to decide on a show.

Good Session suffered no such long, dreary waiting period. The decision to not take the show to series came just a couple weeks after shooting.

Wow. That was fast. Okay, next!

MISSION (OUT OF) CONTROL

Because *Good Session* never got past the pilot, I did what every other actor does that time of year – jump from project to project, hoping to land in a show that "sticks."

I was convinced that *Mission Control* would be that show. This particular TV pilot was the brainchild of Will Ferrell's company, Gary Sanchez Productions – a creative nut I wanted to crack for a while. I was a huge fan of Will and the stuff coming out of Funny or Die, so I jumped at the chance to play Bob Korman, idiot administrator of a band of misfits in the middle of the NASA space race. Conceptually, it was basically *Mad Men* with jokes.

I love the sixties time period – close-cropped hair, skinny ties, the chauvinistic bravado of the guys and the coifs of the women's hair. Some time periods suck for an actor – I never dug the sword and sandal stuff or WWI wool uniforms – but the sixties were cool. Pipes and Zippo lighters and dial telephones heavy enough to kill someone were bizarre reminders of distant childhood memories.

I still love going to the backlots of major studios. It never gets old. Going to the Edith Head building (named after one of the great costume designers of the golden era) on the Universal lot for a costume fitting was awesome, because they made a custom sixties jacket that fit me to a T. Call me snooty, but every so often it's really nice to work on something with a budget.

The main set constructed was an almost-as-big mission control, duplicated with great detail – including overflowing ashtrays at every console.

The cast – an assembly of young, talented comedians – really gave me hope that this show was going to "go." I also really appreciated how these guys worked, creatively. Don Scardino was the director. We worked together on a pilot called *Missing Links* about fifteen years before and he had

Control freaks.

since become one of the "go-to" guys for directing comedy pilots. His style was light and breezy and he kept our energy up. The cool thing would be that after virtually every take Don and the writers would come in and pitch completely new material. I like things fast and loose, where you collectively look for the best way to play out a scene – especially if you want it to have punch or be funny. I enjoyed going to work every day on that. I envisioned years and years of working with this talented ensemble and basically laughing our asses off.

No such luck.

After a bit of recasting, the pilot came to a halt and then sat on the shelf for the better part of a year, while Universal tried to find a slot for it. Eventually, time expired and the network had to shit or get off the pot. Farewell, *Mission Control.* I hope the pilot leaks somewhere so people can actually see it.

Every actor I know has a dozen of these strange projects under their belt that nobody will ever see – some of it really good stuff that just didn't catch on for whatever reason.

LOOSE BRUCE

"Operation Gainful Employment" continued with a little indie called *The Escort.* I was enjoying just being an actor for hire again. Living in Los Angeles, you are way more likely to do small projects, just because you are already here. Living on an Oregon mountaintop, I might as well have said, "No thanks – too much hassle to haul my carcass down there for some little bit."

Hippie dad redux.

Indies are fun, but it usually means that the budgets are low and the personnel are less experienced. As an actor, you have to put that all aside and participate because the role is good. Again playing a hippy-dippy father (maybe the feature on me in *High Times* had an influence on casting), I enjoyed the efforts of its star, Michael Doneger, who was also producing. I always respect when actors get fully behind what they are doing. More and more are producing these days and it makes total sense. If you want control, you need to be a producer and you need to be good at finding money.

Like so many flicks these days, *The Escort* dropped on pay-per-view and Video on Demand (VOD). The film business is adopting a whole slew of new terms for distribution in the digital age. Presumably, the film did okay for what it cost.

No harm, no foul – on to the next venture.

GAME OFF

I had agreed to host a charity game show for troops at the Sam Houston base in San Antonio, Texas. I hate war to the core of my being, but I have no issue with the soldier willing to put it all on the line.

For some reason, I didn't want to go. I was tired, I wanted to kick back and do nothing after a busy year or so, but a commitment is a commitment. So, I donned the silliest red, white and blue outfit I could find and hosted *Quest for the Best,* a military-themed trivia game show where everyone in the audience gets to compete until one soldier wins it all.

The theater where this event took place was beautiful – a fully restored thirties-era showplace, seating six hundred. It was fun performing in front of soldiers who were mandated to be in attendance – they *had* to be there. Nothing like a captive audience. The game and its design unfolded really well and the soldiers were getting quite verbally engaged as the game went on, down to the last four contestants. In a real nail-biting fight to the finish, the soldiers erupted in joy when the final contestant, a woman, took the prize.

This format works, I told myself. *This sucker could be adapted to be done live at conventions – just make it all fan-based, pop culture trivia. A game show for geeks!*

I pitched the idea of *Last Fan Standing* (new name) to Steve

Sellery, the developer of the game, and he bit right away. I then pitched it to John Macaluso, the CEO of Wizard World Entertainment, one of the biggest convention promoters, whom I was doing a lot of business with and he jumped on board.

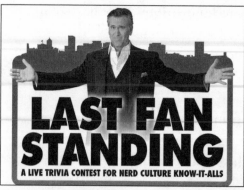

Eventually, the show wound up in the hands of CONtv, an Internet-based network that specialized in movies and TV shows for genre fans. On paper it all sounded great and we made a preliminary deal. The only problem was that CONtv was in no position to finance the actual ten episodes they'd just negotiated to get, so myself and three other partners formed a company and put up the money. That was a neat trick – get the people who make the show to pay for it, too! What a great business model!

The ten episodes of *Last Fan Standing* were filmed live at a couple different conventions and it was a lot of fun. Staging shows at an actual convention, packed to the gills with geeks, made for great contestants. As the episodes played out, there were dramatic upsets, come-from-behind wins, total humiliation – the whole gamut of emotions on display. Generally speaking, the format "worked" and seemed worth the effort.

To this day, I couldn't tell you what the "ratings" were for *Last Fan Standing*. Honestly, I wonder if CONtv even knew. Gone are the Nielsen boxes of the old days. Now we're counting clicks or subscriptions or hits. I hope they figure it all out one day.

Needless to say, CONtv and *Last Fan Standing* had reached the end of the line. It's actually fine, because it freed Steve and me to take the game to various cities and do it live, which is always the most fun anyway.

KICKING THE BUCKET

As an actor, you want to touch all the bases – drama, comedy, action, genre, musicals (okay, maybe not those) – you want to do it all and you want to pepper your résumé with as many portrayals of iconic characters as you can. What else is the point of being an actor?

I was contacted by my *Burn Notice* alumni Marc Roskin and Jonathan Frakes about coming up to Portland to play Santa Claus in the new show *The Librarians*. Every actor has a bucket list. Santa Claus was on mine – and how nice to actually work in the state where I live.

"Where do I sign?"

Even if Christmas isn't your bag, everyone has heard of Santa Claus. He's a worldwide phenomenon. What was nice about this particular Santa was that the writers spun him to be a little edgy, sometimes naughty – but a hero in the end.

Portland, Oregon, is one of my favorite cities on the planet. It's big enough to provide anything you're looking for but small enough to give a shit. The town is run by soul patch–wearing twentysomethings who don't really care what they do for a living. In Los Angeles bartenders can be a snotty, self-important bunch, but in Portland they dig the craft cocktails and really get into the history of adult beverages. I back that approach to life.

Jonathan Frakes, directing this episode, was one of our favorites on *Burn Notice*. We could only get him for one or two episodes a year, because Miami got too hot for him. Frakey-Pants, as I came to call him, was always a delight to work with.

Some directors don't get it. Some don't know how to talk to actors. Frakes was an actor, so he knew all of our foibles and our tricks and could see trouble coming.

Some directors get buried under the workload. The joke on set about such directors is *"Gone with the Wind* in the morning,

Dukes of Hazzard after lunch" – meaning that they got a little too self-important out of the gate and fell behind during the course of the day. Television is a train that needs to run on time. Frakes was a brilliant conductor. He was very happy to print a first take or a partial take and move on to the next. He never simmered or doubted – he just plodded ahead. In television, that's exactly the temperament you need.

He knows if you've been groovy...

The cast of *The Librarians* made shooting a delight. Rebecca Romijn was a great leading lady – funny, professional and striking. The rest of the actors, rounded out by the great John Larroquette, were eager and fresh.

You want to work on a TV show early on, because it's still a fun voyage of discovery. "Old" TV shows can devolve into plodding, humorless affairs, like my guest-star experience on the last season of *The X-Files*, where it felt like the entire company would rather have been anywhere else.

Once I crossed Santa Claus off my actor bucket list, another work call came in – this time from longtime friend and collaborator John Cameron, whom I have known since high school. Beginning as an assistant director, John soon found himself running major movie sets, including *Men in Black* and *The Hudsucker Proxy*. He began producing with the Coen brothers shortly thereafter and I wound up with cameos in *Ladykillers* and *Intolerable Cruelty*, so we kept bumping into each other.

John's most recent gig was producing the Coens' adaptation of *Fargo* for FX and the first season had taken off critically. For his efforts, John walked away with both an Emmy and a Golden

Globe. I got a kick out of going over to his house and making a big deal about it in front of his seemingly unimpressed teenage kids.

"Come up to Calgary and play Ronald Reagan," John said, over the phone.

Knowing full well that we had both imitated Reagan mercilessly during his stint as president, John felt confident that I could fake an imitation, but the trick was to make him a full-blown character, not an *SNL* sketch.

In anticipation of joining this highly regarded show, with a first-class writer in Noah Hawley and Emmys in its wake, I got nervous, so I wasn't going to take any chances. A local rehearsal space in Hollywood is known as The Complex. This jumble of a half-dozen mini-theaters and rehearsal rooms is my favorite place to prep. Each of the small spaces has a different name and feel – they come with sparse furnishings, lighting and a bare stage with about twenty seats in miniature auditoriums. Whenever I go there, I feel like a real actor, with zero distractions.

I dragged my filmmaking buddy Mike Kallio along to shoot a demo of Reagan giving a speech in the opening of the episode. I wanted to show John and Noah what I was gonna do before I got in front of their Emmy-winning cameras. That way, if they wanted to make adjustments – or freak out and recast – they had the time to do it. Fortunately, their response was positive, so I went up to Calgary and my bucket list got a lot smaller.

HOLLYWOOD IN PONTIAC!

Even though I was born and raised in Michigan, I only worked on a handful of movies there. The original *Evil Dead* was filmed in Tennessee because we were trying to avoid a brutal Midwest winter. Our second film, the disastrous *Crimewave,* was shot all over the city of Detroit, but trying to make a movie in the dead of winter left a very unpleasant taste in our mouths.

The next film I produced in Michigan was *Lunatics: A Love Story.* The suburban town of Pontiac was selected, mostly because it was a tiny, more manageable version of Detroit, with plenty of funky old buildings. A large, recently abandoned middle school became our base of operations.

To give you some background, Pontiac was an automotive powerhouse in its post–WW II heyday, kicking out cars and even busses for decades before the industry took its business else-where. A one-horse town, Pontiac – and a lot of other towns like it in Michigan – never fully recovered. For as long as I have known it, Pontiac was always a "sketchy" place.

As we were filming on the streets of Pontiac, the local police were very helpful keeping curious types at bay. My favorite character strolled by late one night, wearing a gloriously ratty tuxedo.

"Hollywood in Pontiac!" he bellowed. "We got white stars, black stars, *polka-dot* stars!"

The only other recent experience I had with Pontiac was being rousted by their Law Enforcement Officers on a bike path. Apparently, some nervous Nellie called in about two people "waving pistols around."

Mind you, riding around on bicycles Ida and I didn't exactly look like Bonnie and Clyde. Ida was sporting a white, Burberry trench coat and I looked like a model out of an Eddie Bauer catalogue – and this wasn't some dark alley or mean street; this was a bikes only, bucolic path on a beautiful Michigan fall day.

As we rode, we could see a police car block an intersection coming up in front of us, with two anxious officers leaping out.

"I thought the guy had to take a leak," Ida later recalled.

We looked behind us and another police car had pulled in to block our retreat.

"Looks like they're after someone," I said, not overly concerned. We thought we were caught in the middle of *something else* going down.

The cop in front of us, gun drawn, approaching "with purpose," shouted with great authority, "Put your kickstands down and put your hands in the air!"

I looked at Ida, incredulous. "Holy shit, he's talking to *us*!"

We complied with his demands and got a quick, unsympathetic

pat-down for our efforts. Thankfully, Pontiac was not in any immediate danger. Neither of us was, in fact, armed and we were allowed to go along our merry way.

Jesus Christ.

After that alarming incident, I had no desire to return to Pontiac – ever again. Imagine my surprise (and delight?) to learn that the prequel to *The Wizard of Oz,* one of the most endearing and enduring classics of American cinema, was going to be filmed – not in Los Angeles or New York or Toronto or New Zealand or even Bulgaria but *Pontiac,* Michigan!

Ironically, the choice made sense. Penny-pinching production practices had sent film and TV projects to Canada and Eastern Europe for decades. To stay relevant, states began implementing their own incentive/rebate programs to entice producers back stateside and it worked.

Michigan knew how important it was to fight the flight of domestic industries, so they jumped into the incentives program with a vengeance and started subsidizing Hollywood movies. I was living out west by this time and started hearing stories about Robert De Niro, Clint Eastwood and Drew Barrymore shooting in Michigan. It seemed like "everyone" was working back in my home state.

The truth was, Michigan's incentives were among the best around. A production could expect to get a refund of almost 40 percent of the money spent *in the state.* When a certain Disney movie had an estimated budget of "well north" of $200 million, it's easy to see how incentivized both state and studio would be to work together.

WINKIE GATE KEEPER

Most of the guys who made Super-8 movies with me in high school went on to become professionals in film, television, writing and photography. I've known guys such as the Raimi brothers, Rob Tapert, Josh Becker, Scott Spiegel, Mike Ditz and John Cameron for most of my adult life, but we don't exactly text each other every time some new project falls into our laps. I don't always know what "the boys" are up to and I don't tend to read the trade magazines such as *The Hollywood Reporter* or *Variety*. I actually heard about Sam doing *Oz* from a friend of a friend of a friend.

It was bizarre to imagine that Sam was chosen by Disney to revisit such a classic. The original *Wizard of Oz* was truly an icon of filmmaking with some of the most recognizable imagery in cinematic history. When you look at Sam's early work, it's easy to appreciate him as a horror director, but let's not forget that he also directed a stylish Western, the wonderfully restrained *A Simple Plan* and the *Spider-Man* movies (the first three anyway) – proving that what defined him most was a varied, fanciful, visual style. *Oz* was bound to be a playground of eye candy and visual quirks, so Sam was perfect for the job.

In order to be involved, I knew that I had to hound Sam relentlessly. The irony of working on a successful multi-season TV series was that people tend to think you're unavailable.

"Sam, come on," I implored. "There's gotta be, like, *seven thousand* roles. Just gimme a little one."

"All right, buddy. Yeah, I'll think about it," he replied, placating me for the time being.

I knew the second Sam hung up he wouldn't remember talking to me. That's how he gets when he's waist deep in a big project and this was the biggest of them all. To keep the pressure on, I dusted off my agent's number and urged him to "track" the lumbering project.

Eventually, Sam tossed me the nebulous role of a Winkie – one of the numerous big, mean, ugly guys who guard the castle.

I felt special that Sam included me, but in retrospect, I can't feel *that* special. It turned out that Sam gave virtually everyone *he ever met* in Michigan a part in the film. Next time you're bored (or stoned), cross-reference the end credits of *Oz the Great and Powerful* with the 1976 Groves high school yearbook and you'll see what I mean.

Even the Ladies of the Evil Dead got a cameo.

OZ, THE SLOW AND POWERLESS

The timing was perfect. *Burn Notice* was over for the season and I had some time to kill. My mom, brothers and some old friends still lived in Michigan, so I decided to rent a place there for a month. I'm glad I did because various production delays kept me on hold and threatened to scrap my "pivotal" scene entirely.

Oz was the biggest-budget project I had ever been a part of. A gigantic former bus-manufacturing facility was completely refurbished (to the tune of a couple hundred million dollars) into a state-of-the-art Hollywood studio – now the largest such space between New York and Los Angeles.

I've seen big, sprawling sets before. Hell, for *Army of Darkness* we built a castle. But the sets for *Oz* were unique, in that they were only partially built. In the modern world of digital compositing, you didn't need ceilings – or a second story – anymore. Mr. Digital took it from there. So, while a castle entrance would boast an impressive, sweeping staircase, you wouldn't see where it leads until the movie was almost finished.

A "production schedule" is a color-coded calendar of interiors, exteriors, location days and studio time. This schedule has to factor in actor availability, budget restrictions, unpredictable weather and a slew of other external factors. It is by no means etched in stone, but much effort is made to never let it get out of control. *Oz* was a big movie, with a big, complicated schedule – therefore, when it had problems, they were big.

FROM THE DIRECTOR OF SPIDER-MAN

Trapped in Oz.
Surrounded by wickedness.
Huge friggin' budget.

OZ *the* GREAT *and* POWERFUL

A SAM RAIMI FILM

Some fans noticed similarities to another Sam Raimi film.

My little cog, a two-day part, was caught somewhere in that big wheel, so when I was told that my first shooting day had been pushed back I didn't think anything of it.

No big deal. Part of the process.

The second time my scene got delayed, I thought, *Okay, well, Sam's doing complicated stuff and it's taking more time than they thought...*

When I got the third call, I knew something unforeseen was causing a big speed bump in the schedule. It wasn't an actor problem (rehab or injury); it was just the scope, size and difficulty of the undertaking, squeezed through a Sam Raimi kaleidoscope.

My Name Is Bruce was shot in the newish HD format, which resulted in what I called HDelay. *Oz* was being shot in 3-D with state-of-the-art cameras. I could only imagine the complications of "3-Delay."

I was beginning to get a nagging feeling that my silly little scene was going to get the axe. It wasn't a particularly crucial scene. I wasn't launching the story by leading a doomed expedition through the jungle or helping reveal a major plot twist by standing next to Billy Bob Thornton. I was expendable.

Then the phone rang.

"Bruce, Sam wants to talk to you," said the ominous, familiar voice of a Raimi assistant.

Getting Sam on the phone was a rare feat since he only came up for air for a few minutes at a time between camera setups.

"Ah, hey, buddy," Sam said, "I've got good news and bad news."

"O-kay," I replied guardedly. "Shoot."

"The *good* news is we're going to pay you."

"That *is* good news!"

"The *bad* news is we're cutting your scene."

"That *is* bad news!"

For *Oz,* I was officially contracted and scheduled. I had already gone through a couple wardrobe fittings and an effects makeup session. I knew Sam must have been deep in "the weeds" to pull the plug after all this.

"No worries, pal," I consoled him. "You've got bigger problems."

FRANCOPHILE

Being cut from the biggest-budget movie to ever film in my home state by one of my oldest friends was deflating, but then the phone rang again. This time, it was James Franco, the star of *Oz.* For some inexplicable strange reason, he had enough spare time during the production to star in a student film for an NYU class he was teaching, called *TAR.*

"Bruce," he offered, "since you're, um, available now, would you be willing to do a gas station scene with me and Goody before you leave town?"

"Goody!?"

That's right, David Goodman, the "filmmaker's burden" and fellow *Man with the Screaming Brain* survivor. Incomprehensibly, Sam had picked Goodman, a chronically lousy driver, to shuttle around James Franco, the star of his massive-budget blockbuster.

Despite Goody's piss-poor driving skills, Franco had become

pretty enamored with him. The "filmmaker's burden" is a very funny guy and the fact that he's so easily tormented is one of his more likable quirks.

I told Franco, "I'll do the scene on one condition."

"What is it?"

"Goody has to drive me to set."

In the spirit of good-natured sacrifice, Franco conceded and loaned me his affable, if distracted, chauffeur for the day.

When an obscenely large Cadillac Escalade pulled up to my rental house the morning of the shoot, I sauntered to the rear passenger door, opened it and smiled. "Goddamn right, Goodman."

"Shut up and get in the fuckin' car," was the surly response.

As we drove through Detroit, Goody and I discussed the history of our troubled home city. Franco's film was set in the 1970s and our scene was all about two guys complaining. Goody and I knew the time period and what the residents would complain about – which was mostly the mayor, hockey and whatever "those jerks were doing to Telegraph Road."

Franco gave us carte blanche to ad-lib in the scene, so Goody and I maxed out. After half a day of filming us bullshitting, Franco pleaded, "Guys, you have to shut up at some point. I've got to get my lines in there somewhere."

After a fun, low-key day of shooting, Franco cracked a crooked grin. "Sam may have cut you from his movie, but I didn't cut you from mine." We shared a knowing laugh, but I suspected that Mr. Franco was up to something.

By this point, I had relocated to a hotel near the Detroit Metropolitan Airport in anticipation of an early flight out of Michigan. At 10:30 that night, the phone rang. Caller ID pegged it as Sam's number. I assumed that Sam either had butt-dialed me, thought he was calling *Neve* Campbell, or was just taking a moment to say, "Happy trails, dear old friend."

However, the voice on the other end was Bob Murawski, Sam's editor. Bob, to put him in historical context, also edited *Army of Darkness* and the *Spider-Man* trilogy. Pause. Oh yeah, he also won an Academy Award for editing *The Hurt Locker*. Affectionately, he's known among us as "Bob the butcher."

"You know what," Bob declared, "you gotta be in this movie. I don't know why they cut you out. What the hell's the problem? Why don't you just – you gotta be in it."

"Bob," I replied, "I'm not the guy to make that decision. Talk to your pal Sam. I have a flight tomorrow at eight. That's all I know."

"This is bullshit," Bob barked. "We gotta change this. Just make it one scene. Just shoot one day."

"Bob, that's a decision above my pay grade –"

"Okay, fine. Bye."

Click.

Moments later, my phone rang again and this time it was actually Sam.

"Yeah, listen, pal, we thought about it," he explained. "I don't know, you know, it's a good idea...Maybe we'll try and do something. Anyway, see ya. Bye."

Click.

Contrary to popular belief, I'm an old man and 10:30 p.m. was past my bedtime. I was getting both drowsy and weary of these interruptions.

Again the phone rang – again showing Sam Raimi, but this time James Franco was on the other end. My mind was racing.

Did my breakout, ad-lib–fueled performance in his NYU experi-
mental film cause him to "need" me in his huge, albeit largely
existential, film? Let's go with yes.

"You know what?" he declared. "This is bullshit. We're
shooting that scene on Monday."

"James, I'm supposed to get on a plane tomorrow at eight a.m.
Am I getting on that plane? Yes or no?"

"No."

"Are you standing next to Sam?"

"Yeah."

"Ask him if I'm getting on the plane."

On the other end, I could hear their muffled ramblings.

"No, you're not getting on that plane," Franco finally
announced. "We're shooting it on Monday."

"Okay, are you sure?" I could hear loud music (probably
"Brick House" or "Macarena") in the background and had little
confidence that any conversation would be remembered in the
morning. "You're *sure* this is happening?"

"Yeah, you know [gibberish] and shit –"

Click.

I transferred to a different hotel and waited for the truncated
version of my clearly expendable scene. It was now going to be
one shooting day – a long, Sam Raimi shooting day. That meant
in addition to the prosthetic makeup process and my time in
front of the camera, I could also expect to get both physically and
psychological abused for the director's amusement.

In the magical land of Oz, it's not enough to be merely
humanoid. Featured characters were given crazy noses, ears,
eyebrows and hairstyles to establish the fanciful universe on the
other side of the tornado. My role as the "Winkie Gate Keeper"
required enough effects makeup that I was glad my two days had
been cut down to one.

The makeup team was composed of Sam Raimi veterans, including Greg Nicotero, Robert Kurtzman and Howard Berger. As the "K," "N" and "B" of KNB Effects, they had been collectively applying toxic substances to my face since *Evil Dead II*. Howard had since won an Academy Award for his work on *The Lion, the Witch and the Wardrobe* and was my official makeup homey.

You Winkin' at me?

I looked around their giant facility. Rows of makeup stations stretched across the room. "How many Shemps come through here every day?" I asked.

"On average? About ninety."

"Christ. Each with a fake nose or bald wig or facial hair?"

"Or all three," Howard said, nonplussed. He had seen a lot since *Evil Dead II*.

In addition to the prosthetic nose, eyebrows, handlebar mustache and chin extension (?!), I was outfitted with a forty-pound Cossack jacket (not much exaggeration there), an eighteen-inch-tall hat and eight-inch boots straight out of a Kiss concert.

I wasn't on set for long before Sam and I fell back into the same old routine. He prodded, goaded and insulted me in front of his now-massive crew. He even made sure to yell at me when somebody *else* made a mistake.

The fun was tossing back an insult, just as loud as his, like, "Sorry, Sam, I was waiting for some direction."

After this zinger, the gasp among the crew was audible. This "day player" had insulted the Grand Poo-Bah. It was only when Sam laughed heartily that they assumed we were old pals. Not surprisingly, Sam also delighted in tormenting James Franco.

"That just means he likes you," I explained to James.

It was all Sam's special treat for the crew – a show for the folks making the show.

Half of the material in my scene was improvised on the fly by Sam, James, myself and Tony Cox – some of which involved a random fly that would land on each of our faces, to different effect. I thought it was really funny, but this sort of unrehearsed nonsense drives visual effects guys crazy. There were something like fifteen hundred effects shots in the movie and each one needed to function in 3-D.

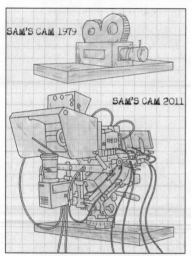

SAM'S CAM 1979

SAM'S CAM 2011

"Video Village" is where the director, script supervisor and key camera technicians "watch" a scene unfold in front of one or two HD monitors. It's like watching television, only you determine the content.

The *Oz* Video Village, being both 3-D and very effects laden, needed *three* different main monitors: one for seeing what the camera sees, a second for "pre-compositing" the foreground action with what will digitally become the elaborate background scenery. That kind of technology, where you could meld the live with the animated, blew my mind.

The third monitor was fuzzy for some reason.

"Put the glasses on," advised a nearby script supervisor.

"Okay," I agreed, putting them on. "Ahh! It's coming right at me! Oh, it's 3-D."

It was almost ridiculous how well the 3-D effect worked in real time. The on-set camera, with coaxial cable tentacles spreading out everywhere, actually utilized two lenses to create the stereoscopic result. The complicated rig looked like something on loan from NASA. Seeing Sam next to that extraterrestrial camera made me think back to the days of him strapping a camera to his hand to get a desired visual effect.

Still, shooting *Oz* was a very intimate experience. Sam was the hometown hero, a big shot Hollywood director with millions and millions of dollars at his disposal, but he was still just an old friend poking me with sticks. I was glad to see that some things never change.

HARDLY FUNCTIONAL

Thanks to Mom, I've always loved the American West and Western movies. She dragged me to the last of the John Wayne movies when I was a kid and instilled a sense of awe in the West – like it was a mythical place. For those of you who have actually *been* to the West – it *is* a mythical, sometimes-mystical place. All the superlatives and clichés apply: thundering rivers, soaring mountains, sweeping, inhospitable deserts. The American West has it all. So, when I got the word about a new project to be filmed in New Mexico, I might have been more excited for my mother than myself.

In truth, Tom Dibble's script for *Highly Functional* was right up my alley. The character Chili Youngfield, a cynical, over-the-hill country singer, was pretty much written for me – aside from the singing and guitar-playing part. I flamed out playing drums for *McHale's Navy* and faced rejection by an Elvis impersonator for *Bubba Ho-Tep,* so my self-confidence in mastering two new artistic skills at the same time was minimal. I was interested in the part – *as long as I didn't actually have to sing or play!*

I met with director Marc Forby and we agreed that, if necessary, the "country-western" part could be faked, so we would instead focus on the story, which was wonderfully eclectic. In it, a country-western singer is kidnapped by a young man with Asperger's syndrome (nicely played by James Frecheville) and forced to play a song for his dying caretaker, Dan – a song that is loathed by the singer as his only hit, yet it's also the only song in his repertoire that he didn't write. Aside from quirkiness, there were elements in the screenplay that very much appealed to me – namely the redemption of a character after enduring a trial by fire.

Before we got any further along in pre-production, I wanted to offer up whatever I could do vocally so the producers would know which way to go. If my singing sucked, they had time to pre-record somebody else and I would lip-sync to their track. If my vocals were useable, they would know that going in and I could sing to a playback of myself – which would be delightful, but either way was okay by me.

I enlisted trusted *Evil Dead* composer Joe LoDuca to help with a demo. Joe had relocated to Los Angeles recently and was keen to jot down some country words and help me record one song. I got a taste of modern musical-recording methods in the process, which is really an art form now. Old-time singers were recorded with the full band or orchestra and they would do the entire take without stopping because there was no "editing" available. Singers had to get it right – and often.

Today, almost any hack can go into a studio with a competent engineer and bluff their way through a song – syllable by syllable if necessary. In my case, I started by laying down a couple of wobbly takes. Joe then worked with the engineer to fix or repair any glitches, false starts or off-tempo singing. Once they were satisfied with the Frankenstein-ish assembly, I then watched in both glee and horror as they changed the pitch of my voice to put me "on key." This career-saving/making program would literally bend my notes up or down until they were where they needed to be and voila – I was a country singer!

There are no Grammies in my future, but the demo was enough to convince both Marc and Nigel the producer to record the songs with my voice, so I happily laid new tracks down with the actual lyrics, written by composer Christopher Bangs.

Knowing that I had to at least *look* like I could play the guitar, I was paired up with singer-songwriter Dave Bernal to guide me through the process. Dave was a great teacher with a mediocre student and I clunked my way through chord progressions for weeks. When I think of a guy playing guitar, I see images of a slightly scruffy dude in torn jeans sitting cross-legged, singing Jim Croce songs to all the pretty girls.

I was never that guy.

I was never musically inclined. The only accessory I took on location was a brief-case, because it was "practical." Accepting this fact, I announced to all creative types that they should not plan on me "playing for real" and we ended up with a hybrid situation – real singing combined with fake playing.

Not pictured: glass shattering and dogs howling.

Back during my *Adventures of Brisco County, Jr.*, days, I started to listen to country music for the first time. Among the annoying patriotic rambles or liquor-soaked bemoaning, country is a great genre for singer-songwriters to tell a story. I wasn't a Garth Brooks or Shania Twain country guy – they were too mainstream to catch my attention. I started to listen to the old-timers like

Hank Williams and Conway Twitty. George "No Show" Jones became a favorite of mine – as much for his colorful lifestyle "off mic" as his rich, authentic singing style. He got the "No Show" nickname for his propensity to get too drunk to perform. An early hit, "White Lightning" – a song about moonshine – had to be recorded over fifty times because he was so wasted. George had a great look, which I adopted: Long, mutton-chop sideburns, which almost reached his jawline. I combined George's facial hair with Glen Campbell's standard wardrobe of jeans, vest and tied neck scarf and I was almost there. A trip to my local Western wear store in Van Nuys, California, finished me off with a sharp hat, a couple pairs of boots and a fat-ass belt buckle.

Sideburn Notice.

I had the country-western thing under control. Now it was time to dive into the acting thing. I retreated with buddy Mike Kallio to The Complex, my favorite rehearsal space and we worked the shit out of the lines. This was a fat role. Chili had a lot of colorful dialogue that was really well written. Admittedly, I have shown contempt to lazy writers in the past by butchering their precious words, but I felt like I owed it to the good writing to get it right.

Learning lines thoroughly isn't just an admirable acting discipline – it's also the first line of defense against inexperienced or indecisive directors. Be sharp on every take, every angle and you'll be okay if you have to go on auto-pilot with no input – or poor input. Marc Forby was new to the directing game but not to producing and he was very sympathetic to the material. This was an important project to him, so we were both on the same page.

The prospect of shooting a movie in the West again was exciting. The last time for me was in Utah for *Sundown: A Vampire in Retreat* back in 1988 and it fueled my love of wide-open expanses. I had passed through New Mexico on road trips a couple times, but never stayed to experience the Navajo lands there. Gallup, New Mexico, was a weird place – a crossroads in the middle of nowhere. Route 66 went through the middle of town and it was founded as a railhead for the Atlantic and Pacific Railroad. Like so many new towns out west, Gallup was named after a railroad official – in this case, David Gallup. When a lumbering freight train eased its way through, you could be stuck at the crossing for a half hour – or hightail it to the other end of town to the solitary bridge over the tracks.

The Navajo Nation was the principal tribe in this "Heart of Indian Country." The experience of shooting in New Mexico enlightened me to the fact that you can't just drive around the Navajo Nation lands and "see what's going on." Tribal land is not only sacred – it's private. Some Navajo sites are open to non-Navajo visitors, but otherwise outsiders are not welcome without a guide.

One such site I visited with Ida was Canyon de Chelly National Monument, which is managed in conjunction with the Federal Park Service. The monument is unique in that it repre-sents an area that has been continuously inhabited for some five thousand years. Most places with ancient ruins are now barren, with no inhabitants for miles around. In Canyon de Chelly and other monuments on tribal land, Navajo families still lived on the land. At the bottom of the canyon, dwellings hundreds of years old would remain frozen in time, while up on the mesa the ances-tors' modern-day Navajo relatives resided in trailer homes.

Life in the beautiful canyon wasn't entirely bucolic. In 1864, Colonel Kit Carson and the Federal Army forced the Navajo into a last stand at the end of the box canyon. After a long winter the Navajo surrendered – ending the last major engagement between their tribe and the Feds.

In discussions with our Navajo hosts, who were most gracious, you couldn't escape the conversation about what had happened before any of us was around and the horrible way the Native Americans were treated. Most conversations about the topic usually ended with non-natives looking down at the ground, nodding, and saying, "Yeah, boy, you guys really got *screwed*."

It was ironic that the Navajo, given their size and successful implementation of gas and oil extraction – not to mention casinos on their sovereign land – were considered the "rich" tribe. In the week that we were shuttled around to various locations, I sure as hell didn't meet anyone who was rich. To illustrate the point, a Native American crew member, hired to drive one of the actor campers, got a little too excited about the weekly paycheck and took off to party with friends – in the camper! It took some back-channel searching, but the woman was eventually located. When she was asked what happened, her excuse was as shocking as it was simple: She had never seen that much money before.

The location was right up my valley.

The first half of the shoot was in and around the city of Gallup, but the latter part was on actual tribal lands. Knowing this, I asked the producers to reach out to the Navajo location guides to see if they could arrange for a "holy man" to come and bless our production. To my great delight, the producers agreed and a blessing was arranged.

The morning of the first day shooting on Navajo lands was

shockingly cold – hovering right around eleven degrees. Our van steered into a nearby Conoco gas station. This was the rendez-vous point to pick up our shaman – who was also the location guide's uncle. This small, smiling man hopped in our van and we rode to the location, mostly in shivery silence.

At the base camp, we gathered the crew around in a large circle and the shaman did his thing, blessing the four directions and passing around a modern-day "peace pipe," containing a sage-like herb. I took a hit and coughed my brains out, but I was honored to participate in this ancient ritual. I asked the holy man if he could do something about the cold. He said it was already taken care of and the crew shared a good laugh – their billowing breath backlit by the orange-tinted morning sun. Mercifully, each day got warmer for the next three days we filmed at that location, so it seemed our guy did something right.

Shooting the actual film was mostly uneventful. I enjoyed working with a diverse cast, from James Frecheville to Judge Reinhold to Annabeth Gish. We were all trying to make the best out of an oddball situation. I use that term because the setup of this project was something out of an international financier's text-book. The main creative types involved – the writer, composer, producer and director – were English in nationality yet were all based in the United States. The rest of the crew came from Ottawa, Canada, yet we filmed in New Mexico. The strange grouping of nationalities and locations must have met some international requirements for funding, so there we were, shivering in beau-tiful New Mexico in November.

But then things got even weirder. About four hours after my last day of filming, our director Marc was, to the best of my understanding, "involuntarily removed" from the project. *They still had a week of shooting to go back in Ottawa. Why now, after all this?* I had no issue with Marc, so it wasn't any of my doing – it would take a lot for me to recommend the actual sacking of a director, as crucial as they are to the process.

Shrugging it off to a potential rift between the director and producers – which happens often – I returned to Los Angeles. A couple of weeks later, after checking on the status/results of the project, I was informed that the producer Nigel had also left *Highly Functional.* That was a first – losing both the director and producer of a project *after* it was filmed, but *before* it was completed.

Who the hell was going to see this through? The caterer?

These are the times that try one's patience with "showbiz." This movie provided a perfect opportunity to strut my stuff doing something that was in my wheelhouse but completely different at the same time – there were no demons, no blood, just good old-fashioned acting and storytelling. What a delight! So, the idea that this movie, after all of our collective efforts, would get held up in international hell was a really disturbing thought.

Highly Functional sat on a shelf from 2014 to the last quarter of 2016, when, miraculously, Marc resurfaced to let me know he was back on board to finish editing and see it through to completion. Some dispute had been resolved and the movie would actually see the light of day.

Fingers crossed.

KISSIN' HANDS AND SHAKIN' BABIES –
THE CON GAME

In 1967, my hometown of Medford, Oregon, held its annual Pear Blossom Festival parade. This particular year, the grand marshal was Leonard Nimoy, dressed as Spock from the new TV show *Star Trek*. Though Medford was expecting hundreds, thousands showed up and Leonard had to be rescued by police. This was the first, unofficial, large gathering of "Trekkies."

Star Trek conventions took hold in the 1970s and the world of pop culture has never looked back. What was once a "fringe" industry or a "cult" phenomenon is now coming to a town near you almost every weekend. Conventions are the modern-day combination of county fair and traveling circus, with cosplay, celebrities, merchandise, comic books, gaming, tattoo and piercing stations – everything but the bearded lady.

Conventions have morphed tremendously since my first Fangoria Weekend of Horrors in Dearborn, Michigan, back in 1988. I was there to promote *Evil Dead II* and it was fun to see which actors were in attendance. Early on, cons were full of older guests who had appeared in popular TV shows or movies years ago and now signed keepsakes for adults who were once their childhood fans.

The biggest change in conventions, aside from their sheer proliferation, is that guests are now actors from both old and *current* shows. Now, you'll have convention mainstay Lou Ferrigno from television's *The Incredible Hulk,* sitting across from Norman Reedus, living legend from *The Walking Dead.*

I have to say, I prefer the new, mixed-bag approach to convention guests – it makes the actors' greenroom so much more interesting to hang around in. Grabbing a cup of coffee, I might bump into Elvira – who is really just shy and delightful – or share a point and a wink with the *Duck Dynasty* clan, who seemed completely out of place.

Like any fan, I love shooting the shit with the Old Guard, the guys who headlined TV shows when I was a kid. It was a thrill to finally meet Adam West and Burt Ward – the original Dynamic Duo. Adam, now late-eighties, always has a smile on his face. I asked him how he was doing in passing one day and he replied, "I'd be doing a lot better with an ice-cold martini in my hand!"

Stan the Man.

Comic book legend/convention staple Stan Lee, mid-nineties now, is a blast. Having appeared in the first three *Spider-Man* movies, Stan and I had the web slinger in common and we always enjoyed talking – which was only for a few minutes at a time between signings. Stan strikes me as a guy who, back in his comic book writing swingin' heyday, would put a jazz record on the turntable in his groovy Manhattan apartment, don his aviator sunglasses and cut the rug with some hot babes.

The *Star Trek* actors, being the first and the biggest, were always popular at conventions. I worked with Walter Koenig ("Chekov") on a movie back in 1988, so we've been friendly ever since and I still see him at cons to this day. I think Walter is a little mystified by all the *Star Trek* stuff. He doesn't really get it, but it doesn't concern him either.

Leonard Nimoy ("Spock") was always hugely popular, so I only met him once. At some sci-fi con, our tables were back to back with a thin black drape between us. At one point, I simply reached through the curtain, introduced myself and shook his hand. That was that.

My meeting with George Takei ("Sulu") was just as brief. At a convention outside of London, he was getting off a freight elevator as I was getting on. We nodded, exchanged a "Hello" and "Good morning," and we were on our way.

Shatner ("Captain James T. Kirk") was the big fish. I had to meet him at all costs because my brother Don and I were ardent fans of the original *Star Trek* series. When I finally had the chance to meet the man/myth, I wasn't going to use the *Star Trek* card. I knew better. I had to try a different angle. Because I had actually studied the TV show *T.J. Hooker* – for my own personal, mostly amusing reasons – I could throw out enough details and delights so that he would know I actually watched the show. My plan worked, and we struck up a lively, non–*Star Trek* conversation, which I think he appreciated.

Bill did not disappoint. Though he is in his mid-eighties, his energy is astounding. He must do twenty conventions a year, not to mention a gaggle of charity events and a one-man show. Guys such as Bill and Stan and Adam have all been a great inspiration – not just in my formative years but presently, because none of them has any intention of slowing down. Shuffling from convention to convention provides their aerobics. Answering questions onstage and having a laugh with fans keeps them sharp and gives them a needed shot of adrenaline every now and again. This is what keeps these old geezers alive and I have taken note. I doubt you'll see me disappear from the convention circuit anytime soon.

Conventions have also been a great way to meet the fine leading ladies from days gone by, like Barbara Eden from *I Dream of Jeannie* and Julie Newmar from *Batman*. Nothing gave me more pleasure than to sneak up behind their signing tables, grab a handshake and flatter them with sexually undertoned admiration. These women gave a young mind much to think about in my formative years and each left an indelible impression.

Robert Englund and Kane Hodder, two of my horror peers from *Nightmare on Elm Street* and *Friday the 13th* respectively, make the convention rounds as well. We've done special photo ops together and it's always fun to watch fans and their tormentors interact. Robert, on the one hand, brings his Freddie glove with him and holds it menacingly close to the fan's throat. Kane, on the other hand, grabs his captives by the back of the neck with one hand and begins to continually apply pressure until the picture is taken. Look closely at the faces of fans in Kane Hodder photos – they all have a slightly alarmed expression. Kane isn't kidding.

The modern-day bad boys of conventions are Norman Reedus, Michael Rooker and Jon Bernthal. Each guy has lots of impressive credits, but they're all part of the *Walking Dead* juggernaut – a status that alone guarantees them con bookings until the end of time.

Jon Bernthal is a sweet beast of a guy. Tough, funny, open. He scowls on-screen, but he's a lot of laughs behind the scenes.

Rooker I already knew of and worked with. His first convention appearances were because of *Henry: Portrait of a Serial Killer* and now, between *The Walking Dead* and *Guardians of the Galaxy,* he's more popular than ever. Michael did an episode of *Burn Notice*, so I got to witness his intense focus and approach. He's a first-rate actor and a fun-loving guy. In shooting the bull I asked him what it was like to work opposite Tom Cruise in *Days of Thunder* and he replied, "It was fine, because I knew I could act."

Ash vs. Walking Dead.

Norman Reedus is the Elvis of the convention scene. He plays a badass on *The Walking Dead*, but he'd walk right past you on the street. Unassuming, seemingly shy and very nice, Norman manages to beguile his fans. I've seen the pile of gifts left for him at each signing; I've witnessed the trembling hands, the tears pouring down the cheeks of mesmerized fans who finally meet their messiah. Norman manages this by hardly saying a word and never taking his sunglasses off. Neat trick!

Most actors I know will never turn down a free meal. For lonely thespians on the road, a meal with a table full of their peers is a welcome event. Over the years, a tradition has evolved whereby I invite roughly ten hooligans, ruffians and scoundrels to a Saturday night dinner in the city of the moment. We tend to take over the private room of a steakhouse – not because we think we're cool, but so we can actually hear the conversations. On the convention floor or in a frantic greenroom, you're not going to have any worthwhile visits – but at a slow, libatious dinner, it's a different story.

During the evening, after ordering, we'll go around the table and play some innocuous game, like "Tell us something nobody knows about you." It's a daring challenge for people in the arts and in the public eye, because many of them don't want to reveal anything about themselves. Mystery is their friend.

Whatever the case, as long as everyone's game some fun facts come out. An actress revealed that for the first ten years of her life she grew up mostly naked in a commune. An actor regaled us about the time his parents got married in Cuba – the night of the Castro revolution. Curious tidbits like that can jump-start other tangential stories and off you go.

One Saturday night in Chicago, we had a large, eclectic group, including Kevin Sorbo, the great director John Carpenter and Erin Gray (*Buck Rogers* hottie). Erin had watched the convention and pop culture world generally explode and very cleverly formed her own representation company – Heroes for Hire. Erin is smart and tough and she has built up quite the stable of celebrity clients.

That particular night, we started by going around the table introducing ourselves and explaining what we did for a living. Granted, most of us knew or knew "of" each other, but it was still fun to hear what people say about themselves. It was a long, raucous night and I became *very* knowledgeable about *everything* on the ride home. As I pontificated, a voice from the backseat stopped me cold.

"Campbell. Shut. The. Fuck. Up."

The cool, measured voice of John Carpenter was unmistakable. "You have no idea what you're talking about. Spare us all and shut up."

John wasn't a guy to mince words and of course he was right. Like a good little actor, I followed his direction and didn't say another word for the rest of the ride.

I like to have fun and entertain my fellow actor buddies, but the guys at Wizard World Entertainment took it to a new level. Wizard started as a comic book buying guide in the early nineties, eventually got into the convention business and went public as a company. I had heard of them but never booked an appearance at one of their cons.

In 2010, John Macaluso, "Johnny Mac," took over the company and shifted things into high gear. Wizard began to add cities left and right, so I decided to book a few dates and see what they were all about.

The first time my right-hand man, Mike Estes, met Johnny Mac, they almost got into a fistfight. Mike is my advance man. He goes a day ahead to scope out the floor, the greenroom situation – even mapping out the bathrooms. I try to be Captain Smiley at conventions, so I rely on Mike to be Bad Cop if needed.

Wizard was new to us and likewise. We had a laundry list of how everything was to be done – the table setup, the location, blah-blah-blah. Over dozens of convention appearances Mike and I had figured out a routine that worked very well for us – and we weren't about to change it.

"Bad Cop" and "Captain Smiley."

As Mike was doing his prep on the floor, he happened to ask a Wizard rep how pre-sales were going. The answer was good news – they'd sold a lot of autograph tickets. In fact, based on my agreement with Wizard, they'd oversold about 250 tickets.

Mike explained this to me and, since Wizard was an unknown entity, I decided to stick to the terms of our deal. I would be happy to stay longer so the fans didn't get stiffed, but it would cost Wizard.

When Mike told Johnny Mac the figure, that's when the fists almost flew. He was very displeased with our number – which was calculated in the same fashion as the original contract – yet

Mike remained firm. The terms were the terms. After a few more words, the tense situation diffused, all parties agreed to the new arrangement and we finished the rest of the con without incident. I'm happy to report that Mike and Johnny Mac are now good buds. I don't want to get in anybody's face and, for the most part, these cons are smooth as silk.

This isn't to say that there isn't strife behind the scenes at conventions. This wasn't the first time guests and promoters had been at odds. What recourse does a promoter have when a head-lining actor, horribly hungover, shows up three hours late for their appearance on a Saturday, the biggest day? Not much, other than not booking them ever again, which happens. Conversely, conventions are shunned by celebrities for slights, poor attendance, non-existent logistics or crappy accommodations.

Actors liked Johnny Mac because he liked them. A lot of corporate types don't know what to say to actors, but Johnny was very inclusive and he likes to laugh and pal around. He was also a sharp and fair businessman – and you don't always find that on the convention circuit.

"Yes, of course this is my car. Check the registration. First name: Bruce..."

Wizard, under John's leadership, was growing by leaps and bounds. Richmond, Virginia, was a new market and they wanted to make a big deal out of it.

It can be difficult for a conventioneer to secure a solid "roster" at an "unproven" market. Johnny Mac made us all think twice with his offer of a private jet ride there and back.

Okay, twist my arm.

The jet, Jim Carrey's former Gulfstream V, was loaded with

a geek's wet dream: Norman Reedus, Michael Rooker, Jon Bern-thal, Dean Cain – and that *Evil Dead* guy.

It was a pretty festive atmosphere, with poker, food and hooch. After we got cranked up, about the only subject *not* discussed was religion. The *Walking Dead* alumni are all into guns of every kind.

"It's not anything ideological," Rooker explained with a laugh. "I just like 'em!"

Dean loves guns and politics and was happy to spar or explain his positions. Look for him on the political circuit one day.

Eventually, we landed in Richmond and poured ourselves into bed. For a flight that's hard to remember, it's one that I'll never forget.

CRAWLING BACK INTO THE WOMB

Ash died.

That's the one thing that everyone overlooks. In all of the questions, discussions and forums about the *Evil Dead* films, nobody seems to remember that the ending of the original movie wasn't a wink, a cliff-hanger or a setup. It was a finale. The hero was killed off by an unseen demon. Case closed. We weren't laying the foundation for a franchise; we were just trying to make and sell our first feature film.

Ready to ditch horror for humor, we went back to our goofball comedy roots with our second film, but the *Crimewave* experience was a horror itself. We were desperate to reclaim the thrill and pride we had while making *Evil Dead*, so we did it again.

Is *Evil Dead II* a sequel or a remake? Is there such a thing as a "requel"?

Ash was supposed to die, not live on for decades in comic books, video games, action figures and tattoos. I never set out to become a B movie actor, but fake blood doesn't wash off so easily.

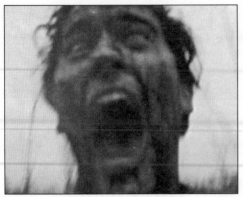

The End...or so we thought...

Ash has been very good to me and I'm thrilled at the longevity and the loyalty that our films have cultivated.

During the twenty-five years after *Evil Dead 3: Army of Darkness* – the third and last of the series – I zigzagged my way across the country, going to horror, sci-fi and fantasy conventions of all stripes. At each one, the same thing occurred – questions about another *Evil Dead*. It was hard telling fans over and over that their beloved movies were finite in number and that they were only going to get three of them. It wasn't something fans would or could wrap their collective head around, so they never stopped hoping.

Somehow, time and technology became our friend. DVDs made it possible to shove huge amounts of content on the disc and the image and sound were much better. This prompted a lot of "revisiting" on the part of video distributors to go back through their catalogue, pull out the golden moldies of yesteryear and reissue them. The *Evil Dead* films fit the bill.

Anchor Bay, a company in Troy, Michigan, of all places, sub-licensed all three of the *Evil Dead* movies. In a groundbreaking repackaging, they shot new interviews, recorded commentary tracks, found deleted scenes, put together "making of" documentaries and assembled obscure photo galleries – a fan's wet dream, all in one package.

Whatever Anchor Bay did, it worked. Fans loved seeing the sausage being made and it put *Evil Dead* back on screens in home theaters for the first time in decades. Naturally, this reemergence fueled plenty of interest at conventions and the questions continued, unabated: "When are you going to make another *Evil Dead*?"

THE ROAD TO REMAKE

The possibility of expanding the *Evil Dead* universe took an interesting turn when filmmaker Fede Alvarez made a short film from his home in Montevideo, Uruguay, and posted it on YouTube. The short was called *Panic Attack* and it was a beguiling story about giant robots attacking a city, with a small boy looking on in wonder. There wasn't much of a story, but the sophisticated special effects and clever assemblage made a very positive impression on Hollywood – and very quickly.

"I was in front of Steven Spielberg two weeks later," Fede explained, still amused at the recollection. "I basically met everyone in Hollywood all at once about developing *Panic Attack* or whatever. Sam Raimi was one of my stops because I wanted to meet him."

Sam was very impressed, like most of Hollywood, and the two hit it off immediately. Fede opted to let Sam and Rob Tapert's company develop *Panic Attack* into a feature, with the short acting as a de facto calling card since Fede had never directed a full-length film before.

It didn't take long before *Panic Attack* got the Hollywood treatment known ruefully as "Development Hell." The idea was bandied about at numerous studios, got bogged down with needless baggage (everyone wants to be part of a "hot" project) and got stuck in the creative mud.

Welcome to showbiz, Fede!

Sam must have seen the signs that *Panic Attack* was fading out, so he offered Fede the opportunity to direct an *Evil Dead* remake. Honestly, Rob and I were surprised that Sam would bite on such a proposal since the *Evil Dead* franchise was his "baby," but Sam was a big champion of Fede and we got on board.

Sam may have been intrigued by recent trends in the world of horror filmmaking. Some of the most iconic horror franchises ever produced were getting rebooted for "modern audiences." Suddenly the same slashers, freaks and zombies that had terrified audiences in the 1970s and '80s were too dated or old-fashioned. All of *Evil Dead*'s peers were getting remade, including *The Hills Have Eyes, Piranha, Friday the 13th, Nightmare on Elm Street* and *The Texas Chainsaw Massacre*.

Because the *Evil Dead* movies had a worldwide "brand," albeit a humble one, it wasn't hard to assemble a modest budget for the remake, between Sony Studios and foreign sales advances. Rob thought it best to take Fede under the Kiwi wing and shoot it with his TV crew in New Zealand. It was a great decision, because it meant that filming would move at a decent pace. As producers, schedule and budget mattered to us.

Once we got the green light to shoot, we had to find a new, five-person cast. As a producing trio, we're not interested or good at every aspect of filmmaking, so we tend to focus our efforts where we can have meaningful, constructive input.

Rob has always been the budget and money guy – Mr. Hands-On. Sam is the Grand Poobah from on high, who makes sure the overall project stays true to the original material. As for me, I'm an actor, so I'm always involved on the acting front and I love the world of post-production editing and sound.

I was curious to see how Fede was going to handle and run auditions. As an actor, I hate auditioning. I find the process uncomfortable, sometimes humiliating and not always the best way to showcase my talent. So, whenever I'm on the producing or directing side I always make actors feel at home auditioning. I was also watching Fede, because at auditions directors do give actors direction between takes. I was curious to see what his notes would be, how he communicated them to the actor and whether the notes led to a better subsequent performance.

In every case, Fede's words to the actors were reassuring, insightful and successful. By the end of the first day of casting, I knew he was going to be just fine at the helm. The cast he chose, led by the very unique Jane Levy, all did a great job.

I was still doing *Burn Notice* by the time shooting rolled around, so I missed that part, but Rob kept us informed of the daily progress. Between Rob's seasoned production skills, Fede's pragmatic approach and a great Kiwi crew, filming was completed without any major injuries or feuds. The actors were each put through some pretty fresh hell, but they were all troupers about it.

I saw my first "director's cut" down in Miami and was immediately relieved. Young filmmakers generally love their own work and find it impossible to trim or remove their precious material. Early edits are usually exasperatingly long, boring, awkward and amateurish. Fede didn't seem to have any of those issues, because the version he turned over to us was already a tight ninety-four minutes – with pace, style and impact. What a relief!

The next time I saw Fede was in the dubbing stage for the sound mixing process. Because of my love of all things sound, I got the nod to be the "overseer" of the mix. Fede was a big fan of sound as well and put folks through their paces trying to match effects to his eclectic descriptions.

With Fede Alvarez, the new "Boy Genius."

"I want the door opening to sound like a baby sighing," Fede would implore the sound designers. "But a sad baby, who is irritable and weak."

A month later, we got what we set out for – a dynamic sound mix that helped establish and maintain the mood and give the gore an unmistakable kick in the pants. Previews went very well, word of mouth was good and the reviews, for an *Evil Dead* film, were not unkind.

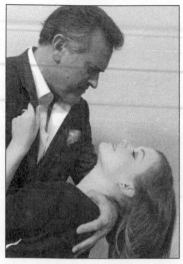

Passing the torch?

Fede, of course, was being compared to Sam Raimi, but to his credit he kept the tone of the film similar to the original – not a joke fest – and carved out his own visual style. For a first-time filmmaker, Fede showed remarkable poise and turned in a solid, effective horror movie.

I always get asked what I thought about the remake. I tell people, "Great, because we produced it!" Some folks assumed that we watched the remake happen from afar, which often happens. At least in this case, we were remaking our own movie!

As far as box office goes – the great Hollywood barometer of success – the 2013 *Evil Dead* remake made around $94 million worldwide and because of its modest budget was an unqualified success. Fede's next film, the taut thriller *Don't Breathe*, was even more successful. I think we'll be seeing more of this Alvarez fellow.

The only "negative" to be gleaned from doing the *Evil Dead* remake, aside from feeling a bit like we were "jumping on the remake bandwagon," was that die-hard fans weren't 100 percent satisfied. Those familiar with the lighter tone of the franchise found the remake too melodramatic and not as much "fun." I got the sense overall that fans felt like the movie was "close, but no cigar" – they wanted the Ash character and they wanted Sam Raimi.

Note taken.

ASH VERSUS TELEVISION

Meanwhile, Sam Raimi and his brother Ivan were semi-secretly writing another *Evil Dead* movie. Sam had become newly energized by the idea and got around to it whenever he and his emergency-room doctor/writer brother could schedule a writing session, which was not very often.

Scripts written on "spec," as in "speculative," tend to take a lot longer because there is no deadline. This was no exception. How much longer would it take? Where would we shop it when it was done? How much would it cost?

"Too damn much," was Rob Tapert's answer.

Rob has always been the fiscal voice of reason in our three-way partnership. It's virtually impossible for him to hold his tongue if he feels that financial doom is gathering on the horizon.

"If Sam directs this as a feature film, it's gonna cost seventy-five million dollars," Rob intoned matter-of-factly. "And if it bombs, the series is dead as a doornail."

Rob is subtle like that.

Should an *Evil Dead* movie cost $75 million? Should it even be a feature? Exploring it in other forms – like as a TV show – caught Rob's eye and certainly mine. Since *Army of Darkness*, both Rob and I had spent several decades mainly doing television. We understood it. We liked the speed and the no BS of it all.

Rob was the first to verbalize it: "How about *Evil Dead* as a TV show?"

Convinced that this was the way to go, I called Sam and arranged to come to his house. It may not seem like a big deal, in this age of texting and e-mail, but sitting in front of a person is still different, still way more real, impactful and immediate. Sam and I have known each other for four decades, but we still had the ability to get "all businessy" if the situation arose. This was a business call – not a personal one.

Sam had produced plenty of television in partnership with Rob, but always once removed, with other directors, writers and production types doing much of the day-to-day. This time, we were asking him to create a story "bible," which lays out multiple seasons' worth of plot, direct the pilot and generally dive into the TV world headfirst.

I'm happy to say that Sam got on board and we began retooling *Evil Dead* as a TV show, framing the action in a much larger context and filling the gaps in what had been a twenty-five-year absence for the character Ash.

What had he been up to? What was he doing now? Let's face it, I wasn't any younger or skinnier by this point, so we would have to play Ash as more of a middle-aged loser than the hero type he was decades ago. Would that new approach work?

Script issues aside, putting a deal like this together would be even more daunting in that all three previous *Evil Dead* films had been made by three different companies – each with different or overlapping rights to the original material. This was going to take some sorting out and it was all "on the clock," which might go a long way toward explaining why Hollywood lawyers live in big houses and drive shiny, fast cars.

Once the legal stuff was sorted out, it came time to "pitch." Pitching is a frenzied period when agents put the word out about your amazing new project and you make the rounds, trying to persuade potential buyers to part with millions of dollars.

Personally, I like pitching. Back on the original *Evil Dead*, we pitched to Detroit investors who didn't know anything about movies and they were hardly receptive. At least network execs were in the same industry and we spoke the same language, so pitching to the suits was never a hassle to me. In the room, I always felt that the network needed us as much as we needed them. Television is the great gaping maw and the vast blank spots have to be filled in somehow.

Sam is always great at pitches. He's very charming and P. T. Barnum-ish, with bold statements and unending enthusiasm. Rob, as the money guy, would give them the bad news – we wanted to be paid adult money and have an adult budget. Asking for specific monetary commitments and creative control quickly weeded six potential suitors down to three – Starz among them.

Budgets are one thing. Creative control is another issue entirely. Sam, through vast box office success and tough negotiating, had won the right of "final cut" on his movies – meaning that he would be the final arbiter of what went in the movie or what did not – a coveted and rarely assigned

The plot thickens: scanning the storyboards.

privilege in Hollywood. Maybe a dozen directors have that much clout. Hell, Sam had it – why not use it to our advantage?

At one particular meeting, Sam broached the topic of creative control, gingerly explaining that final cut was a right he now had – and asked if that network would extend the same rights. The CEO leaned back in his chair and said magnanimously, "Sam, we've been doing some amazing television here. We're really good at what we do."

Mr. Executive didn't elaborate further, but it didn't take a genius to read between the lines. His answer was a big fat "no" couched in corporate speak. From the moment I heard that condescending line, nothing else out of the guy's mouth mattered.

Another suitor was wildly enthusiastic but offered us a budget of exactly half of what we were asking for – which left us less than wildly enthusiastic.

Aside from money and control, another big issue was "content restrictions." What could we show on a given network? On broadcast television, there are "Standards and Practices," a lengthy guide to what you can and can't show or say – as in boo-boo words or excessive sex or violence. On cable television, you have more leeway. You can say some spicy words and characters can be slightly unsavory and drink or smoke to their hearts' content. *Burn Notice* was a good example of that. We had some flexibility, but it was certainly not unrestricted.

Of all the interested parties, Starz was the only one to offer up "zero" content restrictions. That was amazing to consider. From a true horror fan's perspective, it's even more appealing than an R-rated movie, something *Evil Dead* would surely have been subjected to had it been released in feature film form. Through Starz, we had the creative control, the right budget and no restrictions.

How fast can we close this deal?

STARZ IN OUR EYES

I had only heard of Starz in passing at that point. I knew that they were a premium channel and had plenty of subscribers, but they were foreign to the new network mantra: own the intellectual property (although costing considerably more cash up front) instead of airing *someone else's* intellectual property. AMC pretty much invented that dynamic. Netflix, Amazon, Hulu and a slew of others quickly followed suit.

Rob had worked with Starz before on the TV reboot of *Spartacus*. Often in the film business, when a new Head Honcho arrives, they will bring in their own "people" and they can be ruthless in shuttering existing projects (even beloved ones) that didn't bear their personal imprint. Chris Albrecht was new at Starz and *Spartacus* wasn't his baby. He had great programming success at HBO and wanted to repeat that with his new company, so he cleaned house and began to develop projects from scratch.

Timing can be important to a project. A network on a downward path is always nerve-wracking, because they are more prone to be cautious, cheap and regimented. New networks can be great, because they are filled with hope and cash – *initially* – but they can also be prone to wild mood swings as they try to carve out an identity.

Thirty Years Later...

The USA Network is a good example of this. They started with a perfectly plausible "blue sky" concept behind all their shows – upbeat concepts with attractive people in nice, mostly exterior locations. That formula worked great for probably five years and *Burn Notice* was certainly a main benefactor of this approach – hitting the air just as USA was growing and establishing a cable format that was *working*.

But, as happens with all things, change came knocking, and soon USA seemed a little tired, doing the same thing over and over. Viewers seemed to sense that this was all a big "branding" thing and began to check out other viewing options.

The timing with Starz seemed just right and we got the coveted "green light" to make the show – a pilot episode directed by Sam Raimi, followed by nine half-hour episodes.

But where would we shoot it?

Naturally, since I had moved back to Los Angeles, I assumed we would shoot there. Reality dictated that we get the most bang out of our buck and all signs pointed back to New Zealand. Rob had pretty much laid the foundation of a permanent existence in

Auckland. He'd married Lucy Lawless, had two Kiwi sons and has produced a half-dozen shows in his adopted homeland. I still love tormenting Rob that his children talk with a "funny" accent.

Although I was averse to going back down to the Southern Hemisphere, it made the most sense. On top of a healthy "rebate" from the Kiwi government to boost production, the monetary exchange rate was very favorable: Every U.S. dollar was worth $1.25 Kiwi and it made just enough difference in the budget to seal the deal.

BACK WITH THE OLD MAN

Twenty-five years had passed since we made *Army of Darkness*. Sam Raimi had since become one of the biggest directors in Hollywood and I had learned a few new tricks myself. One of the best things about getting the band back together was to share how each of us had grown into our current selves.

Sam had become a master director – cajoling, joking and bullying his way to what he needed and demanded from the crew. Rob was completely comfortable in his own skin and with the talented people he assembled from all of his past shows, such as *Spartacus*, *Legend of the Seeker*, and even alumni from the *Hercules* and *Xena* days. Since *Army of Darkness*, I had put in my leading man time on big and small screens, working with directors such as John Carpenter and Don Coscarelli, so I was eager to see and share what we each had learned.

The overriding joy of this undertaking was in knowing that we were still, after all these years, together as partners and friends.

The family reunion was further fleshed out with Sam's co-writer/
brother Ivan on the writing staff, original composer Joe LoDuca
doing the music and *Army of Darkness* editor Bob Murawski to
keep everyone in line.

But reality soon descended. Sam was not a "typical" TV
director. He doesn't shoot wholesale – he's a meticulous, detail
kind of guy, who has never had a keen sense of shooting time. In
order for Sam to get the days he needed to pull off a believable
pilot episode, we had to effectively "steal" a shooting day from
each of the remaining episodes – a horrible price we would pay
further down the line.

Working with Sam was a treat. The time melted away and you
never really thought about the shooting days, mostly because he
didn't either. But once Sam left town, the atmosphere devolved
into a low-grade panic.

EVIL DEAD VERSUS US

We still had the same challenging material to do but *way* less
time to do it. While the pilot was filmed in twenty-four days, each
subsequent half-hour episode had to be done in roughly six days
with a few special effects and stunt days tacked on the end, but
it was a cruel change of pace. From what started out as a country
club atmosphere under Sam, life on set became a furrowed brow
of buzzing activity, with department heads smiling tightly while
they figured out how in the hell to pull this new reality off.

I was an old hand at the TV pace by this time, but I was not
ready for the shift into ultrahigh gear – right after Sam had just
put us through our serious paces – and I had a rough couple of
episodes. I pitied the incoming director, Michael Bassett, but he
did a great job under enormous pressure to keep the creative bar
up where Sam had left it.

Like any TV show, the first few episodes or half season or

even a *few* seasons are needed to establish what a show is – the tone, the pace and, in our case, the gore factor. *Ash vs. Evil Dead* was no different.

Show runner Craig DiGregorio and his team of writers had their work cut out for them – tasked with compellingly telling the updated story of Ash reengaging the Evil Dead. It wasn't a perfect season, but we launched the ship and it was staying afloat.

PARTNERS IN GRIME

I was delighted to witness the generally good behavior of newcomers Dana DeLorenzo and Ray Santiago. When you get involved with a group of actors for an extended period under trying circumstances, you get to know each other real quick and sometimes those people aren't who their cheery auditions led you to believe. In this case, both actors were not only talented but also patient and very tough.

Lucy Lawless is the silent queen. On a film set, particularly a Kiwi set, she is the calm, easygoing professional, knowing everyone's name and asking about family members – some of whom she has known for two decades.

Ironically, before *Xena* started filming, Rob Tapert made me spend an afternoon with Lucy, jogging along a local Auckland causeway and tutoring her about what makes a good TV star. I had just finished a stint as a leading man on an action-oriented TV show, so I had a lot of "intel" to share that was relevant. I'm not sure what she thought of my all-knowingness, but she was very gracious about it.

Flash forward to twenty years later. We now get the great Lucy as an addition to our show as the character Ruby – a strange and untrustworthy character. Honestly, I didn't much care who Lucy played – I just wanted her on the show.

"Rob, at dinner tonight, ask your wife to do the show, will

you?" I implored Rob, who has been married to Lucy since *Xena*.

I'm grateful to Lucy for reminding me about set etiquette, particularly with the often overpolite Kiwis. Lucy is very careful with her words so as not to offend, no matter how pissed off she gets. I'm a little different. I consider myself

Ray and Dana lent me a hand.

plenty professional, but I can get prickly and impatient if things get bogged down. After getting pissy about something, I have often caught Lucy out of the corner of my eye. Her look of calm cheeriness always mellows me out.

ALL HAIL THE KIWIS!

The New Zealand film crews are amazing. It's always said at acceptance speeches: "Our crew is the best in the world!" On *Ash vs. Evil Dead*, you could make a strong case for it. These skilled men and women from the likes of *Lord of the Rings*, *Avatar* and *Hercules* could do special effects, build special props or re-create rural, low-budget Michigan like nobody's business.

We called upon some of the original *Herc* and *Xena* team to help launch our wobbly ship. Michael Hurst, formerly Hercules' sidekick Iolaus, pitched in to direct. Charlie "Hole in One" Haskell became the hardest working man in show business, keeping our action and special effects unit in top shape. Last but not least, Rick Jacobson, who first directed me on *Xena*, became a great keeper of the franchise flame, directing our most ambitious episodes.

The Kiwis even got "The Classic" back.

Sam's beloved 1973 Oldsmobile Delta 88 and three identical trip-lets were all put in a shipping container and sent to New Zealand for the shoot. Identifying the actual car was not that hard – all you had to do was open the driver's side door and listen to the sound. With a key in the ignition, when the door opens you hear a very anemic *eeeeee-uuuuu-gggg-heeee* sound – like it's trying to tell you that the key is still in the ignition, but it doesn't have enough strength to do it.

When the art department summoned Sam and me to inspect the Delta, now that it was fully decked out, *that* sound emanated when I opened the door to sit inside.

"Wow, Sam, *that sound* – it's exactly the same."

"Yeah," he affirmed. "Kinda creepy."

Creepy and cool. This was the actual car Sam's mother used to drop us off to watch *A Clockwork Orange* during high school. It was the same car we used in *Six Months to Live, The Happy Valley Kid, The James Hoffa Story* – all the Super-8mm

Lucy, Rob and me.

classics we made in the formative years – not to mention every single one of Sam's feature films. This car knew where the bodies were buried. It had some deep history. I'm not a method actor by any means, but it was really cool to have that crappy car back. It meant a lot. It made this real.

The original cabin had to be re-created, both inside and out, to almost full scale. The results were breathtaking. Since Sam had gone back to the States to finish his pilot episode, Rob and I were the only two people, from a crew of three hundred, to have any recollection of what the Tennessee cabin from 1979 *actually* looked like inside.

When I first stepped on the interior set, I felt like I was in a virtual reality video game. What impressed me about the meticulous re-creation was that wherever you went in the interior space, the perspectives were all correct. If I looked to the left of the fireplace, I saw the window that Steve Frankel, our only carpenter on *Evil Dead*, had originally carved out of the wall with a Skilsaw. In the hallway, doors on each side were placed exactly where they had been. The floorboards had the same width and wear; the chairs and even the doilies on the tables were the same as well as the "laughing lamp" from *Evil Dead II*.

All in all, the process of resurrecting this wonky Evil Dead "thing" from our childhood made my head spin. From the time Sam got on board to the time it was on the air was only a year – warp speed in a Hollywood time frame.

For some strange reason, with every opportunity for this to fall apart – legally, financially and logistically – we managed to do just enough right to pull it off. I knew eventually we would face the ratings demon, but for now we had won the battle.

CON OF THE DEAD

Once season one was in the can, we wasted no time at all in beginning the most sustained PR push I have ever been a part of – and I mean that in a good way. Starz got it. They understood that this show was not going to launch itself and that we had to spend money, make the rounds in the right places and get the word out. First stop: San Diego Comic-Con.

Ten years ago, Charlize Theron wouldn't have been caught dead at Comic-Con. Why should she go to that geekfest? Now that geeks run the entertainment world, you bet she's gonna go there – along with every major Hollywood actor trying to launch or promote a show. Cons are here to stay and actors had better get used to it.

The con itself is too big for its own britches. One hundred

and fifty thousand sweaty people are jammed into a teeming showroom over a four-day period, so it's not an event for the squeamish or claustrophobic.

The San Diego Comic-Con isn't really about fan interaction – it's way too big and impersonal for that. When the main ballrooms hold six thousand people, it's virtually impossible to have a one-on-one experience. Actors don't go to the big "cons" to pat little Billy on the head – they go to get their show exposed to the hundreds of media outlets that converge at these events.

As an example, one of our media events is known as a "roundtable" talk – five minutes each at ten different tables, with ten different journalists. At the end of an hour, you've had face-to-face interviews with a hundred outlets. Crazy.

We launched the first *Ash vs. Evil Dead* trailer at Comic-Con and also on Facebook, where we got 10 million views – double the number of any other Starz show – and that got their attention.

At the New York Comic Con (distinguishing its name by using no dash), Sam delighted the crowd by informing them that they were about to see the *entire* pilot episode, not just a few clips. The crowd went ape shit, waving their foam "chainsaw hands" in the air. During the screening, Sam and I stood off to one side behind the stage curtain, taking in both the show and the reactions from the crowd.

Mercifully, the fans ate it up. Starz took note and they planned one hell of a Hollywood premiere. The first *Evil Dead* had what we thought was a fancy affair at the time – spotlights, an ambulance, limos, a cavernous theater – but it was nothing like the *Ash vs. Evil Dead* premiere, when several blocks of Hollywood Boulevard were shut down so Iggy Pop could sing for a thousand screaming fans.

Hollywood, meet *Evil Dead*.

The reviews began to come in. With *Evil Dead*, we always

tended to grit our teeth because half of them were negative, but the feedback on *AVED* was mostly positive – with some of it great. After decades of making fun of the "cheap" this or "cheesy" that, critics could no longer pick on the production values, special effects or even the acting. After four decades, *Evil Dead* had morphed from a homegrown, mostly amateur operation into a respectable affair. Rotten Tomatoes, the modern arbiter of quality, gave *AVED* a 98 percent fresh rating – higher than any of the previous films.

Ash vs. Evil Dead was set to premiere on Halloween 2015, which was perfectly appropriate. Then, in a surprise move, before a single episode aired, Starz pulled the trigger and picked up the show for a second season. This was a remarkable vote of confidence, not to mention a huge relief – my personal jinx of starring only in one-season wonders was broken!

Evil Dead was our first baby. For Sam Raimi, Rob Tapert and myself, it was a professional voyage of discovery – not always smooth, but it got us into the film business and sent us on our way. A lot has happened since the first little movie got a distribution deal,  but there was obviously something about the process of making these that brought us back again – maybe it was the artistic freedom, the over-the-top form of entertainment or the long association with like-minded people. Whatever the case, with *Ash vs. Evil Dead* we had officially crawled back into the womb – and it felt good.

END OF ACT TWO

ACKNOWLEDGMENTS

Since I wrote the first *Chins* book fifteen years ago, there have been several key "passings" in my life that bear mention.

"We're orphans now," old pal Mike Ditz sadly pointed out after I told him that my mother, Joanne, had passed. Mike had lost both of his parents already, so I was just catching up.

"Yeah," I said, the realization dawning. "Feels weird. I feel like I'm untethered now."

It did feel weird. Losing my mother in 2016 represented the new reality of life without parents. Everything I took for granted is now more precious in my mind – the phone calls, the holidays hang time, the shared sense of humor. I knew my parents would die eventually, but it wasn't something I allowed myself to think about.

CHUCK

My dad, Charles Newton, made it to seventy-six. For a former Detroit "Mad Man" in the advertising business, that was a pretty good run. Being a full-fledged member of the cigarette-smoking, coffee-drinking, lunchtime booze crowd, I'm surprised he made it that far. In the end, he had seventy-five good years and one crappy one, when the wheels came off the tracks. Back surgery at age seventy-five was the beginning of the end.

Charlie was definitely from the "older" school view of modern medicine, in that you basically did whatever the doctors told you to do. In this case, he reported back pain and they recommended surgery. The shiny doctor's office brochures claim that you'll be tap dancing again in no time, but it's not always the case. Dad's surgery didn't take and they had to crack him open again. One thing led to another and between sciatic issues and bum kidneys it was game over.

Dad died Election Day, 2006. His last morning was lucid but weak. I leaned close and whispered the boldest lie I would ever tell him. "It's all good, Dad – John Kerry won the election. He's the new president. Isn't that great?"

I figured what could it hurt? Charlie was a shameless liberal and this might put a final smile on his face. He squeezed my hand a little bit.

Aside from his being a generally nice guy, I'm mostly apprecia-tive to my father for being what I call a generational go-betweener. He walked the edge of "toeing the line" and doing whatever the hell he wanted to do like me.

My dad wanted to be a painter, but my grandfather, who *was* old-school, forbade it, so Charlie got into advertising, then amateur theater – edging his way toward creative expression. I'm thankful to him for being accepting of my "wholly creative" pursuits right from the start, as he didn't want the same "half-fulfilled" dreams to plague me. Charlie's frustrations ultimately led to my opportunity and I'll always be grateful for that.

JOANNE

Joanne Louise Pickens passed in her sleep February 1, 2016, in Fenton, Michigan, outliving my dad by ten years. Fewer bad habits, I'm guessing. Mom had eighty-five good years and about three lousy months, which was a decent run by anyone's standards. Being a practicing Christian Scientist, she only went to the hospital three times in her entire life – to deliver three boys.

What started the end-of-days ball rolling for my mom was a fall, followed by a broken hip. It's pretty standard stuff – old folks fall and things break. Naturally, as part of her rehab process she was introduced to pharmaceuticals for the very first time by way of painkillers. In these prescription-drug-addled days, my mother was a revelation to staffers.

"Okay," the nice nurse would ask, "how many drugs you are currently taking?"

"None," my mother would say matter-of-factly.

"None?" the nurse would ask, eyebrow arched. "No aspirin? Advil? Tylenol?"

"No."

"What is the name of your general practitioner?"

"I don't have one," Mom would answer, like it was no big deal.

"You don't have one!?" the nurse would remark, incredulous.

In the medical world, there was a lot more that my mother didn't know – her blood pressure, previous ailments, allergies, you name it. Her lack of a history of even basic medical procedures was met with almost universal disbelief. It was kind of like she was a woman from Appalachia at the turn of the century – only this was the modern era.

With regard to the human body, I did get one useful takeaway from watching my mother go through all this: Use it or lose it. In later years, Mom lived out a lifelong dream to move out west and live the rancher's life – and that's exactly what she did until she didn't want to work that hard anymore.

"I was done by seventy," she would often say and her life did become more sedentary for the last fifteen years of her life.

Mom passed, back at home, sleeping comfortably. I wrote her obituary. Here is a snippet from it that sums her up:

> As a mother, Joanne was kind, fearless and progressive. She was the type of mom who would lash a rope to her station wagon and drag the boys on a toboggan around the snowy Michigan roads a little too fast. She was the mother of three boys, a wife to four men and lover of everything western. Stunningly beautiful, Joanne loved Zane Grey books, Lipton tea and Anderson windows.

LULU

I was sitting in a restaurant with my assistant, Mike Estes, when a text from David Goodman blinked on my phone: "Lulu is gone." Immediately my eyes began to well. Losing Celia Raimi, Sam's mother, was a real knotted fist to the chest.

Lulu, the nickname she used – also the name of her successful lingerie store – was something else. A towering figure in the Raimi household, even though she couldn't have been over five-three, Lulu evoked awe and a bit of fear in the hearts of Sam's friends – or anyone else who entered their house.

Lulu didn't laugh; she cackled. When she told a joke, she would crack herself up so much she could no longer finish the routine. Conversely, her rages, directed at the three fledgling filmmakers, were memorable and quotable. "I don't know which of you is the stupidest," she would often say at the beginning of a lecture about business, raising money or whatever she demanded that we learn.

Lulu's words were sharp, some would say even mean, but she would end each dressing-down by writing a check for the stopgap financing we seemed to always need for *Evil Dead*. Loaning us what would be the last amount of money, she held the check in her hand as she gesticulated. "The well is dry. You understand, you stupid idiots? The. Well. Is. Dry."

My first marriage was meant to be as small as possible. My bride-to-be, Cristine, and I felt that because it was such a personal thing, we should just do it ourselves with a couple witnesses. When I told Lulu of the plan, she looked at me and stated flatly, "If you don't invite me to your wedding, I will never speak to you again." I knew she meant it. Lulu was at the wedding.

Lulu and I had some history, so I knew I had to go to her memorial in Detroit. After a long weekend of signing autographs, doing "photo ops" and generally clowning around at the Chicago Wizard World Comic Con, I only had one outfit left that was worth a damn. To my chagrin, it was the most "used car salesman" of anything I'd brought. This was not a solemn, respectful, "I'm sorry for your loss" outfit – this was a "Hey, where can a guy get a piña colada around here?" kind of outfit.

In a panic, I called another of Lulu's sons, buddy Ted, and asked if he thought it would be disrespectful if I showed up at Lulu's memorial looking like a PGA official. Ted laughed.

"Lulu would have loved that," he said. "And the fact that you came from a job would have made her very happy. Just get here."

So, bright as a peacock, I bid farewell to a woman of great influence. Lulu was insightful, hilarious, a terrible driver but, most important, a second, loving mother.

With the three most influential people in my life now gone, the cutting of a historical, sociological, familial cord was complete and irretrievable. I used to be part of the next generation. Now I'm "it" – nobody outranks me anymore. We are the future old geezers.

Writing this book, it was a little unsettling to relive stories about departed loved ones, even the happy ones, but I was buoyed by the fact that their positive contributions to my life have never faded. I see their influence on a daily basis in the projects I choose, the approach to business I take and the work ethic I apply.

We all know people to whom we owe great debts of gratitude. These were my three.

KNOWN IMAGE CREDITS

Cover Design, Book Composition and Original Artwork
by Craig "Kif" Sanborn

Cover Photograph by Alistair Devine

Contributing Photography by Mike Ditz

Pre-Ramble
Mike Ditz, Renaissance Pictures, Ltd., and Craig "Kif"
Sanborn. Original *If Chins Could Kill* cover design by Philip
Pascuzzo.

1. Exodus
Bruce Campbell and Ida Gearon.

2. Jack of One Season
Geoffrey Short and Craig "Kif" Sanborn. Production image(s)
courtesy of Universal Studios. All rights reserved.

3. Gnome, Sweet Gnome

Bruce Campbell, David Gibb Photography, Mike Ditz and Craig "Kif" Sanborn.

4. A Hunk of Bubba Love

Melanie Tooker and Craig "Kif" Sanborn. Production image(s) courtesy of Metro-Goldwyn-Mayer Studios. All rights reserved.

5. Hello, Neighbor!

Bruce Campbell, Ida Gearon, David Gibb Photography and Craig "Kif" Sanborn. Production image(s) courtesy of Metro-Goldwyn-Mayer Studios. All rights reserved.

6. Getting High

Craig "Kif" Sanborn.

7. Lovemaking

Bruce Campbell, Mike Ditz and Craig "Kif" Sanborn. Original *Make Love! The Bruce Campbell Way* cover design by Howard Grossman.

8. The Big Thaw

Charles Campbell, Rumen Yavev and Craig "Kif" Sanborn. Production image(s) courtesy of SyFy. All rights reserved.

9. Apocalypse How

Mike Ditz, Rumen Yavev and Craig "Kif" Sanborn. Production image(s) courtesy of SyFy. All rights reserved.

10. Attack of the Screaming Brain

Bruce Campbell, Melanie Tooker, Rumen Yavev and Craig "Kif" Sanborn. Production image(s) courtesy of SyFy. All rights reserved.

11. Life on the Wild Side

Bruce Campbell, Ted Raimi and Craig "Kif" Sanborn. Production image(s) courtesy of National Public Radio. All rights reserved.

12. What's My Name?

Bruce Campbell, Mike Ditz, David Gibb Photography, Gary Sauer and Craig "Kif" Sanborn.

13. Rise of the Master Cylinder

Craig "Kif" Sanborn. Production image(s) courtesy of Sony Pictures. All rights reserved.

14. Ashes to Axes

Bruce Campbell, Ida Gearon, E.K. Keratsis and Craig "Kif" Sanborn. Special thanks to William Shatner. Production image(s) courtesy of Twentieth Century Fox Film Corporation. All rights reserved.

15. To Iraq and Baq

Bruce Campbell, Don Campbell and Craig "Kif" Sanborn. Special thanks to James Montgomery Flagg and the soldiers of the United States Armed Forces.

16. Legends of the Fall

Bruce Campbell, John Ales and Craig "Kif" Sanborn. Production image(s) courtesy of Twentieth Century Fox Film Corporation. All rights reserved.

17. Afterburn

Mike Ditz and Craig "Kif" Sanborn. Special thanks to Norman Rockwell. Production image(s) courtesy of The Orchard and Universal Pictures. All rights reserved.

18. Hollywood in Pontiac!

Howard Berger and Craig "Kif" Sanborn. Production image(s) courtesy of the Walt Disney Company and Universal Pictures. All rights reserved.

19. Hardly Functional

Bruce Campbell, Mike Estes and Ida Gearon.

20. Kissin' Hands and Shakin' Babies — the Con Game

Mike Estes, Celeb Photo Ops and Epic Photo Ops. All rights reserved.

21. Crawling Back into the Womb

Acknowledgments

Bruce Campbell and Ann Kelly. Special thanks to the Raimi family.